Poetic Exhibitions

Poetic Exhibitions

Romantic Aesthetics
and the Pleasures
of the British Museum

Eric Gidal

Lewisburg
Bucknell University Press
London: Associated University Presses

Associated University Presses
440 Forsgate Drive
Cranbury, NJ 08512

Associated University Presses
16 Barter Street
London WC1A 2AH, England

Associated University Presses
P.O. Box 338, Port Credit
Mississauga, Ontario
Canada L5G 4L8

The paper used in this publication meets the requirements of the American National Standard for Permanence of Paper for Printed Library Materials Z39.48-1984.

Library of Congress Cataloging-in-Publication Data

Gidal, Eric.
    Poetic exhibitions : romantic aesthetics and the pleasures of the British Museum / Eric Gidal.
        p.   cm.
    Includes bibliographical references and index.
    ISBN 0-8387-5493-7 (alk. paper)
    1. English poetry—19th century—History and criticism.
    2. Antiquities in literature.   3. Archaeological museums and collections—England—London—History—19th century.
    4. Literature and history—Great Britain—History—19th century.
    5. Art and literature—Great Britain—History—19th century.
    6. Wordsworth, William, 1770–1850—Knowledge and learning.
    7. Aesthetics, British—19th century.   8. British Museum—History.
    9. Romanticism—England.   10. Elgin marbles.   I. Title.

PR575.A55 G53   2002
821'.709357—dc21   2001035796

Contents

Acknowledgments

Many people have provided intellectual and profes-sional encouragement as I have worked on this project. I owe much to the professors under whom I studied at the University of Michigan, my fine colleagues at the University of Iowa, and many others at various institutions who have had occasion to comment on aspects of this study and to encourage its completion. I would single out for particular appreciation Teresa Mangum and Judith Pascoe for their collegial support and clarity of critique and Carole Paul for her generosity and excitement.

Gary Thorn and the staff at the British Museum provided critical assistance in archival research and in tracking down hard-to-find images. I also thank the editorial board of Bucknell University Press for their support of this publication and the editorial staff of Associated University Presses for their efforts on its behalf.

I owe a debt greater than words to my wife Jacqueline Briggs who has been an unfailing source of support and assistance, advice and good humor.

Finally, I would thank two teachers from the University of Michigan, Marjorie Levinson and Ralph Williams, who, in different yet complementary fashions, inspired and instructed. Each seems to me a model of scholarly integrity, and I hope this book pays back in some small part a great intellectual debt.

Most of chapter 2 of this book originally appeared as "Wordsworth's Art of Memory" *Studies in Romanticism* 37, no. 3 (1998): 445–75. Reprinted by permission of *Studies in Romanticism*. Portions of chapter 4 originally appeared as "Playing With Marbles: Wordsworth's Egyptian Maid" *The Wordsworth Circle* 24, no. 1 (1993): 3–11, and appear here in revised form. Reprinted by permission of *The Wordsworth Circle*.

Poetic Exhibitions

Introduction

THE OBSERVANT VISITOR TO TODAY'S BRITISH MUSEUM MAY
note the presence of two emblematic designs as he or she
approaches the entrance to Robert Smirke's grandiose
embodiment of neo-classical sensibilities. The first, because of its grander scale and higher position, is the pediment sculpture designed by Richard Westmacott in the
1840s entitled "The Progress of Civilization." This grand
assembly of figures towers over the visitor and seeks to establish both the context and content of what will be found
within. Westmacott himself best expresses its conception
in a description later expanded upon by Sir Henry Ellis,
Principal Librarian of the museum, 1827–55:

> Commencing at the Eastern end . . . man is represented as
> emerging from a rude savage state, through the influence of
> religion. He is next personified as a hunter, and a tiller of the
> earth. . . . Patriarchal simplicity then becomes invaded and
> the worship of the true God defiled. Paganism prevails and
> becomes diffused by means of the arts. The worship of the
> heavenly bodies . . . led the Egyptians, Chaldeans and other
> nations to study Astronomy, typified by the centre statues, the
> keystone for the composition. Civilization is now presumed to
> have made considerable progress. Descending towards the
> Western angle of the pediment, is Mathematics. . . . The
> Drama, Poetry and Music balance the group of the Fine Arts
> on the Eastern side, the whole composition terminating with
> Natural History.[1]

Westmacott's progressive iconography exemplifies the
foundational myth of both Enlightenment rationalism
and Victorian imperialism. Its temporal mapping of
cultural difference onto a progressive model of history
justifies the British prerogative in both empirical classification and material appropriation. But Westmacott's

11

Richard Westmacott, "The Progress of Civilization" on the pediment of the British Museum. © Copyright The British Museum.

sculpture gains its performative power less from the details of its programmatic allegory than from its material personification and elevated location above the visitor's entrance to the museum of the British nation. Though neither the museum nor the nation is directly represented in the sculpture, they connect viewer and form as aesthetic and ideological categories of cohesion and identification. As a spatial topography of natural order and cultural progress, the utopian space of the museum embodies the paradigms of visual exhibition and categorical organization literally and figuratively supporting Westmacott's narrative. As a political category of collective identification, the redemptive idea of the nation analogously unites its citizens within the systems of power and organization that have acquired and displayed these traces of its own development. Having, therefore, surveyed the iconographic progress of human civilization, the visitor is suitably prepared to enter the British Museum, the simultaneous representation and fulfillment of that progression.

Just before passing through the front doors, however, perhaps while having his or her bags checked by security, the visitor might also note a second design positioned immediately above the entrance, shadowed (both literally and figuratively) by the colonnade supporting Westmacott's statuary. This design faithfully reproduces the original seal of the British Museum, designed in the 1750s for the trustees of the newly founded institution. Its designers defend it as follows:

> It need not be observed here, that the word Museum properly signifies a building dedicated to the service of the Muses. . . .

"The seal of the Trustees of the British Museum founded by agreement
of Parliament AD 1753" By kind permission of the Trustees of the British Museum.

But of later times the name Museum has been commonly applied to signify any repository of natural and artificial curiosities ... As the British Museum therefore contains both these,
it was thought not improper to represent it upon the Seal by
the front of a building together with the images of those dei-
ties, and their different attributes, which agreeably to the
antient mythology might emblematically denote the several
parts, of which this Museum consists.

Thus, on the right, the visitor will find Tellus "as representing the natural productions of the earth," and, on the
left, Minerva "as the tutelar deity of arts and sciences."

Presiding over both, in a pediment position akin to the
one now occupied by Westmacott's sculpture, hangs the
emblem of the sun, representative of Apollo, "who was
not only considered as presiding over the Muses, but also
as the inventor of the art of medicine, which is the principle subject of the [foundational] Sloanian library." Beneath the figures reads the motto "BONARUM ARTIUM
CULTORIBUS" [For the Cultivators of the Good Arts]. The
whole image is surrounded by a foundational inscription
"SIGILLUM CURATORUM MUSEI BRITANNICI EX SENATVSCONSVLTO
CONDITI A.D. MDCCLIII" [The seal of the Trustees of the British Museum founded by agreement of Parliament A.D.
1753]. This verbal proclamation of the national institution
was originally served by a fourth figure, that of Britannia
herself "with her proper attributes, as the patroness of
the museum." Because her presence overcrowded the
seal, as well as pitting Apollo and Britannia in competition for the position of precedence, it was decided to drop
Britannia in favor of the aforementioned inscription, so
that "the Sun might stand with greater advantage and
beauty in her place within the pediment."[2]

Here the visitor encounters an alternative sense of the
museum about to be entered. The historical consciousness of Westmacott's design has no place in the seal's association of both the museum and the nation with the
cultivation of the timeless and universal principles of
classical thought. The apology makes apparent the novelty of the institution, which figures less as a culmination
and embodiment of historical progress and more as a
timeless repository of eternal ideals. Like the Renaissance traditions of cabinets and galleries, from which it
draws both its iconography and defense, the seal conceives of the national museum as an Apollonian temple
and a theater of knowledge.[3] The encyclopedic learning
manifested in the museum's material collections mediates between the cultivation of the liberal and mechanical arts and the prestige of public display. Yet, unlike the
earlier traditions of idealized museums, the seal of the
British Museum positions the nation, not the prince, in
the role of political and cultural legitimation.[4] By subsuming Britannia under the sign of Apollo, the seal's de-

signers emphasize enlightenment over polity, even as the
seal's foundational legend establishes the necessary relation between the two. Britannia figures not as a personification of hierarchical power, but as a supplementary
inscription of the social body in its collective identity.
Signifying a system of social relations more than a figure
of political authority, she becomes a subject as well as an
object of exhibitionary admiration.

For the contemporary visitor, however, the architectural juxtaposition of the original seal and Westmacott's
statuary establishes the deepest sense of resonance before he or she even enters the museum proper. The ap-
proximate century that divides the two emblems of
national culture collapses into a few paces, prefiguring
the temporal juxtapositions of the exhibits within. Just as
the visitor's progress from Chinese porcelain to Grecian
marble may produce reactions of aesthetic delight or historical discomfort, so too may the architectural juxtaposition of seal and sculpture initiate a consideration of the
multiform and diverse possibilities of the national museum. This iconographic correspondence of Apollonian
knowledge and progressive teleology unites the aristocratic cultivation of dilettantes and antiquarians with the
political aspirations of a British union. From the modern
and, it should be noted, just as frequently non-British
perspective of the contemporary visitor, either representation of nation and museum seems as intriguing, yet as
contingent, as any of the objects they comprise.[5]

I begin with this approach to the museum's entrance to
emphasize the phenomenological nature of the museum
experience, an experience by necessity both aesthetic
and ideological. As its very name reminds us, the British
Museum manifestly connects political ideology and cultural aesthetics, joining two denominative terms ("British" and "Museum") that, at the time of its establishment
in the middle of the eighteenth century, were far from stable terms of definition.[6] Yet each offered the possibility
that a group of heterogeneous objects might be collected
into a totality, a totality that would simultaneously guar-
antee both categorical coherency and individual autonomy. Each offered a means of linking material experience

with cognitive reflection through a pleasurable and ennobling fusion of reason and sensibility. And each replaced earlier social and visual hierarchies premised upon distinction and coercion with a dialectical communion of harmonious particulars. In allowing for a movement from the fragmentary and antagonistic to the unified and sympathetic, both nation and museum comprised profoundly imaginative acts.

This book offers a study of those imaginative acts, a reading of what I will call the pleasures of the British Museum from its foundation in 1753 to the completion of its current architectural residence and the consolidation of its institutional identity in the 1850s. Evoking pleasure in the eighteenth century signified a range of cultural issues. It spoke to the formulation of taste and the exercise of the imagination, but it also spoke to the critique of luxury and the fear of the passions. Analogously, I employ the term to reflect upon both the aspirations and the anxieties producing national museum culture during the Romantic period. I offer neither a purely ideological critique of the institution's representations of national incorporation and imperial ascendancy, nor a purely aesthetic appreciation of its heterodox collection of antiquities, specimens, and manuscripts. Rather, I offer a reading of the multifaceted experiences enabled within its walls insofar as they both embody and inform a broader culture of imaginative sensibility and Romantic apotheosis.

The poetry and aesthetic philosophy that flourished during the British Museum's first period of major growth offer eloquent accounts of the perception of material objects and the reflective creation of individual and collective identities. Such accounts, while often read as expressions of imaginative autonomy, speak to the very means by which directors and visitors composed visions of cultural unity and invented narratives of historical progress in Europe's first public, secular, and national museum.[7] Far from mere reflections on Miltonic passages, ruined abbeys, and country gardens, Romantic poetry and aesthetics influenced and were in turn affected by the organization of knowledge, the production of visual culture, and the formation of a national consciousness. These cultural and fundamentally poetic activities converged in the discourse and practice surrounding the British Museum. Despite the physicality of architectural form and exhibitionary apparatus, the museum, like the nation, is an imagined establishment.[8] Its signifying power is greater than the sum of its collections and more dialectical than their curatorial organization. As a space of aesthetic reflection, it offers every individual the chance to assume an active part in what Carol Duncan, in discussing the public museum in contemporary culture, has so usefully termed a "civilizing ritual."[9]

In the Romantic period, this ritual fuses aesthetic affirmation with a poetics of cultural and historical discontinuity, offering the nationalized subject as an imperfect reconciliation between the unitary and the divided. The normative category of the nation and the aesthetic authority of the museum promote order and coherency, yet are as threatened as they are enabled by the subjects and objects they comprise. The imperative of public access, the vastness of the museum's collections, and the ruined state of its antiquities continuously disrupt visions of harmonious beauty with the seductive allure of the novel, the oppressive confusion of the sublime, and the melancholic recognition of individual and cultural mortality. The museum's visitors are often diverted and bewildered by the abundance of specimens on display and people gathered to view them. Yet the plenitude of nature and the diversity of the public just as often stimulate pleasure and imagination. Similarly, museum spectators may be separated irrevocably from the conscious enactment of religious and political ideologies that produced the artifacts upon which they gaze. Yet Romanticism's retrospective myths of original genius and transcendent beauty seek less to overcome this separation than to work through it. Converting the displacements of history and the fragmentation of knowledge into the motivations of aesthetic meditation, the imaginative spectator in the national museum pursues an elusive goal of cultural consummation. Such pursuits speak as much to apprehensions of national identity as they do to personal aesthetic desires. The unease felt by the early trustees between Apollo and Britannia as the stabilizing figure of truth and beauty is symbolic of a systemic tension between cultural and political authority in Romantic museum discourse.

The Romantic fascination with the ruined forms of antiquity has been well recognized at least since Stephen Larrabee's *English Bards and Grecian Marbles* (1943).[10] Larabee's important study traced the progress of the Platonic admiration of sculptural forms from its revival in the seventeenth century through its ascendancy and productive flourishing in the eighteenth and early nineteenth centuries. Fusing formal criteria of order and proportion with a faith in humanity's moral sensibilities, this antiquarian aesthetics provided a language for both artistic appreciation and personal reflection. As Murray Krieger has more recently demonstrated, however, the semiotic encounter between poetry and the plastic arts as often ends in exasperation as in communion.[11] Indeed, in the Romantic period, as W. J. T. Mitchell, James A. W. Heffernan, and Grant F. Scott have insisted, the interaction between the verbal poetic subject and the visual aesthetic object is a telling site of personal and political confrontation.[12] Their studies have demonstrated that the impulse towards idealization characteristic of Romantic antiquarianism is predicated upon the need to debase the materiality of its desired objects in a struggle for imaginative autonomy. Philip Fisher, A. W. Phinney, and John Whale have joined these critics in considering the emergence of museum culture in the late eighteenth century as an historical and epistemological influence on these representational struggles.[13] Missing from these varied critical reflections, however, is a sustained account of the manifestly nationalist implications of this institution's paradigms of exhibition. Within the walls of the British Museum, issues of aesthetic communion become inextricable from questions of cultural and political unity. The simultaneously idealizing and debasing tendencies of Platonic criticism towards material forms should be understood not as an isolated aesthetic struggle, but as part of a larger institutional discourse that sought to simultaneously incorporate and differentiate varied classes and nations within a unified exhibitionary experience.[14]

It was, however, a medical botanist and not an antiquarian whose collection founded the British Museum, and it was only as late as 1881 that the museum's natural history collection was finally removed to a separate institution at Kensington. Bemoaning this conflation of cultural objects and natural specimens, Francis Pulsky observed in 1856 that the museum's visitors traveled "from the masterworks of the Parthenon straight up to the stuffed seal and buffalo; and two monster giraffes stand as sentinels before the gallery of vases."[15] Disturbing as this eclecticism might have been to both antiquarians and men of science, it insured that the museum's curatorial practices developed as much from the New Science of the Royal Society as from the neo-classical aesthetics of the Royal Academy. Truth and beauty in this context referred less to the perfection of classical form and more to comprehensive visions of harmonious variety in the natural world. Recent work in the social history of botany, zoology, geology, and the other natural sciences has placed both the private and the public use of scientific organization and display within the ideological programs of national consolidation and imperial control. Expanding upon the insights of Michel Foucault, who in *The Order of Things* (1971), characterized scientific classification as exemplary of the eighteenth century's organization of knowledge and power, critics and historians (such as James L. Larson, Lynn L. Merrill, Mary Louise Pratt, Rhoda Rappaport, Harriet Ritvo, and Ann B. Shteir) have explored the cultural contexts of scientific discoveries and methodologies during the eighteenth and nineteenth centuries.[16] For all of the importance of scientific nomenclature to cultural epistemologies, when displayed under the aegis of the national museum, scientific collections became as much the site for aesthetic reflection and political identification as Egyptian, Greek, and Roman antiquities. As Susan Stewart has noted of collections in general, in the eclectic holdings of the early British Museum, "stones and butterflies are made cultural by classification, and coins and stamps are naturalized by the erasure of labor and the erasure of context of production."[17] In the national museum, this figurative landscape of cultural and natural forms becomes a manifestly political topography. As the collections and practices of the Royal Society were subsumed within those of the British Museum, both the discourse of the aesthetic and the empirical revolution that produced it were incorporated within an exhibitionary production of national identity.

Richard Altick demonstrated some time ago that the British Museum occupies but one position in the larger and more varied space of the shows of nineteenth-century London.[18] Any assertion of its critical importance must account for its often-marginal position within the popular urban culture of the period. One of the points of interest concerning the British Museum, however, is precisely the slow pace at which its cultural and ideological value was recognized and promoted by those entrusted with its administration. Yet its unique conflation of visual culture, scientific organization, and national institution was immediately apparent to those who visited it, making its predicaments of curatorial strategy and exhibitionary reception particularly interesting for considering the relations between aesthetics and ideology. The characteristic Romantic concerns with the imaginative recuperation of the past and the transformation of the material world find a uniquely institutional application within the walls of the British Museum. Aesthetic philosophy from Shaftesbury and Addison to Smith and Burke, and on to Coleridge and Shelley can, therefore, be read as a nascent curatorial theory, a body of work manifestly concerned with questions of visual perception and subjective identity. Poetic meditations on landscapes and ruins, journeys and recollections, from Thomson, Akenside, and Gray through Wordsworth, Byron, Shelley, and Keats, prove rhetorically and ideologically homologous with varied responses in and to the national museum. Indeed, the work of Romantic poetics, like that of the British Museum, may be understood as the formation of identity through the appropriation and delimitation of objects constituted as foreign by virtue of cultural, historical, or ontological displacement. As such, the poetry of the period provides not just occasional records of actual museum encounters, but a basis for understanding the imaginative maneuvers necessary for exhibitionary mechanisms to cohere. Within the walls of the British Museum, nationalist ideology and Romantic aesthetics find a direct and material connection.

I have organized the five chapters that follow in roughly chronological order, but they may be divided more properly into two conceptual categories. In the first two, I consider the arrangement and apprehension of the British Museum's early collections in relation to contemporary aesthetic philosophy and the rhetorical art of memory. As an institution founded "not only for the inspection and entertainment of the learned and the curious, but for the general use and benefit of the public,"[19] the British Museum marked a union of legitimization and freedom both aesthetic and social. The actual composition of the museum's public constituency proved a point of great contention, no more so than how an institution was to appeal simultaneously to the learned and the curious, to open its exhibitions in a manner proper for both inspection and entertainment. In chapter 1, "The Pleasures of the British Museum," I reflect on the language of aesthetics in the eighteenth century as a bridge between scientific inquiry and public display. I compare various curatorial plans and observations with a range of aesthetic theories from such early writers as Anthony Ashley Cooper, third earl of Shaftesbury, Francis Hutcheson, and Joseph Addison to such later mid-century writers as Mark Akenside, William Hogarth, Adam Smith, and Edmund Burke. Akin to the secularization of the newly nationalized collections, the eighteenth-century discourse of aesthetics commenced with the transformation of the rule of moral and political law into an ethical sensibility located in the taste of an idealized individual. In establishing a correlation between visual experience and cognitive reflection, the discourse of the aesthetic offered a ready-made curatorial language by which organizers and visitors might arrange and understand this novel institution. This language was as tied to the polite world of dilettantes and men of science as were the institution's foundational collections, however, and the transition to the public sphere of national exhibition proved systematically disruptive. The aesthetic categories of the novel, the beautiful, and the sublime assume diverse associations with distinctions of education, class, and gender, contesting claims for a unified national identity in debates over public access and exhibitionary design. Nonetheless, the discourse of the aesthetic, like the British Museum and the nation it serves, ultimately proves accommodating to a wide variety of identities and aspirations.

Chapter 2, "Wordsworth in the Museum: A Romantic Art of Memory," considers the power of subjective agency in the museum experience by examining the rhetoric of the museum guidebook in relation to the museum's conceptual origins in the classical art of memory. Adapting picturesque paradigms of longing and gratification to the perusal of a variety of specimens and antiquities, early guidebooks to the British Museum aggressively deploy the rhetoric of curiosity, belittled by more conservative ambitions for the museum's purposes, to expand the parameters of national identification. Their supplementary role as verbal recollections of visual experience joins them to a rhetorical tradition with origins in classical antiquity. Read against William Wordsworth's employment of the museum as a controlling metaphor of visual observation and personal recollection in his autobiographical poetics, accounts of and guides to the national museum and other sites of public exhibition reveal a critical reformulation of the subject in the exhibitionary experience. No longer a passive spectator of princely splendor or encyclopedic knowledge, the national citizen now dialectically engages with categories of political and epistemological identification. Referencing the theoretical writings of John Locke, Edmund Burke, and Samuel Taylor Coleridge, I argue that both the modern museum and the modern nation state depend upon such engagement, even as they underline the personal and historical loss conditioning such imaginative acts.

While my first two chapters witness the transformation of the subject as a political and epistemological identity within evolving notions of curatorial display, the subsequent three chapters consider specific exhibitions of cultural objects within the British Museum. Here I simultaneously explore the temporal mapping of aesthetic paradigms as the national museum spectator attempts to reconcile historical as well as ontological difference. Beginning with what is surely the most contested acquisition in the museum's history, in chapter 3, "Composition and Alienation: The National Reception of the Elgin Marbles," I study a portion of the poetic, pictorial, and political representations of the Parthenon Marbles, purchased for the nation in 1816 from Lord Elgin. The public acquisition of the marbles joined an ongoing debate regarding their aesthetic merits with a political debate regarding the rights of nations to artifacts of their cultural histories, debates informed on both sides by tropes of melancholic loss and aesthetic idealization. I consider the stylistic conflict of the painters Benjamin West and Benjamin Robert Haydon in relation to Sir Joshua Reynolds's prescriptions for academic art, and I examine the poetical reflections of Lord Byron and Felicia Hemans in relation to the traditional eighteenth-century progress poem. For all sides in the artistic and parliamentary contentions regarding their acquisition, the Elgin Marbles provoke a melancholic nostalgia for symbolic communion. Sorrow and sensibility prove multivalent responses in the simultaneously epic and elegiac exhibition of the marbles.

Chapter 4, "Ekphrasis and Empire: Wordsworth's Egyptian Maid," considers the rhetorical and practical links between imperialism and the trope of ekphrasis—the verbal representation of visual representation. This consideration takes the form of a reading of Wordsworth's late poetry in relation to the British Museum's expanding Egyptian galleries and the acquisition of the Townley collection of Greek and Roman statuary. Subsumed within an increasingly programmatic exhibition of cultural progress during the reformist period of the 1820s and 1830s, these collections disturb more than they consolidate the rising imperialist ideology governing the man-

agement and promotion of the British Museum. These
shifting curatorial strategies are akin to late Romanticism's conservative recasting of its earlier imaginative
impulses. In 1835, the same year as Parliament held its
most extensive hearings to date on the purpose and practice of the national museum, Wordsworth's revisionist
self-fashioning culminated in his most popular volume of
poetry *Yarrow Revisited and Other Poems*. This volume articulates the same impulses of medievalist nostalgia and
Orientalist fantasy transforming the national museum.
Both poet and museum construct a romance of national
glory, offering organic paternalism as amelioration to di-
visive political agitation.

The final chapter, "Babel's Curse and the Museum's
Burden: Shelley, Rossetti and the Exhibition of Alterity,"
offers a theoretical meditation on the ironies of this romance. I conclude in the 1850s as the British Museum's
current edifice is completed and the institution becomes
consolidated within a broader series of exhibitionary institutions in London and throughout the British Empire.
Focusing initially on the promotions and critiques of the
Assyrian artifacts brought to the museum in the 1850s by
Austen Henry Layard, I demonstrate the continuing vitality of the museum as a public space for debate and reflection. Turning to Percy Bysshe Shelley's poetry and prose,
I argue for a uniquely Romantic curatorial program, one
that fuses skepticism and idealism, offering a critically
optimistic vision of what museums and nations can imaginatively enable. Though the British Museum offers only a
utopian promise of cultural understanding, I argue that
its potentials lie in embracing such utopian ideals, not in
rejecting them.

As should be clear, this is not a traditional history of
the British Museum. Several excellent histories of the institution already exist. Edward Edwards's *Lives of the
Founders, and Notices of Some Chief Benefactors and Organizers of the British Museum* (1870) remains an impressive
work of scholarship, referencing a wide array of primary
sources, historical and biographical. More recently, Edward Miller's *That Noble Cabinet: A History of the British
Museum* (1973) offers a more comprehensive, if less de-

tailed history than his nineteenth-century predecessor, while J. Mordaunt Crook's *The British Museum* (1972) examines the institution from an architectural perspective, drawing upon the broader philosophical and artistic contexts which produced the exhibitionary apparatuses of the national museum. A. E. Gunther's *The Founders of Science at the British Museum, 1753–1900* (1980) covers the development of the natural history collections and, most recently, Ian Jenkins's *Archaeologists & Aesthetes* (1992) provides extensive information and analysis regarding the acquisition and exhibition of antiquities throughout the museum's history.[20] All of these works, as well as more detailed monographs on individual pieces, personalities, and collections, have been invaluable to me in the writing of this book. While I am much indebted to both their scholarship and critical analysis, in this study I read the British Museum less according to its own terms of empirical science, art history, and cultural archaeology and more as a focal point for varied aesthetic, ideological, and ultimately poetic struggles of the era. I, therefore, not only add some hitherto unconsidered materials to the history of the institution, but also assess the documented accounts of the institution as imaginative acts and encounters in their own right.

To read the museum in this fashion, indeed, to *read* a museum at all, is of course, counterintuitive and may seem to suggest too-easy affinities between institutions and texts and between visual and verbal representation. Here I need to be quite clear. I am not proposing a neo-Horatian doctrine of *ut musaea poesis* that establishes an absolute compatibility of material exhibition and verbal mimesis. Such a methodology, as I demonstrate in the first chapter, actually has a long tradition in art history, the natural sciences, and museum studies, where paintings and sculptures are envisioned as rhetorical signs, natural specimens as metonymies of objective classification, and museums as transparently syntactical arrangements embodying varied cultural, scientific, and historical grammars.[21] Such readings of museum culture are often deployed in critiques of the culture of late capitalism, the imperial projects of acquisition and domination, or the hegemony of Western European forms of aesthetic expression.[22] As a genre of cultural representation, museums certainly may be seen as inscribing economic and political power relations through ideologies of commodification that subsume foreign and ancient artifacts within narrative spectacles of evolutionary progress and Western ascendancy. The project of cultural critique then becomes one of archaeology in the Foucauldian sense, unearthing the historical and ideological maneuvers by which such institutional practices interpolate subjective identity within a social web of power and knowledge.

Museum studies may just as likely, however, service aspirations of universal culture, pluralistic expression, and social and economic empowerment. In this model, the museum as a form becomes amenable to a variety of subjective articulations and performative acts. In this kind of analysis, cultural critique assumes an aesthetic function and aids the institution in realizing its potential for democratic exposition.[23] To argue that the museum has an aesthetic function is not to deny the role of the ideological in the aesthetic experience, but to expand our sense of museum poetics beyond transparent embodiments of cultural epistemologies. Contemporary studies of collections and exhibitions often establish an opposition between the institutional authority of the museum and the eccentric desires of collectors and spectators.[24] Yet, as John Elsner and Roger Cardinal have reminded us, museums and amusement share more than an etymological connection.[25] Despite their architectural trappings of sacred and political power, museums are as much sites of aesthetic pleasure as they are of ideological control. Indeed, one of the key insights of aesthetics as it has been handed down to us from the eighteenth century is the necessary centrality of subjective judgment in forming a coherent vision of nature and society. Even as its narratives spoke increasingly of British ascendancy and imperial sway, the British Museum's curatorial discourse and practice created a space for aesthetic experience that stretched the imaginative possibilities of the national citizenry. Such experiences, in turn, allowed for the articulation of a national body more inclusive and democratic than its more manifestly political institutions. Far from a mere false consciousness obfuscating more insidious methods of ideological interpolation and control, the experience of the aesthetic pushed the British Museum past the limited conceptual confines of its original trustees, curators, and visitors. It enabled these national citizens to imagine a multitude of pleasurable and instructive responses to the objects on display and the subjects gathered to view them.

To recognize the museum's institutional potential for expansive imagination helps to correct the distrust of the aesthetic within contemporary studies in Romantic culture. It has now been some time since Jerome McGann's arguments regarding romantic ideologies brought the apparently transcendent concerns of the Romantics down to a more material realm.[26] McGann challenged the self-promoted autonomy of the Romantic lyrical voice and its institutional reproductions as inhabited formally and thematically by historically specific constructs of subjectivity and power. Recent years, however, have witnessed a critical reaction against what are now orthodox norms of historicist and ideological critique in the humanities. Oscar Kenshur, George Levine, and Thomas Pfau have forwarded dissenting views of the relation of the aesthetic to the ideological that resist what all three view as the tendency to reduce the aesthetic experience to ideology without accounting for what makes the experience intrinsically aesthetic. Kenshur resists a view of absolute co-optation that sees all aesthetic expressions as always and already compromised by the dominant ideology of any given society. He thereby allows for the possibility of opposition within a pervasive ideology through the very ideas and forms it comprises. Analogously, Levine suggests that the modes of imagination and self-regulation necessary to a modern democratic society have freest play in the contested domain of the aesthetic because this domain is the most sensual and least controllable. Most recently, Pfau has argued for a structural homology between the New Historicism and the Hegelian notion of historical totality it seeks to displace. In Pfau's persuasive account, historicist practice claims for itself either teleological fulfillment of a historical development independent of particular ideologies or irremediable compromise within the systems of power. The critical position thus manifests either redemption or despair. All three critics propose different alternatives to the self-contradictory stances of contemporary ideological critique. For Kenshur, the answer lies in careful attention to context; for Levine, the solution is to be found in a non-partisan reclamation of the power of the aesthetic domain; for Pfau, the best available choice is to focus on the functions rather than the attributes of aesthetic pleasure, finding in Romanticism's communal and pedagogical deployments a more satisfying, if only because more provisional, account of its ideological affinities.[27]

In various ways, conjoining Romantic discourse with the institutional practices of the British Museum speaks to all three possibilities. I wish to avoid establishing an inherent relation between aesthetic theory and ideological deployment. As my study repeatedly emphasizes, the various elements of eighteenth-century and Romantic aesthetics were as often tied to modes of liberation as they were to methods of control, as often used to demand inclusion as they were to justify exclusion, as often elements of progressive imagination as of nostalgic reaction. Furthermore, it was precisely their aesthetic quality that gave such moments, whether textual or exhibitionary, their ideological valance. Indeed, it is all in the deployment. The British Museum, like the nation it serves, provides a specific domain of aesthetic pleasure that is informed by its status as a public, national, and secular institution. These characteristics have been far from monolithic categories in the imagination of the museum's trustees, promoters, and visitors, and the aesthetic activities they have enabled have hardly been over-determined. Rather, the British Museum has provided a space wherein a public and secular nation could be imagined and, in part, created, through individual, and thereby contradictory, aesthetic experiences. Hence, when I turn to more manifestly literary works, be they poetic or theoretical, I do not claim an absolute or uniform connection between their representational strategies and various strains of conservative, progressive, or revolutionary nationalism. Rather, I consider their varied homologies and deployments within an expressly ideological and manifestly aesthetic institution.

The reconfiguration of epistemology and ethics enabled by aesthetics as the binding category between experience and reflection is in one respect a truly liberating innovation. It allows independent subjects to imagine a social contract based not on hierarchical authority, but on a homogenous code of ethics rooted in natural and universal law, linking the individual to the collective through an insistence on shared experience and common humanity. Of course, by inserting social order in a subjective and interior "moral sense," the discourse of aesthetics is subject to critique as internalized repression, interpolating subjects so thoroughly within organizations of power that they submit to domination under the illusion of free will. Yet, as even such an arch-materialist as Terry Eagleton has pointed out, an aesthetic ideology is inherently unstable as a program of social control. "The aesthetic as custom, sentiment, spontaneous impulse may consort well enough with political domination," he argues, "but these phenomena border embarrassingly on passion, imagination, sensuality, which are not always so easily incorporable."[28] It is precisely this recognition of the fundamentally sensuous and imaginative pleasures of the museum experience that provides the recurrent point of ideological confrontation in the history of the institution. In the domain of the public museum, a domain whose core experience involves a subjective confrontation with a material object, any ideological mediation remains precarious and unstable. Within the walls of the British Museum, aesthetic ideology finds a simultaneously material and poetic expression.

1

The Pleasures of the British Museum

Robert Hooke, director of the royal society's repository of natural specimens in the late seventeenth century, a collection subsumed into the British Museum in 1779, offered a famous curatorial imperative in service of the mechanistic philosophy of the New Science the Society helped to create and promote:

> It were . . . much to be wisht for and endeavoured that there might be made and kept in some Repository as full and complete a collection of all varieties of Natural bodies as could be obtained, where an inquirer might be able to have recource, where he might peruse, and turn over, and spell, and read the book of nature, and observe the orthography, etymologia, syntaxis, and prosodia of nature's grammar, and by which, as with a dictionary, he might readily turn to find the true figure, composition, derivation and use of the characters, words, phrases and sentences of nature written with indelible, and most exact, and most expressive letters, without which book it will be very difficult to be thoroughly a literatus in the language and sense of nature.[1]

Hooke's ambition for a material dictionary of the natural world emerges from the new scientific methodology promoted by the Royal Society, a methodology whereby discrimination and classification came to provide the means for proper interpretation. Michel Foucault has situated this methodology within a broader epistemological shift in seventeenth and eighteenth century scientific discourse from visions of relationship to projects of discrimination. Moving away from earlier modes of hermeneutics

30

that conceived of the world as an infinite spiral of signs and similitude, the representational dream of the later projects of classification held that, in Foucault's words,

> [a] complete enumeration will now be possible: whether in the form of an exhaustive census of all the elements constituting the envisaged whole, or in the form of a categorical arrangement that will articulate the field of study in its totality, or in the form of an analysis of a certain number of points, in sufficient number, taken along the whole length of a series.[2]

This vision of a complete enumeration sought an idealized relation whereby the ordered taxonomy of the parts would suffice for the representation of the whole. Yet, as Michael Hunter has demonstrated, the Society's actual repository embodied internal divisions between "virtuoso" and "scientific" values, the former privileging the exotic and curious, the latter favoring the common and exemplary.[3] Hooke's aspiration for a complete collection of natural specimens typifies the scientific ambition for comprehensive perspective that opposed the virtuoso predilection for isolated objects of wonder. His conceit of the collection as a dictionary of the book of nature favors a hermeneutics that emphasizes formal system over phenomenological event, insisting that the truth of nature's book may be discovered most truly by the adept and objective "literatus." Indeed, his privileging of grammatical order over imaginative reflection specifically denies the reader a position in the book's syntactic structures. The "literatus" must turn to the repository's taxonomy to discover the true "sense of nature," but the sense exists autonomously from the reader's consultation.

Hooke's imperative does not stop at privileging the grammar of nature's book, but expands to consider the proper manner of reading the repository's collection. His methods rule out affective and imaginative participation and, in so doing, exclude large segments of the population from perusal and observation. "The use of such a Collection," he writes, "is not for Divertissement, and Wonder, and Gazing, as 'tis for the most part thought and esteemed, and like Pictures for Children to admire and be pleased with, but for the most serious and diligent study of the

most able Proficient in Natural Philosophy."[4] Hooke's
prohibition distinguishes modern scientific collections
from the more frivolous and ostentatious cabinets of curiosities that, ironically, contributed the bulk of the repository's initial holdings. Equally intriguing, his distinction
between proficient inquiry and pleasing admiration tellingly privileges textual over visual representation and
refuses the possibility of an exhibitionary aesthetic. His
dismissal of divertissement, on the one hand, and wonder,
on the other, denies the power of novelty and sublimity in
the figuratively literary experience. And his distinction
of the "literatus" from the majority of the population, belittled as juvenile in their literary dispositions, indicates
the social ideologies informing his prescribed reading
practice. One reads not for transport, wonder, or entertainment, but for edification and literacy.

Hooke's ambitions reveal the power and the limitations
of a purely structural account of the museum experience.
Yet, in many respects, modern theorists of the origins and
phenomena of the museum, even at their most critical, remain true both to Hooke's distrust of the virtuosi and to
his corresponding faith in the semantic transparency of
exhibitionary culture. Hence, Mieke Bal, in her generally
fascinating and wide-ranging study of curatorial exposition as a condition of cultural modernity and humanist
scholarship, predicates her analysis by insisting that
"walking through a museum is like reading a book."[5] More
properly, Bal equates the narrative and epistemological
grounds of museum exhibition with the nineteenth-century realist novel and its occlusion of the first person in
constructing the illusion of the real. Both artistic and ethnographic exhibitions employ a mode of display that "is
so rigorously constative that its syntax confirms the structure of the affirmative sentence only, not leaving much
room for other speech acts, such as questions and other
dialogic forms."[6] Bal's critique seeks to expose the
grounds of rhetorical and curatorial authority in order to
advocate a more interrogative mode of museum exhibition. Analogously, Tony Bennett's arch-Foucauldian
reading of the "exhibitionary complex" of institutions
and technologies of public display reads the museum as a

transparently determining space of public regulation and ideological control: "If museums gave this space [of representation] a solidity and permanence, this was achieved at the price of a lack of ideological flexibility. Public museums instituted an order of things that was meant to last."[7] By interpolating the public citizen as both subject and object of a manifestly ideological order, museums form the perfect complement to prisons in Bennett's reading, reversing the principles of the Panopticon so that a large number of people may participate in a normative and unifying gaze.

These critiques are profoundly important in situating the grammar and syntax of the museum within broader structures of power and knowledge and represent much of the best work in current museum studies. Yet both skeptically reject the aesthetic experience as delusion and obfuscation, masking power relations and refusing heterogeneous or subversive articulations. To be fair, Bal devotes a large portion of her work to argue for the potential for such subjective resistance to hegemonic narratives. Yet early accounts of the British Museum and other sites of public exhibition consistently reveal that in the eighteenth century walking through a museum was already an interrogative experience in which various objects found both harmonious and discordant relations in the mind's eye through the sensibilities of the viewing subject. Bennett also recognizes the limitations of his Foucauldian approach in failing to account for just such moments of subjective interrogation and the possibility of resistance to or even departure from managed programs of interpolation they engender.[8] In this chapter, I want to move beyond such grammatical readings by examining the simultaneously determined and determinative pleasures of the British Museum—the fraught intersection of the institution's manifest ideologies of civic republicanism, cultural nationalism, and global imperialism, and its equally manifest aesthetics of material encounter and reflective judgment. Through reading early accounts of the museum and its foundational collection by both visitors and trustees alongside the discourse of eighteenth-century aesthetic theory, I hope to demonstrate the instability of any single ideological program imagined for the museum. An attention to the dialectical poetics of the museum phenomenon reveals the degree to which both the visitors and the managers of the exhibitionary experience participated in a far more eclectic project than a strictly ideological analysis allows. For to understand any modern cultural form, be it a museum or book, a performance or poem, without accounting for the centrality of aesthetics in the production of meaning, is to produce an insufficient account blind to the heterodox possibilities of interpretive acts.

Stephen Bann, following both Michel Foucault's theories of cultural epistemologies and Hayden White's theory of the poetic tropes of historical narration, has articulated a useful but limited conception of museum poetics. Bann premises "that it is possible, in certain special circumstances, to reconstruct the formative procedures and principles which determine the type of a particular museum, and to relate these procedures to the epistemological presumptions of our period." The tropological analysis he develops allows him to trace the development of nineteenth century historiography in the formation of Alexander du Sommerard and Alexandre Lenoir's collections of antiquities and their official adoption by the French state as the Musée de Cluny in Paris. In the rhetorical methodology of the modern museum, Bann argues, the representation of objects moves from chronologically reductive metonymy to historically organic synecdoche, creating a systematic reconstruction of the past. Bann's structuralist critique, like Bal and Bennett's, offers a compelling method for reading a range of cultural and scientific exhibitions. But he excludes what he oddly terms the "pre-history of the British Museum, from the Sloane legacy of 1753 to the opening of the present premises in 1851,"[9] the very period of this study, as insufficiently systematic for his conceptualization of museum poetics. According to his own premises of epistemological transparency, Bann is completely correct. What the formative *century* of one of Europe's first public national museums reveals, however, is the insufficiency of such a purely epistemological critique of material and aesthetic

institutions. As an examination of the discourse surrounding the early British Museum reveals, it is precisely
in aesthetic experience, in the divertissement and wonder
that Robert Hooke and contemporary theory so suspect,
that both nation and museum gain their congregating and,
I will argue, liberating power.

It is useful to recall that the discourse of the aesthetic
emerged out of the same empirical revolution that produced the Royal Society and, subsequently, the British
Museum. In the methodology of the New Science, neither
God nor Church was the guarantor of truthful knowledge.
Instead, man himself became both the source and the
confirmation of understanding, grounding knowledge in
immediate observation and comparison. John Locke's
Essay Concerning Human Understanding (1690) had further
thrown open the relation between sensory experience
and cognitive reflection. Locke denied the validity of received understanding and situated the individual mind
as the primary agent in the perception of ideas and the
construction of knowledge. Yet the methods of empirical
inquiry inevitably turned the eyes of the beholder in-
wards. Skeptical methodology provoked such thinkers as
Locke and Hume to consider the very category of the subject whose activities were to form the basis of all other
branches of knowledge, a potentially futile quest often
ending in abject despair. The pleasures of aesthetic judgment, on the other hand, staved off the ontological and
ethical despondency of absolute skepticism. In response
to the ethical and theological vacuum left by Lockean philosophy, eighteenth-century theorists developed the language of aesthetics to replace the former bulwarks of
social and moral restraint—the Church and the King. In
the writings of such Neoplatonic theorists as Shaftesbury
and Hutcheson, the aesthetic perfectly served the logic of
rationalist Deism, restoring God through imaginative observation. In the writings of other more empirically in-
flected theorists as Addison and Hume, the aesthetic
recuperated the category of the subject as an identity per-
ceptible through the transition from sensory perception
to rational understanding. As a broader discourse, the
aesthetic served to unite perception and understanding

through affective judgment in both epistemology and, just as important, ethics. Whether we consider Addison's celebration of the pleasures of the imagination or Shaftesbury's evocation of divine rhapsody through the contemplation of the works of nature or Burke's account of the pleasing abjection in the face of sublime magnitude, we find an aesthetic discourse fundamentally concerned with issues of truth and power in a skeptical age.[10]

Despite Hooke's curatorial program, the insufficiency of a purely grammatical reading of the book of nature was a centerpiece of eighteenth-century aesthetic theory. Writers throughout the century associated humanity's moral and spiritual elevation with the imaginative contemplation of the wondrous and diverse productions of nature. Theorists of the aesthetic experience were inspired by Longinus's contention that "Nature never designed man to be a groveling and ungenerous animal, but brought him into life, and placed him in the world, as in a crowded theatre, not to be an idle spectator, but spurred on by an eager thirst of excelling, ardently to contend in the pursuit of glory."[11] Major and minor theorists in the Longinian tradition located the true sense of nature neither in the material nor in the spiritual, but in the dialectical communion of the human and the divine. The poet and theorist Mark Akenside exemplified the centrality of imaginative pleasure in reading the book of nature in his 1744 poem "The Pleasures of Imagination." For those properly sensible to the workings of the material universe upon the mental faculties, such a reading experience borders on divine consummation:

> To these the sire omnipotent unfolds
> The world's harmonious volume, there to read
> The transcript of himself. On every part
> They trace the bright impressions of his hand:
> In earth or air, the meadow's purple stores,
> The moon's mild radiance, or the virgin's form
> Blooming with rosy smiles, they see portray'd
> That uncreated beauty, which delights
> The mind supreme. *They* also feel her charms,
> Enamour'd; *they* partake th'eternal joy.
>
> (1.99–108)[12]

"The Pleasures of Imagination" is a secularized Miltonic epic, justifying the ways of the Neoplatonic One to the minds of men. Its indebtedness to eighteenth-century aesthetic theory is evident throughout its three books as it grapples with the position of the imagination within both the mental faculties and the social order. Linking beauty to truth and virtue, in an "open, pathetic and figur'd stile," Akenside seeks a reformation of pleasure towards noble ends. In the passage above, the cultivated mind reads the creation as divine transcript, metaphorically moving from the vehicle of natural forms to the tenor of a benevolent providence. The mind partakes of this benevolence through enamored and affective reading rising to elevated joy, a process Akenside's poem narrates at some length. Joining aesthetic pleasure to moral and political evolution, Akenside first imagines humanity's departure from the state of nature as a rational and moral development:

> For of all
> Th'inhabitants of earth, to man alone
> Creative wisdom gave to lift his eye
> To truth's eternal measures; thence to frame
> The sacred laws of action and of will,
> Discerning justice from unequal deeds,
> And temperance from folly.
>
> (1.537–43)

But, "beyond / This energy of truth, whose dictates bind / Assenting reason," it is "imagination's rays," adorning "the honour'd paths of just and good" (1.543–47), which compel the aspiration towards the social state:

> Where virtue rising from the awful depth
> Of truth's mysterious bosom, doth forsake
> The unadorn'd condition of her birth;
> And dress'd by fancy in ten thousand hues,
> Assumes a various feature, to attract,
> With charms responsive to each gazer's eye,
> The hearts of men.
>
> (1.548–54)

As a curatorial credo, "The Pleasures of Imagination" demonstrates the centrality of aesthetic experience in the secular foundation of a moral society. The discriminating judgment of the heart perceives the beautiful and the good, as the imaginative rays of the mind respond to the seductive charms of virtue. Unlike Hooke's "literatus," Akenside's imaginative spectator must fully participate with subjective feeling to complete the syntax of material exhibition and to read comprehensively the book of nature. If the repository or museum is to exemplify nature's grammar, the spectator must engage in aesthetic divertissement and wonder in order for the exhibition to cohere.

What works in theory often proves problematic in practice. As the rhetoric of divine apprehension through imaginative pleasure was transferred from the private realm of dilettantes and men of science to the public realm of the national museum, the easy fit between pleasure and virtue was compromised by anxieties both aesthetic and social. As an institution founded "not only for the inspection and entertainment of the learned and curious, but for the general use and benefit of the public," the British Museum marked an institutional union of aesthetic pleasure and political organization in the public sphere. Unifying both the variety of the collections and the diversity of the viewing public, the museum's mandate promoted a picturesque composition where, in the adapted words of Pope's "Windsor Forest," "Order in Variety we see, / And where, tho' all things differ, all agree" (15–16).[13] Both the vastness of the museum's collections and the imperative of public access, however, continuously disrupted such a vision of beauty with the seductive allure of the novel and the oppressive confusion of the sublime. Studies of collectors, curiosities, and scientific culture in early modern Europe have demonstrated curiosity's tainted yet central role in the relationships between desire and comprehension, possession and knowledge, and private passion and public display.[14] As Nicholas Thomas has put it, "if not exactly antithetical, curiosity and virtue were far from readily reconciled; curiosity, collecting, curiosities, and licentiousness were uncomfortably connected."[15] Although variety and novelty were recognized in contemporary aesthetic discourse as the foundation of intellectual pleasure, when unrestrained by harmony and order they threatened the autonomy of the idealized spectator with sensuous seduction or confused terror. Within the walls of the British Museum, these aesthetic tensions frequently were displaced onto gendered and class-marked distinctions between a normative national identity and a contested public domain.

II

In his Advertisment to the *Catalogue of King Charles the First's Collection of Pictures* (1757), Horace Walpole eloquently expresses the aspirations of many of his fellow trustees for the newly founded British Museum. Having first surveyed the parallel fates of the Stuart monarchy and their collections through accretion, dissipation, and restoration, Walpole offers a redemptive vision for an aspiring national museum:

> The Establishment of the British Museum seems a charter for incorporating the arts, a new era of *virtu*. It is to be hoped that collections that would straggle through auctions into obscurity, will now find a center! Who that should destine his collection to the British Museum, would not purchase curiosities with redoubled spirit and pleasure, whenever he reflected, that he was collecting for his country, and would have his name recorded as a benefactor to its arts and improvements? And where so fair a foundation is laid, if pictures and statues flow in to books and medals, and curiosities of every kind, may we not flatter ourselves, that a British Academy of arts will arise; at least that we shall not want great masters of our own, when models are prepared; and our artists can study Greece and Rome, Praxiteles and Raphael, without stirring from their own metropolis?[16]

According to Walpole's rhetoric, the British Museum will serve both as an incorporation of collections and as a model for emulation, a school that will revive the ancient

arts of Greece and Rome within the London metropolis.
Placed in a manifestly social context of national display,
the accumulation and preservation of natural and cultural artifacts assumes a distinctly civic function. In a
circular logic of signification and legitimization, the heterogeneous exhibition of pictures, statues, books, medals,
and "curiosities of every kind" enables a collective identification between benefactors and beneficiaries that, in
turn, unifies the exhibition under the coherent rubric of
the nation. An individual's knowledge of the objects' ultimate destination in the national repository inspires him
to increase his collecting activities so that a series of
acquisition and dispersal with no cohesive meaning or
purpose now finds a national "center" to provide a teleological significance for both collectors and artifacts. The
private collections Walpole envisions composing the national museum both memorialize their personal collectors and attest to the higher ideals of *virtu* and the nation
itself, the incorporation, collection, and thereby fulfillment of its participants.

Walpole's concern over material dispersal may be read
as a metonymy for a loss of aristocratic privilege, for in
seeking to incorporate *virtu* within the parameters of national exhibition, Walpole seeks expedience and stability
for both antiquarianism and the leisure status upon
which it depends. As an introduction to the *Catalogue*,
Walpole's celebration of a national museum of memorial
preservation and foundational emulation compensates
for the destruction of the Royal collection and its contemporary system of patronage and cultivation. In a distinctively elegiac tone, Walpole contrasts King Charles's love
and promotion of the arts with his collection's melancholy destiny in the civil war: "the stroke that laid Roy-
alty so low, dismissed the painter, and dispersed the
royal virtuoso's collections: the first cabinets in Europe
shine with its spoils" (ii). The *Catalogue* thus gains power
in indirect proportion to the cohesion of the collection it
represents: "while a collection remains entire, the use of
the catalogue is obvious; when dispersed, it often serves
to authenticate a picture, adds to its imaginary value, and
bestows a sort of history on it" (iii). Hence the simultane-

ously mournful and celebrating tone of Walpole's remarks: for if the *Catalogue* can but trace the glorious royal collection now forever lost, it may also point forward to the British Museum as its redemption. In this novel institution, both the collections themselves and the system of exhibition and promotion that surround them—in short, the practice of *virtu*—are to be reconstituted under the aegis of the nation.

Walpole's public rhetoric concerning the nascent museum stresses *virtu* and incorporation, but his private correspondence satirizes the idle curiosity of its patrons and trustees. In a letter to Horace Mann from 1753, Walpole quipped that, having become one of the trustees to Sir Hans Sloane's foundational collection of manuscripts and natural specimens, he was "at present in the guardianship of embryos and cockle-shells":

> [Sloane] valued [the collection] at fourscore thousand; and so would anybody who loves hippopotamuses, sharks with one ear, and spiders as big as geese! It is a rent-charge to keep the foetuses in spirit! You may believe that those who think money the most valuable of all curiosities, will not be purchasers. The King has excused himself, saying he did not believe that there are twenty thousand pounds in the Treasury. We are a charming wise set, all philosophers, botanists, antiquarians, and mathematicians; and adjourned our first meeting, because Lord Macclesfield, our chairman, was engaged to a party for find out the longitude. . . .[17]

Both of Walpole's descriptions of the nascent museum emphasize the expanse and diversity of its holdings, but where his advertisement to the *Catalogue* links such seductions to cultural preservation and enrichment, his private quips stress only the appeal to curiosity. Walpole's irreverence participates in a common satirical tradition whereby the collector is figured as merely accumulating specimens and artifacts valuable only for their novelty. From the satirist's perspective, the curiosity cabinet is not merely an absurd, but a false representation of the world, failing to draw the attention past initial interest towards any complete vision of natural order. For all his mockery, Walpole's self-abasing emphasis on the mone-

tary worthlessness of such collections actually maintains
the separation between antiquarian and mercantile pursuits that insures the cultural value of such endeavors.
"Those who think money the most valuable of curiosities," are both given their due and kept at arm's length
from the more cultured, if eccentric, "charming wise set"
of dilettantes and virtuosos. Both of Walpole's reflections
circumscribe the national museum as a space set apart
from the social and economic transformations that
threaten the private domain of virtuosity he seeks to reproduce.

For his anxiety over the dissipation of collections stems
not only from the royal collection his catalogue memorializes, but from the auctioning off of portions of his father
Robert Walpole's collection in the preceding decade. Walpole had observed in *Aedes Walpolianae,* his own catalogue of his father's collection at Houghton Hall, that
"commerce, which carries along with it the Curiosities
and Arts of Countries, as well as the Riches, daily brings
us something from Italy," and wondered "how many valuable Collections of Pictures are there established in England on the frequent ruins and dispersions of the finest
Galleries in Rome and other Cities."[18] Faced with a similar fate for his father's collections, Walpole expressed his
dismay that "Gidion the Jew and Blakiston the independent Grocer have been the chief purchasers of [his
father's] pictures sold already."[19] As Cynthia Wall has argued, the rise of the auction house in the eighteenth century stands in sharp contrast to the realm of the private
collection, not only redistributing property in a public
forum, but, thereby, reshaping social identity as well.[20]
Yet, if private collections could no longer provide a secure domain of aristocratic privilege and display, the national museum might refashion that sphere of interest,
both securing the personal prestige of its benefactors and
patronizing the production of new artistic endeavors. If
the auction provides, in Wall's words, a "narrative of dismantling," the museum provides a counter-narrative of
congregation, one in which nation and museum serve as
signs of stability and compensation. Ironically, what remained of the collection at Houghton Hall was sold in

1779 to the Empress Catherine of Russia to pay off the debts of Walpole's nephew George, despite appeals by John Wilkes to establish a picture gallery "for the reception of this invaluable collection"[21] in the very British Museum Walpole had imagined might prevent such national cultural hemorrhaging. If the British Museum were to become a "center" to stabilize the vicissitudes of the auction market, the nation must provide the means as well as the rhetoric for countering the pitiless determinism of the economy.

Preservation and virtue point to somewhat different ends in the will and codicils of Sir Hans Sloane, whose bequest effectively instigated the museum's creation upon his death in 1753.[22] Sloane's rhetoric of rational Deism joins preservation and public access under the rubric of enlightened knowledge:

> being fully convinced that nothing tends more to raise our ideas of the power, wisdom, goodness, providence, and other perfections of the Deity, or more to the comfort and well being of his creatures, than the enlargement of our knowledge of the works of nature, I do will and desire that for the promoting of these noble ends, the glory of God and the good of man, my collection in all its branches may be, if possible, kept and preserved together whole and entire, in my Manor House in the Parish of Chelsea.[23]

Of a piece with Sloane's earlier writings, particularly his major work *A Natural History of Jamaica* (1707), the language of his will contemplates the deity through an inventory of its creation. It allows each piece of the collection to stand both as a metonymy of its natural or cultural origins and as a metaphor of divine wisdom and power. Its rhetoric reveals Sloane's active intellectual and experimental participation in the scientific culture of the Royal Society, founded in 1660, the year of Sloane's birth. Sloane served both as Secretary (1693–1727) and then, following Newton, as President of the Society (1727–41), positions which helped him to earn an association with many of the distinguished scientists of his time. As editor of the Society's *Philosophical Transactions*, Sloane not only came into contact with, but also exerted a stylistic influence on many of the era's most important scientific communications. Though frequently parodied for its increasingly convoluted prose style, a departure from the Society's early insistence on plain style, the *Philosophical Transactions* was viewed by many of his contemporaries as a powerful example of the methodologies of empirical inquiry. John Locke himself praised Sloane's systematic documentation of botanical specimens, concluding "that there is noe thing constantly observable in nature, which will not always bring some light with it, and lead us farther into the knowledge of her ways of workeing."[24] For Sloane, such a progress of observation led inevitably to a contemplation of the Deity. In 1722, entering into agreement on behalf of the Royal Society with the Society of Apothecaries for joint control of and access to the Apothecaries' Garden in Chelsea, Sloane spoke of the garden as "the manifestation of the power, wisdom and glory of God in the works of the Creation."[25] His preface to the *Natural History of Jamaica* registers both the empirical methodology and the unbridled wonder given expression in this philosophical position. "Knowledge of Natural-History, being observation of Matter of Fact, is more certain than Others, and in my slender Opinion, less subject to Mistakes than Reasonings, Hypotheses, and Deductions are. ... These are things we are sure of, so far as our Senses are not fallible; and which in probability, have been ever since the Creation, and will remain to the End of the World, in the same condition we now find them."[26]

The fusion of natural philosophy and aesthetic pleasure witnessed in these remarks exemplified itself in Sloane's activities as a collector. Visitors to his collection, first in Bloomsbury and later in Chelsea, provide us a sense both of Sloane's amazing resourcefulness and of his generosity with educated visitors. John Evelyn offers a description from 1691 which demonstrates the connections between material collection and categorical documentation characteristic of the culture of the Royal Society:

> I went to see Dr. Sloans [*sic*] Curiosities, being an universal Collection of the natural productions of Jamaica consisting of

Plants, [fruits,] Corralls, Minerals, [stones,] Earth, shells, animals, Insects &c: collected by him with greate Judgement, several folios of Dried plants & one which had about 80: severall sorts of Fernes, & another of Grasses: &c: The Jamaica pepper in branch, leaves, flowers, fruits &c: [which] with his Journal, & other philosophical & naturall discourses & observations is indeede very extraordinary and Copious, sufficient to furnish an excellent History of that Iland, to which I encouraged him, & exceedingly approved his Industry.[27]

Evelyn conceptually links the material collection to documentary natural history with ease. For him, collecting and producing natural history are near equivalents. Both are intended primarily as empirical investigations into the terrain, flora, and fauna of this early colonial outpost. As Mary Louise Pratt has characterized the convergence of science and sentiment in a later generation of natural historians, these investigative activities convert the island into a "contact zone" of Europe and the new world, creating it as "a site of intellectual as well as manual labor."[28]

Sloane's collecting activities paralleled his scientific research as he gradually amassed a collection of over 79,000 specimens comprising collections of botany, zoology, shells, minerals, insects, fossils, classical and oriental antiquities, drawings, manuscripts, and seals. Sloane's magnanimity as a private exhibitor matched his diligence as a collector. One contemporary noted that he was "always ready on proper Notice to admit the Curious to the sight of his Musaeum,"[29] and such generosity, fused with his meticulous cataloguing of his possessions, earned his collection a reputation as a stable storehouse of material knowledge. John Evelyn called it a "universal collection,"[30] and this it was in more ways than one. For Sloane's collection not only comprised a vast array of natural specimens and cultural artifacts, but a wide assortment of other men's collections subsumed within Sloane's over the years. The varied holdings of William Courten (1642–1702), Leonard Plukenet (1642–1706), and James Petiver (c. 1663–1718), all major acquisitions of natural specimens and cultural antiquities, found their way

into Sloane's ever-expanding collection. As with the
national museum his collection would found, Sloane's
assemblage grew in size as it grew in reputation. Eventu-
ally, others perceived Sloane's home as a desirable repository for various manuscripts and specimens of
scientific interest. These acquisitions expanded the
range of Sloane's collections to include coins and medals,
manuscripts, prints and drawings, and a host of miscella-
neous curiosities. To all of these items, Sloane brought a
cataloguing energy exceptional for its time, and he has
been described among his many accolades as ". . . a pio-
neer cataloguer who perceived the need to document his
collections in a systematic way."[31]

To understand Sloane's activities simply in terms of rational empiricism, however, is to miss the affective power
such a prodigious collection had on its visitors. Accounts
of early visitors to Sloane's private collections consistently deploy an aesthetic rhetoric of pleasure, wonder,
and pride, a rhetoric that would be adapted to nationalist
ends upon the founding of the British Museum. In 1710,
the German Zacharias von Uffenbach recorded his visit to
Sloane's collection and seems more impressed with its
size and variety than with its attestation to divine wisdom. "Not only is a large quantity here," von Uffenbach
writes, "but they are for the most part extraordinarily curious and valuable things." Curiosity and value are the
twin standards by which von Uffenbach lavishes praise
upon Sloane's collections, referring to the "great quantity" and "prodigious variety" of Sloane's "handsome collection," and noting "that the Venetian Ambassador had
offered him fifteen thousand pounds sterling for this collection." Repeating a common complaint, von Uffenbach
laments, "we were very sorry that this large and wonderful collection had to be seen in such a comparatively
short time, but he has so very little leisure because of his
medical practice."[32] The wide variety of Sloane's ever-
expanding collection insured that most visitors would be
more taken with the expansiveness of the whole than with
any particular specimen or artifact. Accounts of the collection by the French traveler Sauveur Morand from 1729
or Linnaeus's pupil Per Kalm from 1748 do attempt to pro-

vide some catalogue of their brief experiences with Sloane's collection. Yet a sense of accumulative wonder, rather than taxonomic mastery, emerges from these accounts as the prolific enumeration of Sloane's specimens and curiosities defies any categorical coherency in favor of the glory of the whole. Gazing with equivalence upon anatomical specimens, medals, preserved animals, Egyptian antiquities, minerals, shells, ethnographic artifacts, and manuscripts, the writers of these accounts offer a vision of material plenitude that points less to the grammatical precision of the collection than to the divertissement and wonder its apprehension affords. Such affective descriptions easily slip into praise of the creator, understood less as a master designer and more as a sublime power, incomprehensible to the mind of man.

An account of a visit to Sloane's museum by the Prince and Princess of Wales in 1748 emphasizes the awe induced by the massive breadth and variety of the collection which "delighted the eye, and raised the mind to praise the great creator of all things." Portrayed alternately in this account as a sumptuous banquet and a "noble vista," the collection surpasses any coherent or categorical description ("Fifty volumes in folio would scarcely suffice to contain a detail of this immense museum, consisting of above 200,000 articles") adding, not subtracting, from the instructive power of the collection. In the description's conclusion, the wonder of the collection is converted into the honor of the nation through royal appreciation:

Their *royal highnesses* were not wanting in expressing their satisfaction and pleasure at seeing a collection, which surpasses all the notions or ideas they had formed from even the most favourable accounts of it. The Prince on this occasion shew'd his great reading and most happy memory; for in such a multiplicity, such a variety of the productions of nature and art; upon any thing being shewn him he had not seen before, he was ready in recollecting where he had read of it; and upon viewing the ancient and modern *medals*, he made so many judicious remarks, that he appear'd to be a perfect master of *history* and *chronology*; he express'd the great pleasure it gave him to see so magnificent a collection in *England*, esteeming it an ornament to the nation; and expressed his sentiments how much it must conduce to the benefit of learning, and how great an honour will redound to *Britain*, to have it established for publick use to the latest posterity.[33]

The auspices of the royal family convert wonder and pleasure into honor and pride for the nation. The prince's sentiments regarding public access look forward to the foundation of the British Museum yet already give indication of the conceptual challenges made manifest after the collection's public opening. While the public might hope for equal access to Sloane's collections, they could by no means expect to rise uniformly to the Prince's "great reading and most happy memory." Conceiving of the collection as both an ornament and an honor, the Prince joins pleasure and virtue in a tribute to both divine providence and national glory.

The ultimate fusion of Sloane's collection with the Cottonian Library, the Harleian Manuscripts, and the Old Royal Library and their collective removal to Montagu House in Bloomsbury did not contradict provisions made in Sloane's Will and Codicils. To a certain degree, the tenor of the parliamentary act that founded the British Museum maintained his emphasis on preservation and public access, approving of its relocation "if such removal shall be judged most advantageous to the public, so as the said collection be preserved entire without the least diminution or separation, and be kept for the use and benefit of the public, with free access to view and peruse the same."[34] Yet Sloane's conception of the collection's signification of divine providence and wisdom is markedly absent. It is replaced with a recognition of the interconnection of "all arts and sciences," and a conception of the museum as "not only for the inspection and entertainment of the learned and the curious, but for the general use and benefit of the public." The interconnection between the arts and sciences no longer establishes a divine plan manifesting itself in its creation, but becomes the foundation of the advancement, improvement, and entertainment of all members of the public body, learned and curious alike.

Once the category of the nation serves to compose the idea of the museum as a functional institution, then the implications for formal composition are complex. A decade after the museum opened its doors, *A Description of Middlesex* from 1769, echoing the Prince of Wales's sentiments, noted of Montagu House that "the building is finely ornamented with paintings, and the disposition, in which this noble collection is arranged, is so orderly and well designed, that the British Museum may be justly esteemed an honor and ornament to this nation."[35] Ornamentation, disposition, arrangement, and design convey a sense of national honor, a representation of national identity. In line with Walpole's public aspirations for "a new era of *virtu*," the description joins aesthetic pleasure with social nobility. In both aesthetic theory and curatorial practice, however, pleasure was not so easily contained, nor did it necessarily lead towards such moral or even patriotic ends. Writing in a letter of her privileged visit to Montagu House during its conversion towards its new identity as the British Museum, Catherine Talbot delights in the visual wonder of the scene before her: "I was delighted to see Science in this Town so Magnificently & Elegantly Lodged; perhaps you have seen that fine House & Pleasant garden: I never did before, but thought I liked it much better now, inhabited by Valuable Manuscripts, Silent Pictures, & Ancient Mummies, than I should have done when it was filled with Miserable Fine People, absent of gayety on the inside, & a place of [] without." Her social barbs contrast the frigid decorum of aristocratic society with the magnificence and elegance of the newly nationalized collections. The pleasure of the viewing experiences leads her thoughts not towards public *virtu*, but towards political agitation: "Indeed in another Reverie I looked upon the Books in a different view, & consider'd them (some persons in whose hands I saw them suggested the thought) as a Storehouse of Arms open to every Rebel Hand, a Shelf of Sweetmeats mixed with Poison, set in the reach of tall overgrown Children."[36] Ornamentation and honor are by no means naturally aligned. In Talbot's good-natured satire, pleasure easily leads to sedition, destabilizing social propriety and national unity through its seductive charms. As aesthetic theory becomes exhibitionary practice, its potential for populist liberty is as realized as its potential for hierarchical control.

III

In 1755, a letter appeared in the *Weekly Advertiser and Inspector* for December 6–13, promoting the British Museum as an institute for the advancement and dissemination of biological knowledge. Though praising Britain's position in the forefront of scientific inquiry, the writer critiques the seductive charms of Linnaean classifications and cautions that

> in the Thirst of Improvement, let us be careful we do not overrun Discretion. The Love of Novelty extends itself even into these serious Studies; and if we cast our Eyes upon the Face of Science throughout Europe, we shall have the Mortification to see, that Philosophers, tho' wise Men, are but Men; and that what the Poet limited to the weaker Part, might be extended to the Whole of our Species; for 'tis not Fools alone, who in avoiding one faulty Extream, run into its contrary.[37]

Revealing a simultaneously scientific, aesthetic, and sexual anxiety, the writer seeks to guard the noble practices of the national institution against the feminine seductions of mere novelty. Such seductions, when multiplied, threaten to overwhelm the judgment of the philosophical viewer. Heightening the pitch of his warning, the writer goes on to speak of "the Terror that arises to the Student from the Number of Plants" and cautions that "the great Care will then be, that in establishing a Method, we do not, in avoiding the Quick Sands of antient Ignorance, overwhelm ourselves in the Whirlpools of modern Distinction." The writer constructs biological knowledge as the building up of distinction where before was mere chaos; but the sheer abundance of distinction produces abject terror if untempered by the controlling mediations of uniformity and relation. Guarding against both a sublime "terror" and a novel "thirst," the exhibition of specimens must achieve a tempered balance of ordered distinction.

These cautions were not entirely unwarranted and might have extended well beyond the early museum's biological specimens, for the records confirm Walpole's vision for the British Museum as a central repository for private collections. In 1756 alone, three years before the museum even opened its doors, they show the donations of

An Aegyptian mummy in its sycamore coffin . . . A bird of Paradise, and a small bird's nest in a glass case . . . The Bible in 11 Volumes elegantly bound in Turkey leather . . . The skin of a large Surinam serpent . . . Various plants for the garden . . . Tiles taken from Roman baths at Bath . . . A large hunting piece painted in oil . . . Copies of two original letters from the Duke of Buckingham to King James I. . . . Designs of Chinese buildings . . . The horn of a rhinoceros . . . An Indian idol from Jamaica . . . Two teeth of the sperma ceti whale . . . and Medical Observations and Inquiries in the name of a Society of Physicians in London.[38]

The many writers who dubbed the institution a "noble cabinet" or "grand repository" surely were not mistaken; for the early British Museum far more resembles the curiosity cabinets of the previous centuries than the modern museums of the nineteenth and twentieth. In description after description of the early museum, variety and novelty seem the guiding principles. After all, this was an institution whose three departments were simply labeled Coins and Medals, Books and Manuscripts, and Natural and Artificial Productions. Clearly, as the correspondent in the *Weekly Advertiser and Inspector* warned, some discretion was called for.

How was such a collection to found "a new era of *virtu*"? In principle, there was nothing wrong with such various holdings. Aesthetic theorists had long recognized the importance of variety in gratifying an imaginative spectator. Addison had, perhaps, put it most succinctly when he noted that "every thing that is new or uncommon raises a Pleasure in the Imagination, because it fills the Soul with an agreeable Surprise, gratifies its Curiosity, and gives it an Idea of which it was not before possest. . . . It is this that recommends Variety, where the Mind is every Instant called off to something new, and the Attention not suffered to dwell too long, and waste it self on any particular Object."[39] Hogarth had placed Variety at the center of his *Analysis of Beauty* (1753), illustrating the concept on its title page with the image of a snake curved inside a regular pyramid and Milton's description of Eve's specular seduction: "So vary'd he, and of his tortuous train / Curl'd many a wanton wreath, in sight of Eve / To lure her eye."[40] Even Addison and Hogarth, however, recognized the need to contain the curiosity provoked by such novelty within the higher aesthetic experience of beauty. For Addison, beauty "in the several Products of Art and Nature" consists "either in the Gaiety or Variety of Colours, in the Symmetry and Proportion of Parts, in the Arrangement and Disposition of Bodies, or in a just Mixture and Concurrence of all together."[41] And despite his delight in the seductions of variety, Hogarth praises chiefly "composed variety; for variety uncomposed, and without design, is confusion and deformity."[42]

Uniformity in variety, *discordia concors*, was the hallmark of the aesthetic philosophy of moral-sense rationalism. Francis Hutcheson makes the principle a centerpiece of his *Inquiry into the Original of Our Ideas of Beauty and Virtue* (1725) holding, in his first treatise on "Beauty, Order, Harmony, and Design," that while "there are many Conceptions of Objects that are agreeable upon other accounts, such as Grandeur, Novelty, Sanctity, and some others . . . what we call Beautiful in Objects, to speak in the Mathematical Style, seems to be in a compound Ratio of Uniformity and Variety."[43] This conception of beauty allows Hutcheson, in considering the natural world, to counter the terror of excessive distinction with harmonious relation:

If we descend to the minuter Works of Nature, what great Uniformity among all the Species of Plants and Vegetables in the manner of their Growth and Propagation! How near the Resemblance among all the Plants of the same Species, whose Numbers surpass our Imagination! And this Uniformity is not only observable in the Form in gross; (nay, in this it is not so

very exact in all Instances) but in the Structure of their min-
utest Parts, which no Eye unassisted with Glasses can discern. In the almost infinite Multitude of Leaves, Fruit, Seed,
Flowers of any one Species, we often see a very great Uniformity in the Structure and Situation of the smallest Fibres.
This is the Beauty which charms an ingenious Botanist. (22)

Hutcheson formulates these aesthetic principles in the
world of botanical science, but he extends his formula-
tions to the animal kingdom as well as to the arts, geome-
try, and scientific theorems. "The Beauty of Theorems,"
he holds, surpasses all others in having the most "amazing Variety with Uniformity: and hence arises a very great
Pleasure distinct from Prospects of any farther Advantage" (30). Hutcheson recruits this concept of beauty to
temper the multitude of scientific distinction with an underlying vision of harmonious order:

That we may the better discern this Agreement, or Unity of
an Infinity of Objects, in the general Theorem, to be the Foundation of the Beauty or Pleasure attending their Discovery,
let us compare our Satisfaction in such Discoveries, with the
uneasy State of Mind when we can only measure Lines, or
Surfaces, by a Scale, or are making Experiments which we
can reduce to no general Canon, but are only heaping up a
Multitude of particular incoherent Observations. Now each
of these Trails discovers a new Truth, but with no Pleasure
or Beauty, notwithstanding the Variety, till we can discover
some sort of Unity, or reduce them to some general Canon.
(31)

Hutcheson's conceptions of Beauty, Order, Harmony, and
Design temper the terror arising from the excess and multitude of distinction and variety with the pleasurable vision of beautiful order. In line with his broader equation
of beauty and virtue, the vision of unchecked variety,
however potentially productive of truth and beauty, may
also produce a vision of deformity and incoherence.

Adam Smith had likewise made botanical investigation
the test case for the evaluation of wonder as a motivating
experience of aesthetic and philosophical inquiry. In his
Essays on philosophical subjects (written c. 1758; published

1795), he meditated on the dynamic relation between the effects of novelty and the establishment of categorical coherency:

> With what curious attention does a naturalist examine a singular plant, or a singular fossil, that is presented to him? He is at no loss to refer it to the general genus of plants or fossils; but this does not satisfy him, and when he considers all the different tribes or species of either with which he has hitherto been acquainted, they all, he thinks, refuse to admit the new object among them. It stands alone in his imagination, and as it were detached from all the other species of that genus to which it belongs. . . . But to some class or other of known objects he must refer it, and betwixt it and them he must find out some resemblance or other, before he can get rid of that Wonder, that uncertainty and anxious curiosity excited by its singular appearance, and by its dissimilitude with all the objects he had hitherto observed.[44]

Smith's rhetoric of desire and gratification is of a piece with his aesthetic rendering of imaginative knowledge. Wonder is experienced as agitation, and must, therefore, inevitably lead towards the repose of categorical positioning. Hence, the proliferation of distinction loses efficacy as amelioration to the anxious spectacle of novelty, requiring the counterbalance of relation to soothe the agitated mind. Yet "Wonder," Smith insists, "and not any expectation of advantage from its discoveries, is the first principle which prompts mankind to the study of philosophy, of that science which pretends to lay open the concealed connections that unite the various appearances of nature; and they pursue this study for its own sake, as an original pleasure or good in itself, without regarding its tendency to procure them the means of many other pleasures."[45] Curiosity for its own sake thus holds a highly ambivalent status in the discourse of the aesthetic, for though it must be perpetually generated by novelty and variety, it must lead towards a higher knowledge of system and relation for its ultimate justification. Otherwise, it either degenerates into mere pleasure and divertissement, or perpetuates itself into an infinite spiral of division and agitation.

Indeed, the characterization by the letter writer in the *Weekly Advertiser and Inspector* of the abundance of novel distinctions as productive of "terror" allows us to recognize the affiliation of seductive novelty to the sublime. Edmund Burke had also denigrated mere variety as infantile while simultaneously recognizing that "some degree of novelty must be one of the materials in every instrument which works upon the mind."[46] He had likewise located the sublime in the infinity of biological distinction as well as in the magnitude and obscurity of dimension:

> when we attend to the infinite divisibility of matter, when we peruse animal life into these excessively small, and yet organized beings, that escape the nicest inquisition of the sense, when we push our discoveries yet downward, and consider those creatures so many degrees yet smaller, and the still diminishing scale of existence, in tracing which the imagination is lost as well as the sense, we become amazed and confounded at the wonders of minuteness; nor can we distinguish in its effect this extreme of littleness from the vast itself. For division must be infinite as well as addition; because the idea of a perfect unity can no more be arrived at, than that of a compleat whole to which nothing may be added.[47]

Such a definition of the sublime is essentially a proliferation of novelty, an affinity that was remarked upon by many theorists of the aesthetic. As Ronald Paulson has noted, for Addison "the Great is only an expansive version of the Novel."[48] "We are flung into a pleasing Astonishment at such unbounded Views," Addison says of vast prospects, "and feel a delightful Stillness and Amazement in the Soul at the Apprehension of them . . . the Pleasure still grows upon us, as it arises from more than a single Principle."[49] In his 1716 essay on epic poetry, Richard Blakemore had praised the wondrous power of uncommon objects and declared that "novelty . . . is the parent of admiration,"[50] and Joseph Priestley had opened his lecture on the sublime later in the century by declaring that "great objects please us for the same reason that *new* objects do, viz. by the exercise they give to our faculties."[51] Whether perceived as abject terror or magnanimous exaltation, the experience of the sublime was frequently associated with the agitation of novelty and wonder. Either experience would seem both to promote and to undermine the philosophical goal of unification and composition, for though the imagination might be agitated by infinite variety, it must find composure in an ever-elusive vision of beautiful harmony. If a "perfect unity" is an impossible goal in such a divided multitude as composed the holdings of the British Museum, exhibitionary plans must capitalize on the sublime power of such insatiable novelty all the while tempering it through recourse to intermediate categories and relations.

Various exhibitionary plans submitted and suggested to the early trustees sought to do just this, to both emphasize and temper the diversity of the museum's collections through recourse to strategies of harmonious variety and ordered composition. A plan submitted by Under-Librarian James Empson in 1756 observed that "how much soever a private Person may be at Liberty arbitrarily to dispose & place his Curiosities; we are sensible that the British Museum, being a public Institution subject to the Visits of the Judicious & Intelligent, as well as Curious, notice will be taken, whether or not the Collection has been arranged in a methodical manner."[52] Recognizing both the liberties of the museum's potential benefactors and the disparate composition of the museum's intended public, Empson seeks a course "most simple & most natural," attempting to find a common ground of observation for the exhibitionary experience. While grounding his plans in the "methodical manner" of categorical divisions, he nonetheless privileges aesthetic pleasure as their primary goal. He states his rationale for the arrangement of Natural Productions as follows:

> We intend, according to the Nature and Characteristick of each of these Matters, to subdivide them & in disposing of each Subdivision, to take particular Care, that those matters may be brought nearest the sight, as are most pleasing to the Eye and of most consideration; placing the Rest, in proportion as they are less so, higher & higher on the Shelves above

them and those that are still inferiour, in the Drawers under each Subdivision. We conceive, that such a Disposition will afford great Ease to the Spectator and be no less convenient to the Officer in Shewing them.[53]

In Empson's plan, categorical divisions highlight the variety of the collections, emphasizing such variety as the key principle of aesthetic pleasure. He notes that "the Vegetables, though of equal Value and full as interesting will not, by themselves, make an appearance sufficiently pleasing to the Eye" and therefore proposes "to add to them Part of what belongs to the animal kingdom." The aesthetic principles informing such combinations become explicit in his discussion of the arrangement of fossils: "If the apartment just before mention'd on account of a great variety of pleasing objects, will make a beautiful appearance, as it really will; this last one will be yet more so, as a still greater variety will be contained in it, and as the far superior number of agreeable objects will more strongly attract the Eye of the Spectator."[54] Seeking to both attract and guide "the Eye of the Spectator," Empson's plan finds a balance between novelty and beauty, variety and order. His proposed exhibition fuses didactic and aesthetic arrangement, equating the contemplation of order and harmonious variety with an affective perception of the beautiful. Akin to Akenside's aesthetic reverie, this plan will dress knowledge "in ten thousand hues / . . . to attract, With charms responsive to each gazer's eye, / The hearts of men" (1.551–54). Unifying both the variety of the collections and the diversity of the viewing public, such a beautiful composition produces an affective pleasure capable of uniting erudition and curiosity in the "Eye of the Spectator."

In an alternative plan presented to the trustees in the following year, Empson conceives of the exhibitions in more explicitly didactic terms, yet maintains a predisposition for the production of aesthetic pleasure. Dividing the sub-department of Natural Productions into "the three general divisions of Fossils, Vegetables, & Animals," Empson opines that "Of these the Fossils are the most simple; & therefore may properly be disposed in the first rank: next to them the vegetables; & lastly the animal substances. By this arrangement the Spectator will be gradually conducted from the simplest to the most compound & most perfect of Nature's Productions."[55] The visual ordering of classifications will in this plan emphasize not variety and distinction, but relation and comprehension, yet the difference in the two reports lies more in their emphases than in their objectives. Both seek a composition that stresses uniformity in variety. Empson reasons in the latter report that "since there is found in Nature a gradual & almost insensible transition from one kind of natural production to another, I would endeavour both in the general & particular arrangement to exemplifie those gradual transitions as much as possible."[56] If the variety of the holdings might agitate the imagination of the spectator, their exhibitionary composition may soothe his faculties and produce a pleasurable vision of harmonious variety. As Adam Smith had reasoned,

> When objects succeed each other in the same train in which the ideas of the imagination have thus been accustomed to move . . . such objects appear all closely connected with one another, and the thought glides easily along them, without effort and without interruption. . . . The ideas excited by so coherent a chain of things seem, as it were, to float through the mind of their own accord, without obliging it to exert itself, or to make any effort in order to pass from one of them to another.[57]

Burke had argued similarly that it was precisely this form of composition which might soothe and quiet the disposition of a spectator: "nothing long continued in the same manner, nothing very suddenly varied can be beautiful; because both are opposite to that agreeable relaxation, which is the characteristic effect of beauty."[58] The ideal museum experience imparts the truths of scientific categories through the aesthetic pleasure and relaxation attendant upon a beautiful exhibition. While both the novelty of the various holdings and the grandeur of the collections as a whole inspire and excite the interest of the spectator, the beauty of their composition provides pleasure and gratification and cultivates the *virtu* of learned observation. Aesthetic pleasure would seem to allow all visitors, "the Judicious & Intelligent, as well as Curious" to find common ground as spectators in the national museum.

IV

Despite the aspirations of such exhibitionary plans for a pleasing and instructive visual experience, their dependency upon a unified "Eye of the Spectator" for cognitive and aesthetic comprehension introduces a site of profound anxiety for representational cohesion in the public and national museum. In 1755, the same year in which the author of the letter in the *Weekly Advertiser and Inspector* warned of the "Terror" of the multitude of biological specimens and the subsequent need to steer a narrow course between ignorance and excessive distinction, Dr. John Ward presented to the trustees his "Objections to the appointing Public days for admitting all Persons to see the Museum without distinction."[59] Arguing that "General liberty allowed to ordinary people of all ranks or denominations is not to be kept within bounds," Ward spoke for a significant number of trustees and members of Parliament concerned about what John Fuller, speaking in the House of Commons fifty years later, would refer to as "promiscuous access" to the national institution.[60] "The day must be published in the newspapers," Ward reasons, "& will be considered by ordinary people as an holiday, no persons of superiour degree will care to come on such days, so that this low Class with the lowest of all, 'the Mobb,' will make the Museum that day a place of diversion." Ward concludes his dire predictions with a vision of the complete degradation of the noble institution:

> If the common people once taste of this liberty, & it should be attended with inconvenience or even mischief, it will be very difficult afterwards to deprive them of it; it will therefore be better never to let them have any admittance at all, & admit

only such who in all probability, will conform to the rules &
orders which may be prescrib'd for the purpose, a great con-
course of ordinary people will never be kept in order, they
will make the apartments as dirty as the Street, impair &
spoil the furniture, make a havock of the Gardens, & put the
whole Oeconomy of the Museum into disorder.[61]

Reactionary rhetoric to be sure: but we must note that
Ward's argument reproduces the fraught balance between novelty and beauty in the exhibitionary experience in a tension between liberty and economy among the
viewing public. Such liberty presents a dual threat of su-
perficiality (transforming the museum into a place of
mere "diversion") and confusion (disrupting the whole
"oeconomy" of the museum); in aesthetic terms, the degeneracy of mere novelty and the abject terror of sublime
disorder. The configuration of the national museum as
"an honor and ornament" to the nation it serves depends
upon an orderly "oeconomy"; an "oeconomy" based in
distinction both amidst the objects on display and among
the subjects viewing them. While aesthetic theorists
could reconcile these various orders of experience, for
Ward the commingling of desire and edification threatens
to disrupt the entire exhibitionary project.

Ward's denigration of novelty and terror at the prospect
of access without distinction reveal the limitations of
Walpole's hopes for a reconstitution of polite collections
in the *virtu* of a national institution. The aesthetic fusion
of virtue and curiosity that attempted to bring together
"the Judicious & Intelligent, as well as Curious" just as
frequently provided yet another means of distinguishing
among the social classes in the national museum. The
French writer Pierre Jean Grosely, in speaking of Montagu House itself, could note in 1772 that "the Museum, independent of what it contains, is of itself capable of
exciting the curiosity of strangers,"[62] yet it was precisely
this curiosity that was often used to distinguish between
the learned and the idle, between the scholar and the
tourist.

Such distinctions continued well into the nineteenth
century. A listing of sights and institutions in London
from 1823 remarks that

For the admission of companies to a sight of the Museum (a popular, though far less useful application of the institution) various regulations have, from time to time, been formed, every successive alteration having had for its object to add to the facility of access, and in every respect to the accommodation of the public. . . . In general, every practicable facility is afforded that may render this institution really useful to science and the arts, for which it is chiefly intended, as well as gratifying to the curiosity of the multitude, who incessantly resort to it in quest of amusement.[63]

It is precisely this "curiosity of the multitude" which is simultaneously a boon and a threat to proper representation in the national museum. Aesthetics of containment and order depends upon pleasure and beauty as affective means of conveying proper distinction, scientific or social, but the curiosity grounding such aesthetics is not so easily contained. "Curiosity almost universally prevails," writes Edmund Powlett in the preface to his *General Contents*, but the common attribution of universality to such properties as curiosity makes the containment of such categories as the nation, the public, and the museum ultimately impossible, both materially and discursively.

Echoing Ward's fears of the breakdown of proper distinction, a trustee report of May 18, 1801 announces itself as "A draught of some arguments against admitting all persons gratis who apply for permission to see the British Museum."[64] The report addresses the problem faced by officers when confronted by the lower classes "claiming a right . . . to an equal participation of his attentions, with those of the highest rank or of the deepest erudition." The mixing of "persons of low education, who visit the collection from mere motives of idle curiosity . . . with those who have prepared themselves by reading to receive usefull information" derives from an erroneous confusion concerning the role of the national museum:

This perfect equality in the rights of those who chuse to visit the Museum, is said to have originated in an opinion, that being purchasd with the money of the people, those who have paid for it, are intitled to the free use of it, but this idea (which will not in any case stand the test of argument) is quite unfounded in that of the British Museum.[65]

The report reasons that while the British Museum, like the Royal Academy, was established for the advancement of knowledge for the overall benefit of the nation, such a pursuit can only succeed through maintaining the museum as a private resource for an educated elite. It argues for the levying of an admissions fee to simultaneously raise funds for the functions of the museum and to discourage the less educated classes from interfering in these pursuits. The uneducated resort to the museum merely "to satisfy a fruitless curiosity, from the gratification of which, neither they nor the Public can ever hope to derive the least portion of permanent advantage."[66]

The abstraction of "the Public" from the common masses and their "fruitless curiosity" rhetorically correlates with the representational logic of the argument. The economy of the national museum signifies mimetically the national body it both honors and serves. The maintenance of distinction, both within the walls of the museum and between the interior and exterior of the institution, constitutes the museum as a space of social practice separate from, *and thereby representative of*, the larger category of the nation. Just as the museum will best serve the Public by maintaining its separation from the people, so too will it best represent the nation as mental construct by maintaining its separation from the nation as social practice. The national museum is safely contained in an economy of regulated and orderly exhibition as a necessary prerequisite for the production of visions of harmonious variety.

Nowhere are these social and aesthetic tensions more dramatically negotiated than in the nascent genre of the museum tour. Seeking both to encourage and to contain the excitement of novelty and the wonder of grandeur within the pleasures of beauty, early guidebooks to the museum staked out an important rhetorical position as both companion and guide, mediating between the arrangement of the exhibitions and the desires of the spectators. The original *View of the British Museum* (1760) seeks to gratify the public with an account "of very great use to the judicious and curious, giving a general notion of the whole, and a better insight into the nature of things." It therefore aspires to "serve as a director in viewing the collections; as a memorandum to recollect it afterwards; and . . . [to] give great instruction to those that have not the opportunity of seeing it."[67] As verbal supplements, these guidebooks aggressively supplant not only the material exhibition of natural and artificial productions, but also the unformed desires of the viewing public, offering rhetoric of simultaneous seduction and constraint. Edmund Powlett, in the introduction to his *General Contents of the British Museum: With Remarks. Serving as a Directory in Viewing that Noble Cabinet* (1761), proclaims a public debt to George II, Sir Hans Sloane, and the British Parliament for this "lasting Monument of Glory to the Nation."[68] He echoes Horace Walpole's aspirations in his hopes "that the time may soon come, when every public-spirited Collector of rare Medals, Minerals, Animals, Plants, Insects, or Stones, and, in fine, of every thing that either Nature or Art produces worthy the Observation of the Curious, will deposit the Produce of his Labour in this most valuable Cabinet" (vi). Powlett figures the museum as the culminating feat of the progress of learning. "Nothing," he claims, "can conduce more to preserve the Learning which this latter Age abounds with, than having Repositories in every Nation to contain its Antiquities, such as is the Museum of Britain" (vii).

Powlett's self-congratulatory aspirations echo the general tone of the promotions surrounding the early British Museum, but his guidebook also reflects the anxieties surrounding the actual experience of the museum that motivate the need for a guide in the first place. Repeating the supplementary logic of the *View of the British Museum* from the year before, Powlett both engages and deflects the curiosity of his audience. Reproducing the traditionally gendered relation of novelty and order, Powlett conceives "that my Readers among the Ladies will be very numerous, many of them having, in my Company, lamented the Want of something of this Kind, to direct their Observations, and give them a general Idea of the Contents of this Collection" (xii). He frequently takes pains to guide the ladies' attention to the beauties of the British Museum that their intemperate love of novelty might have overlooked. Such a role seems potentially questionable, as Powlett immediately defends "the Uprightness of my Intentions, meaning only to oblige the Public" (1). The actual contents of both of these early guides offer little more than paratactic enumeration of the various specimens and artifacts on display as well as the varied frescoes and portraits on the gallery walls, thereby recreating in print the leveling randomness of the exhibitions. Although Powlett offers much more detail than his predecessor, his guide offers little apparent discrimination by which the viewer might arrange, or reflect upon, the museum's contents and the reading experience produces more enervation than mastery.

Subsequent guidebooks from the 1760s, however, drew upon other generic protocols in mediating the museum experience, experimenting with dramatic staging and epistolary meditation as affective means of negotiating between desire and edification. Powlett's rhetorical fusion of masculine didactic virtue and feminine aesthetic curiosity finds a more comically exaggerated manifestation in the Reverend Warden Butler's "A Pleasing Recollection, or A Walk Through the British Museum" (1767). This unpublished drama introduces a host of young ladies and their matron as a pair of alternatively flirtatious and instructive male guides leads them through the museum. Upon viewing a group of shells, the instructive Dr. Gifford[69] informs the young women that

> these shells are the Cochloa or Screw Shaped: You observe they wind in the Mannerosa Staircase. This white Shell under my Finger is esteemed the most beautiful and curious of the whole Series. This distinct Curve into Seven Intervals, and the transverse addition of that thin Braid, which as it were connects the Curls together from the aperture as the point render it a very singular phenomenon.

To which the ladies respond collectively:

Very pretty!	Extremely fine!
Excessively curious!	Wonderfully disposed!
Amazingly elegant!	Strikingly beautiful, indeed![70]

Powlett had also conceived that the collection of shells would "particularly attract the Attention of the Ladies,"[71] but similar exchanges between male science and female aesthetics appear throughout Butler's play, often leading to rhapsodies about the wisdom of the creator. While we can dismiss such exchanges as bad drama, they manifest more a difference in degree than one in kind from Powlett's fraught promotion of the national museum. In both works, the aesthetic desire of the female visitors is encouraged and contained by the masculine guide. Like the more sober exhibitionary plans considered by the museum's trustees, the truths of science are manifested in the arrangement of the exhibitions, but realized in the aesthetic pleasure of the "Eye of the Spectator."

Such dramatic negotiations between liberty and restraint could be displayed just as effectively through epistolary meditation. Alexander Thomson, in his *Letters on the British Museum* (1767), offers his tour as a sequence of letters to a gentleman obliged to leave London without having seen the British Museum. Thomson thus plays two roles simultaneously, writing as both a curious spectator and a reflective guide. Thomson's truly supplementary letters vacillate from description to reverie and offer a curious juxtaposition of novelty and grandeur. He hopes his epistolary meditations on "antiquities, natural curiosities, and animals" will offer at least "the smallest amusement" even as he praises "the stately edifice in which that noble collection of rarities is deposited."[72] Mirroring his own vacillation between pleasure and order, Thomson notes, "the whole economy of the Museum is conducted by the best regulations; which indeed are necessary to preserve order, where the public curiosity is so much concerned" (4). If the economy of the museum requires regulation, the guidebook itself may serve as the ideal enforcer, mediating between observation and reflection in the production of aesthetic pleasure. Nonetheless, Thomson himself admits to "being . . . more inquisitive after such objects as amuse the eye, than those that gratify the understanding" (36) and confesses at one point to "a rambling curiosity, more than any philosophical motive" (38). His letters, more whimsical than informative, support this confession. He offers panegyrics to Cleopatra, wondered descriptions of the fossils and shells, and transcriptions of pastoral poetry. He is just as capable of falling into melancholic meditations over the fate of empires and the vanity of human aspirations as he beholds the ruins of Egypt and the manuscript records of English history and literature. Aesthetic desire and rational improvement, visual seduction and verbal reflection, novelty and beauty, play out a complex drama in these early guidebooks as they describe a sequence of natural and cultural objects and prescribe the means for their national appreciation.

V

Early guides to the British Museum display a dramatic tension between inclusion and distinction, a tension expressed in terms both aesthetic and social. Despite the anxieties they reveal regarding the diversity of the public and the abundance of objects gathered under the twin rubrics of the British Museum, these guides are essentially promotional, eager to accommodate both virtue and curiosity. Yet, in the face of such diverse immensity, both in the collections and in the public gathered to view them, many observers reacted not with delight but with horror, viewing the museum as a microcosm of the nation itself and not appreciating what they saw. In his *Travels in England, Scotland, and the Hebrides* (1799), the French traveler Faujaus Saint Fond reacts strongly against what Hogarth characterizes as the "confusion and deformity" attendant upon "variety uncomposed"[73] or what Burke terms the sublime resultant from obscurity. Burke claims, "the mind is hurried out of itself, by a croud of great and confused images; which affect because they are crouded and confused."[74] Saint Fond desires no such mental agitation in contemplating a national museum. Finding the museum's organization lacking in any degree of sufficient system or method, he states, "nothing is in order, every thing is out of its place; and this assemblage appears rather an immense magazine, in which things have been thrown at random, than a scientific collection, destined to instruct and honor a great nation."[75] Saint Fond views a beautiful union of order and distinction as the proper means by which both to memorialize and to found a proper representation of the nation.

In Saint Fond's view, the central cause of the disorder in the British Museum stems from its effacement of its individual founders through the fusion of their collections: "But I am not pleased that the collection of a private individual, to which there has been since added a crowd of heterogeneous objects, calculated rather to distract, than to command the attention, should possess the title of The British Museum" (1:63). Unwilling to group the "crowd of heterogeneous objects" under the national category, Saint Fond's perception of disorder alerts us to the correlation between his categories of cognitive understanding and his particular conception of the nation itself:

> A nation, respectable from the highly perfect state of her commerce and manufactures, and the importance of her navy, the results of a multitude of difficult combinations and profound knowledge, ought to have monuments worthy of herself, and more analogous to the grandeur and stateliness of her character. (1:63)

Saint Fond's characterization of the nation corresponds to his conception of a well-ordered museum: clarity of distinction that allows for a comprehension of the whole. Holding that a nation is only as great as the sum of her parts, Saint Fond notes "that England has reaped more real glory and distinction from the uncommon geniuses which she has produced, than from her conquests in both the Indies, her fleets, her battles, or her eternal parliamentary discussions" (1:63–64). Saint Fond views the lack of order in the museum, resultant from the attempt to fuse the accomplishments of individual geniuses into a categorical whole, as a hindrance to the arts and sciences. No artist, painter, or physician will resort to the museum, as they will be helplessly frustrated in their pursuits by the lack of proper distinction:

> Neither will the philosopher, who loves to behold nature on a great scale, nor he who delights in studying the details of

that immense chain which seems to connect every species of being, and to unite its last link to the first, find any thing to interest them in the midst of such disorder. (1:65)

As with the display of natural specimens, whose composition both represents and enacts the idea of the Chain of Being, the collections of the British Museum must maintain an order based in distinction in order to mimetically represent the nation they purport to instruct and honor. For Saint Fond, the nation amounts to no more and no less than the sum of its parts, understood and arranged through proper distinction.

But Saint Fond's preface to his travelogue alerts us to another source of his concern. "The following Tour was prepared for the press in the second year of the revolution," we are told, "but the troubles of that period rendered it necessary to delay its publication. The laws have, however, at length, resumed their empire, and the sciences will soon follow in their train." Saint Fond then adds that

> [t]hese painful recollections [of the revolution] have given to some of the notes that have been added to this work a melancholy, or perhaps, a peevish tone, which the reader, it is hoped, will excuse.—The injuries done to myself I bury in oblivion, but the sufferings of others I have not been able to forget. (1:ii)

Saint Fond links the lack of proper representational order and distinction in the scientific collections with the breakdown of social order set in motion by the French Revolution. The anger and melancholy resulting from his experience of these social upheavals informs, among many observations, his assessment of the British Museum. The "Terror" against which Saint Fond reacts is not that of the multitude of distinction, but rather the breakdown of distinction itself that he has so recently witnessed in France.

We may take Saint Fond at his word and attribute his mimetic analogy as overly melancholy and peevish, but his cognitive leap from a disorderly collection to a disorderly nation participates in a broader discourse of discrimination surrounding the British Museum. In surveys of the pageantry of London street life, the British Museum often appears as a microcosm of the aesthetic and ideological confusion exhibited within the metropolis. Matthew Bramble, Tobias Smollett's melancholic alter ego in *The Expedition of Humphry Clinker* (1771), provides the first literary account of the British Museum.[76] True to most early views of the institution, he notes peevishly that while the museum might be considered "noble" and "stupendous" as the product of "a private man, a physician, who was obliged to make his own fortune at the same time," as a public institution it is sorely lacking:

> great as the collection is, it would appear more striking if it was arranged in one spacious saloon, instead of being divided into different apartments, which it does not entirely fill—I could wish the series of medals was connected, and the whole of the animal, vegetable, and mineral kingdoms completed, by adding to each, at the public expense, those articles that are wanting.[77]

Bramble offers analogous suggestions for the library, desiring a more coherent and comprehensive system of catalogue and an addition of professors in the major fields of practical knowledge "who should give regular lectures on these subjects." Bramble's hopes for such plans are slight, because he views the condition of the museum as a synecdoche for the larger nation whose practices he finds severely wanting:

> But this is all idle speculation, which will never be reduced to practice—Considering the temper of the times, it is a wonder to see any institution whatsoever established, for the benefit of the public. The spirit of party is risen to a kind of phrenzy, unknown to former ages, or rather degenerated to a total extinction of honesty and candour. . . . (96)

Bramble links the dispersal of the collections and the lack of comprehensive knowledge in the British Museum to the fragmented condition of the social body. These passages on the British Museum occupy a central position in a series of melancholic letters from Bramble to his doctor

that represent the entire spectacle of London as a symbol
of a degenerate society. "The capital is become an overgrown monster," he bemoans, "which, like a dropsical
head, will in time leave the body and extremities without
nourishment and support" (82–83). Luxury and corruption
are evidenced everywhere, leading to a complete breakdown of social order: "there is no distinction or subordi-
nation left—The different departments of life are
jumbled together" (84). Sublime confusion reigns, and the
essence of this disorder is quickly identified: "The diver-
sions of the times are not ill suited to the genius of this
incongruous monster, called the *public*. Give it noise, confusion, glare, and glitter; it has no idea of elegance and
propriety" (84). Bramble's employment of the "public" as
both the goal of enlightened exhibition and the source of
degeneracy is of a piece with his ambivalent stance
towards the museum itself. He reserves his most caustic
remarks for the gardens and amusements at Ranelagh
and Vauxhall, which he equates with Bedlam for their absolute subversion of rational social order, and describes
in terms homologous with Saint Fond's depiction of the
British Museum. "It is an unnatural assembly of objects,"
he writes, "fantastically illuminated in broken masses;
seemingly contrived to dazzle the eyes and divert the
imagination of the vulgar" (84). Indeed, all of London's institutions provide grist for his melancholic mill. The lack
of comprehension and coherency he finds obtaining in
the British Museum is but a microcosm of the larger disorder he observes in the social body, where novelty and
diversion, rather than beauty and edification, rule the
day.[78]

A similar analogy between the museum and the social
body appears in *The Ambulator* of 1774, which offers itself
in its subtitle as *The Stranger's Companion in a Tour Round
London; Within the Circuit of Twenty-five Miles: Describing
Whatever is remarkable, either for Grandeur, Elegancy, Use,
or Curiosity; and comprehending Catalogues of the Pictures
by Eminent Artists. Collected by a Gentleman for his private
Amusement.* Noting that "of all the public structures that
engage the attention of the curious, the British Museum
is the greatest," the gentleman author observes that "this

foundation is altogether for the use of the public and the only one in London free for their reception, without any expense."[79] He nonetheless is quick to make a distinction between members of that public in direct relation to his conception of the museum's purpose:

> This is certainly one of the most valuable institutions for promoting literary knowledge in the universe, and the vast number of valuable manuscripts has already thrown great light on the history of England. But when we consider the vast number of idle people, who come to view the curiosities, and who by their ignorance can never relish their beauties, we cannot help applying to it the following words of the poet. (19)

The gentleman's figurative contrast between valuable manuscripts and idle people, between the relish of beauty and the vision of curiosity, is followed by the passage from Alexander Pope's "Epistle to the Earl of Burlington" mocking aristocratic dilettantes who collect without knowledge or appreciation, including a pointed reference to Sir Hans Sloane ("Old monkish manuscripts for Hearne alone, / And books for Mead, and rarities for Sloane"). The author expands further on his distinction between the educated and the idle:

> There are but few people, even in this age, who can relish all, or even any of the beauties of those curiosities in the British Museum. Idle girls, or, which is still worse, idle men and women, may go there and admire, for a few minutes, the colour of a snake, or the enormous jaws of a crocodile! but they will return neither wiser nor better; the image will soon be effaced from their minds their understandings being as much darkened as their memories are unretentive. (20)

The gentleman author argues that the admission of such idle persons is simply a waste of time as they are ill-equipped to "relish" what they view. What is particularly intriguing about this gentleman's dismissal of a vast number of the visitors to the British Museum is that he also argues for the need to replace the brick wall surrounding Montagu House with an iron fence to increase the public's interest: "Were it laid open to public view, with a fine

iron rail placed before it, many people might resort to see
its outside from motives of curiosity" (21). While the interior of the museum is to remain the domain of an educated elite, a vision of the exterior should be open to all
so as to excite their "curiosity." "[W]hereas at present,"
the gentleman adds, "it appears as a prison before, and a
palace behind" (21). The gentleman's opinions regarding
the surrounding wall were not uncommon. As late as 1817,
a J. Horne wrote the trustees with the same recommenda-
tion noting that, the museum "being now appropriated to
National purposes, there is not that occasion for privacy,
which perhaps there might be when designed for a Family Residence. I was lately told," he adds, "that it has been
taken for a Prison."[80]

To confuse the museum for a prison seems to confirm
Tony Bennett's contention that where the prison ends, the
museum begins. But to distinguish between these two institutions of national power on the basis of access to external view corresponds with the diverse inventions of
the nation as a category of identity and difference, both
within and outside of the walls of the museum. In its interior practice, the museum serves as a separate, yet mimetically representative symbol of the national body as a
category of the beautiful. Uniformity in variety is the
rule, both for the individual objects and those who would
view them. As a category of national signification, however, the British Museum must be open to the gaze of all
whose curiosity is sufficiently raised. Both as a cognitive
category for those inside and as a physical edifice set off
from surrounding Bloomsbury, simultaneously hidden
and signified by its surrounding wall, later clearly visible
yet separated by its iron fence, the museum increasingly
comes to figure the nation as a sublime object of desire,
simultaneously unattainable yet constitutive of understanding.

Despite the desire of some curators and visitors for an
exhibitionary experience of composition and beauty,
both the vastness of the museum's collections and the imperative of public access insured the predominance of
the novel and the sublime in the national museum. These
seductive and dizzying aesthetic experiences began to

offer an alternative means of conceiving not only the value of the museum's exhibitions, but also the nature of the nation it honored and served. In aesthetic theory, the novel and the sublime had long been associated. Addison had stressed the connection in his description of a sublime "Horison . . . where the Eye has Room to range abroad, to expatiate at large on the Immensity of its Views, and to lose it self amidst the Variety of Objects that offer themselves to its Observation."[81] This is precisely the experience Ward and the correspondent in the *Weekly Advertiser and Inspector* are concerned about; but for Addison, such a "spacious Horison is an Image of Liberty . . . as pleasing to the Fancy, as the Speculations of Eternity or Infinitude are to the Understanding."[82] Burke would later privilege this experience, holding the sublime combination of astonishment and desire as the means by which the contemplative soul was elevated to the apprehension of grandeur.

John Van Rymsdyk would certainly concur. His *Museum Britannicum, Being an Exhibition of a Great Variety of Antiquities and Natural Curiosities, Belonging to That Noble and Magnificent Cabinet, The British Museum, Illustrated with Curious Prints* (1778), conflates novelty and grandeur, desire and nobility, from its opening pages: "When first the Museum opened for the good of the Public, it elevated my Mind with great Conceptions; nothing would have made me more happy than Drawing and Studying these Curiosities; having always had a great Veneration and Taste from my Youth, for all manner of Learning, being like a Luxurious Banquet, to me indeed the most voluptuous Entertainment."[83] Echoing Catherine Talbot's remarks regarding the subversive temptations of the museum's holdings, Rymsdyk perceives the collections as a sequence of enticing sweetmeats. In the midst of such seductions, Rymsdyk finds the sublimity of the collections in the insatiability of his own curiosity:

> The present Age is certainly the Happiest the World ever saw, if we consider the infinite Number of fine Productions in all Arts, &c. and the Multitude of Books published since the Invention of Printing, being so long known to all the Polite

Nations; which productions may be looked on as so many
Roses, Lillies, Honeysuckles, and other innumerable Flowers, from whence the industrious artful Bee, or studious En-
quirer may Feed, Load, Provide, and Improve their Combs
with sweet Knowledge.[84]

In the midst of such rapture, Rymsdyk curiously echoes
Walpole's memorial and foundational aspirations for the
institution, but with a decidedly more inclusive vision:
"What Improvements in Arts, Sciences, Manufacturies;
&c. every Individual may reap from this Harvest of Learning, must strike every one at first View!—O Happy Nation!
Where there is such Liberty granted, and such Generous
Benefactors, whose Names will be convey'd with Honour
to succeeding Generations; nay, be made Immortal."[85]
Again the British Museum memorializes its private benefactors and foundationally produces national honor; but
where Walpole stresses *virtu*, Rymsdyk stresses Liberty,
rejoicing in the very freedom, both aesthetic and civic,
which informs the national museum. The novelty of the
museum's holdings, like the variety of its attendant public, is not only seductive, it provides the compelling and
often overwhelming power to the spectacle of national exhibition.

The configuration of both the museum and the nation
within the category of the beautiful presents us with a
particular aesthetic and ideological response to transformations in cultural and social representation. Shaftesbury had many decades earlier made the theoretical
connection, arguing that "the admiration and love of
order, harmony, and proportion, in whatever kind, is naturally improving to the temper, advantageous to social affection, and highly assistant to virtue, which is itself no
other than the love of order and beauty in society."[86] And,
as Burke would note, an exhibition of beauty allows the
spectator a position of power within the cultural and social complexes enacted in the museum space. But in its
infinite divisibility of parts, as well as its magnitude as a
whole, both nation and museum increasingly come to resemble a sublime object of desire, positioned as simultaneously visible, yet unattainable.

In the next chapter, I will return to the rhetoric of the guidebook as a dialectical model for ideological identification. As supplementary signs of exhibitionary experience, these escorts mediate between curious spectators and various objects, employing the aesthetic tropes of novelty, beauty, and sublimity in nationalist productions of knowledge and value. They must, as both companions and tutors, simultaneously promote and contain the curiosity of the museum's visitors through recourse to aesthetic gratification and pedagogical control. Yet, as literary responses to a materially sublime experience, guidebooks participate in the broader Romantic project of recreating the material world through recuperative self-identity. As novelty and variety merge into sublimity and vastness, the economy of the British Museum is indeed disrupted, and in its disruption is its regeneration.

2
Wordsworth in the Museum:
A Romantic Art of Memory

I

THE READER IS ASKED TO SYMPATHIZE WITH EDMUND POWLETT, author of *The General Contents of the British Museum: With Remarks. Serving as a Directory in Viewing that Noble Cabinet* (1761). "Among the Numbers whom Curiosity prompted to get a Sight of this Collection, I was of Course one," he notes in his introductory remarks, "but the Time allowed to view it was so short, and the Rooms so numerous, that it was impossible, without some Kind of Directory, to form a proper Idea of the Particulars."[1] Powlett is able to provide to others what he himself lacked, a summary of the general contents which he "can offer . . . as a Kind of Directory to those who are inclined to see the Museum; it will likewise serve to give a tolerable Idea of the Contents to those who have no Opportunity of seeing it, and to refresh the Memory, where perhaps it hath been viewed in a cursory Manner."[2] As a guide, a substitute, and a revision to, for, and of the national museum, Powlett's *General Contents* will allow the reader "to form a proper Idea of the Particulars," where Powlett's own experience was one of insufficient time and overabundant rooms.

Powlett's situation "among the numbers" of the curious and his oscillation between a contemplation of the particulars and an apprehension of the museum as a whole elucidate the form and function of the guidebook with particular clarity, but are by no means unique to his pen or his object of contemplation. *A Companion to every Place of Curiosity and Entertainment in and about London and*

76

Westminster (1767) offers itself as "a Directory to Strangers to make Choice of Objects suitable to the Time they have to spare, and to enable them to relate what they have seen," and it notes in its preface that "the Desire which leads us to see whatever is Antique, Remarkable, or Uncommon, being commended by all; and that Desire almost universally prevailing, a Compilation of this kind must be very acceptable to the Inquisitive." Powlett's vacillation between novel seduction and sublime agitation is obviously not uncommon, for the *Companion* also notes that "it has been a general Complaint, that in viewing so many different Departments, the Time allotted is so short, and the Objects so numerous, that it was impossible to form a proper Idea of the Particulars."[3] The urban areas of London and Westminster, like the British Museum, present to the viewer an abundance of objects and departments with little time for sufficient contemplation. In both the national museum and the larger world of social practice, curiosity and the desire for entertainment may be "almost universally prevailing," but without such companions and directories, forming "a proper Idea of the Particulars" proves a hard task indeed.

An Historical Account of the Curiosities of London and Westminster (1777) gets even more to the heart of the matter. Having also noted that "the Desire of seeing the Antiquities and Rarities of our Country is allowed by all to be a laudable Curiosity," the guide notes in its preface to the Tower of London that "it is a general Complaint, that the Mind, being crowded with too many Objects at once, cannot distinguish, amidst so great a variety, what is worthy to be dwelt upon, and what is not."[4] These guidebooks, like many others of their time, offer themselves figuratively as ameliorations to this complaint, directories that may guide, supplement, and revise in memory the raw experience of the collections. These collections may be actual specimens and antiquities on exhibition in the museums, abbeys, and towers of London, or simply the lived experience of its urban dwellers, transformed into curiosities by the desiring spectator.

This problematic of specular curiosity was also elucidated by another museum guide, William Wordsworth,

who defended his sonnet "With ships the sea was sprin-
kled far and nigh" to Lady Beaumont in 1806 by asking
"who is there that has not felt that the mind can have no
rest among a multitude of objects, of which it either cannot make one whole, or from which it cannot single out
one individual, whereupon may be concentrated the attention divided or distracted by a multitude?"[5] The sonnet itself joins desire with observation as a means of
soothing the restless mind, as the poet singles out a ship
among the many and "pursue[s] her with a Lover's look /
This Ship to all the rest did I prefer" (10–11).[6] The alternative to such an amorous preference would be what Wordsworth in another context defined as the consummation of
the sublime: "whatever suspends the comparing power of
the mind & possesses it with a feeling or image of intense
unity, without a conscious contemplation of parts, has
produced that state of mind which is the consummation of
the sublime."[7] As a matter of course, either solution to the
mind's agitation will eliminate the representation of either the part or the whole and bring an end to the guidebook's narrative. The challenge to the guidebook is to
mediate between these two poles of specular fulfillment,
maintaining the "general complaint" as a means of perpetuating itself as amelioration.

When the poet turns to his autobiographical identity,
exhibiting his very memory itself as a formal structure,
guidebook and museum are joined and the dialogue between complaint and amelioration moves from a rhetorical maneuver to a production of subjective identity itself.
As a simultaneous guide, substitute, and re-vision to, for,
and of his childhood years at Cambridge, the third book
of the 1805 *Prelude* serves as both museum and guide for
the poet's recollection and establishment of self:

> Carelessly
> I gazed, roving as through a cabinet
> Or wide museum, thronged with fishes, gems,
> Birds, crocodiles, shells, where little can be seen,
> Well understood, or naturally endeared,
> Yet still does every step bring something forth
> That quickens, pleases, stings—and here and there

A casual rarity is singled out
And has its brief perusal, then gives way
To others, all supplanted in their turn.
Meanwhile, amid this gaudy congress framed
Of things by nature most unneighbourly,
The head turns round, and cannot right itself;
And, though an aching and a barren sense
Of gay confusion still be uppermost,
With few wise longings and but little love,
Yet something to the memory sticks at last
Whence profit may be drawn in times to come.

(3.651–68)[8]

Richard Altick has characterized this passage as an early instance of museum fatigue.[9] As I hope to demonstrate, such fatigue, understood as a simultaneous stimulation and overpowering of the imaginative faculties, plays the same rhetorical function as the citation of the "general complaint" by the earlier guidebooks, namely as a longing informative of both the structure and function of the museum guide. Wordsworth's passage brings together many central thematic and formal elements of his autobiographical poetics: the distinction between careless vision and mature poetic insight, the tyranny of the eye over the imaginative faculty, the endless dialectic between longing and affection, and the recuperation of past events as symbolic capital whose profit is the very emergence-through-articulation of poetic identity. Understood as informative elements of a museum guide, Wordsworth's poetic maneuvers may be seen to correspond structurally, and functionally as well, with modes of ideological identification enacted in sites of public exhibition. His characteristically Romantic movements from questions of identity to processes of identification, from being to becoming, join these questions explicitly with issues of representation. This connection finds a cultural counterpart in the modern national museum, a microcosm of broader cultural transformations in which new patterns of ideological identification and aesthetic representation are brought into direct and material relation.

Indeed, Wordsworth's articulation of "an aching and a barren sense / Of gay confusion," is matched rhetorically by the German writer and traveler Carl Philip Moritz who, in 1782, visited the British Museum as part of a larger tour of England. Though anticipating a leisurely tour through a sequence of specimens and antiquities, memorial representations of silenced contexts that he might reconstruct through informed imagination, Moritz, like so many others, is frustrated in his attempts at disinterested contemplation by the vastness of the collections and the logic of the museum tour:

> The rapidly passing through this vast suite of rooms, in a space of time, little, if at all, exceeding an hour; with leisure just to cast one poor longing look of astonishment on all these stupendous treasures of natural curiosities, antiquities, and literature; in the contemplation of which you could with pleasure spend years, and a whole life might be employed in the study of them—quite confuses, stuns, and overpowers one.[10]

From the vastness of space to the frustration of leisurely observation and pleasurable contemplation, from the longing gaze of astonishment to the overall experience of confusion and awe—the rhetoric informing this passage throughout is that of the experience of the sublime. Moritz is able to single out the occasional rarity by means of a German guidebook, which enables him "to take a somewhat more particular notice of some of the principle things; such as the Egyptian mummy, an head of Homer, &c." (68), but his experience of the institution as a whole corresponds with what Edmund Burke would term the sublime resultant from obscurity in which "the mind is hurried out of itself, by a croud of great and confused images; which affect because they are crouded and confused."[11] This oscillation between the comprehension of memorial objects and the apprehension of a categorical sublime structures Moritz's account of both the institution and his fellow visitors.

In relating his rushed tour through the museum, Moritz makes a curious remark. "I am sorry to say," he states, "it was the rooms, the glass cases, the shelves, or the repository for the books in the British Museum which I saw, and not the Museum itself."[12] While this comment seems to denaturalize the institution and the constructed nature of its exhibition in calling attention to the very mechanisms of that construction, it simultaneously sublimates "the Museum itself" as an ideal greater than the sum of its exhibited objects or institutional apparatuses. Moritz's frustration and longing in viewing the objects on exhibition turn his attention to his fellow visitors where he observes the same diversity of parts, but is now able to comprehend the whole through recourse to the concept of the nation. He notes that "the company, who saw it when and as I did, was various, and some of all sorts; some, I believe, of the very lowest classes of the people, of both sexes; for, as it is the property of the nation, every one has the same right (I use the term of the country) to see it, that another has" (68). The social standing of the collector signified by earlier private collections is now made available in imaginative form to a larger public through their identification with the nation whose material acquisition and exhibition they may view. Differences of class and gender become secondary to the company's status of national citizenry, a status obtained through their participation in the exhibitionary rite. The shared time and manner of viewing the collected specimens forges and defines national identity through the dynamics of observation, a point which is brought home to Moritz when he supplements the brevity of the tour with notes from a German guidebook which he shares with his fellow visitors. Moritz's actions cause a display of nationalist contempt from the guide "when he found out that it was only a German description of the British Museum" (68). Just as "the Museum itself" is, for Moritz, a category greater than the sum of its exhibitionary apparatuses, the nation is experienced emotionally and symbolically in the longing and confusion obtaining in the museum experience.

For both Wordsworth and Moritz, museum fatigue registers a dialectical relation between fragment and totality, between insufficiency and anticipation, in which the discursive production of a subjective or national self-identity emerges in the passage between. Within the poetic logic of *The Prelude*, such dialectic reproduces the gap between experience and memory as poetic identity. Within

the logic of the British Museum and other sites of public
exhibition, the signifying gap between memorial objects
and their re-collection in public institutions is the constitutive means by which social and national identity is both
posited and redeemed. Susan Stewart has theorized that
in the collection, "each sign is placed in relation to a
chain of signifiers whose ultimate referent is not the interior of the room—in itself an empty essence—but the interior of the self."[13] In the national museum, this self is a
distinctively national self, an identity formed through a
mediation both aesthetic and ideological. The rhetorical
affiliation between exhibitionary guidebooks and Wordsworth's autobiographical poetics allows us to rethink the
centrality of memory as a transforming presence not only
in Romantic poetics of self-reflection, but also in the institutionalization of the museum as a public resource for
an idealized national unity. In what follows, I explore the
exhibitionary representation and enactment of individual and collective memory as a process of imaginative
and ideological identification. To understand and position this congruence between poetic and ideological
identification, I consider the writings of one of the most
popular guides to London in the late eighteenth century
alongside the aesthetic and political theories of Edmund
Burke and Samuel Taylor Coleridge. I then return to
Wordsworth's guide to the museum of his self and explore
how his establishment of poetic self-identity is informed
by his appropriation of the traditional art of memory and
the representational trope of personification. What
emerges is an understanding of the interplay between
imaginative and ideological productions of individual
and national identity in a peculiarly Romantic museum
discourse.

II

The French writer and traveller Pierre Jean Grosley's
*Tour to London; or, New Observations on England and its In-
habitants* (1772), one of the most popular foreign guides to
England in the later eighteenth century,[14] contains an ex-

tensive survey of public exhibitions in a chapter entitled "National Pride—How far Melancholy may be productive of it. Effects of this pride, with regard to England." Its opening paragraph is worth reprinting in full:

> The impetuosity, and the perseverance, with which melancholy dwells upon such objects as interest and engage it, are the principles which induce the English to concern themselves so much about public affairs. Each citizen identifying himself with the government, must of necessity extend to himself the high idea which he has of the nation: he triumphs in its victories; he is afflicted by its calamities: he exhausts himself in projects to promote its successes, to second its advantages, and to repair its losses: he may be compared to the fly in the fable, which, when it approaches the horses, "Thinks to animate them by its humming, stings one, then another, and imagines every moment that it makes the carriage go forward; it sits upon the pole, and upon the coachman's nose: and no sooner does it see the carriage driven on, and the people continuing their journey, but it arrogates the glory of the whole movement to itself."[15]

Foundational to Grosley's theory of national pride is the disposition of melancholy and its relation of mutual engrossment and production with "such objects as interest and engage it." The national body may be located neither in its citizens nor in the "high idea of the nation" to which they aspire, but in the passage between the form and the ideal, between the parts and "the glory of the whole movement" which such objects seem to embody. National pride and the nation itself are, in Grosley's terms, inextricable. He compares this pride with that of antiquity and characterizes it as "a pride, which being the first foundation of public strength, and multiplying it *ad infinitum*, subdivides, and in some measure, distributes itself to every citizen" (192). Grosley even goes so far as to quote the sixth book of the *Aeneid* regarding the Neoplatonic union of souls as an analogy for this process of identification: "Totam diffusa per artus / Mens agitat molem ac magno se corpore miscet" (192).[16] Within this dynamic of national pride, such exhibitionary institutions as the British Museum and Westminster Abbey stand out for

Grosley as consecrations to melancholy, productively mediative forms between a citizenry and a national ideal:

> This ardour, which warmed Rome and Greece, is to be found in England, and must necessarily produce the same fruits in that kingdom. The British Museum, the palaces of great noblemen, the cabinets of the curious, the houses of citizens, those dark and solitary grottos which people of fortune consecrate to melancholy in their country retirements, the taverns and inns, the houses where people meet for public diversions, are all adorned with figures painted or engraved, and with busts of all sizes, made of all sorts of materials, of Bacon, Shakespeare, Milton, Locke, Addison, Newton, and even Cromwell himself: I could not without astonishment see a fine bust of the latter fill a distinguished place in the British Museum. (196–97)

Grosley's expostulation reaches its climax as he considers Westminster Abbey which he characterizes as "the grand depository of the monuments erected to the glory of the nation" (204). While he bemoans the fact that the various monuments within the abbey were not "raised by a public decree, at the expense of the nation," but rather "by the family or friends of each personage," this fault is more than made up for in Grosley's mind by the reception and attention paid to these monuments by the national public:

> The abbey in which they stand is incessantly filled with crowds, who contemplate them: the lowest sort of people shew also their attention: I have seen herb-women holding a little book, which gives an account of them; I have seen milk-women getting them explained, and testifying, not a stupid admiration, but a lively and most significant surprise. (205)

National pride is not an ideal pressed upon a stupid and passive populace, but is an active apprehension of a sublime totality by a melancholic disposition. While the individual memorials signify the particular heroes of British national culture, the apprehension of the collection as a whole astonishes and surprises, establishing a proud ardour of national glory. In the exhibitionary sites of the

British Museum and Westminster Abbey, the nation is posited synechdochally through a sequence of memorial objects, but the "high idea . . . of the nation" is redeemed in the citizenry which, like the fly in Grosley's fable, sees only the representational parts, yet "arrogates the glory of the whole movement to itself."[17]

Identification as such had been a central characteristic of the sublime experience since Longinus who argued that "the mind is naturally elevated by the true sublime, and so sensibly affected with its lively strokes, that it swells in transport and an inward pride, as if what was only heard had been the product of its own invention."[18] Longinus was describing aesthetic experiences while Grosley is considering a process of nationalist identification, but the connection was already well established by eighteenth-century theorists of the aesthetic, most notably Edmund Burke, who cites Longinus in the section of his *Philosophical Enquiry* concerning Ambition:

> Now whatever either on good or upon bad grounds tends to raise a man in his own opinion, produces a sort of swelling and triumph that is extremely grateful to the human mind; and this swelling is never more perceived nor operates with more force, than when without danger we are conversant with terrible objects, the mind always claiming to itself some part of the dignity and importance of the things which it contemplates. Hence proceeds what Longinus has observed of that glorying and sense of inward greatness, that always fills the reader of such passages in poets and orators as are sublime; it is what every man must have felt in himself upon such occasions.[19]

The "swelling and triumph," the "transport and . . . inward pride," the arrogation of "the glory of the whole movement" to the subjective viewer of the sublime is, for all three writers, a process of identification. The objects themselves are not the objects of identification, but supplementary mediations for a true object of desire that is the very breakdown of the division of subject and object itself into a unified totality. Whether that totality is manifested in the "high idea of the nation" or the "glorying and sense of inward greatness," the transport of the sublime pushes beyond the representational mode of such objects of desire to an absolute identification between subject and object.

Such objects, for both Burke and Grosley, are objects that address themselves to a peculiarly melancholic disposition. Burke's subject who is "conversant with terrible objects," is engaged in a conversation which mixes pleasure and pain in the production of social love: "The passion of love has its rise in positive pleasure; it is, like all things which grow out of pleasure, capable of being mixed with a mode of uneasiness, that is, when an idea of its object is excited in the mind with an idea at the same time of having irretrievably lost it" (47). Burke elaborates on this relation between social love and the lost object earlier in the same part of the *Enquiry*:

> It is the nature of grief to keep its object perpetually in its eye, to present it in its most pleasurable views, to repeat all the circumstances that attend it, even to the last minuteness; to go back to every particular enjoyment, to dwell upon each, and to find a thousand new perfections in all, that were not sufficiently understood before; in grief, the pleasure is still uppermost; and the affliction we suffer has no resemblance to absolute pain, which is always odious, and which we endeavor to shake off as soon as possible. (34–35)

He cites the example of Homer's depiction of Menelaus bemoaning his fallen friends: "He [Menelaus] owns indeed, that he often gives himself some intermission from such melancholy reflections, but he observes too, that melancholy as they are, they give him pleasure" (35). The mix of joy and grief, pleasure and pain, which attend to moments of the sublime, is a dynamic obtaining between two poles, a melancholic subject and an idealized form. Mediating between these two poles is the experience of the sublime that simultaneously embodies presence and absence, insufficiency and anticipation.

Yet both melancholic subject and idealized form are produced as much as they are mediated by this sublime valence. In Burke's broader argument, the dynamic nature of this relation serves as a catalyst to higher social

achievement and imaginative production, curing the inevitable stagnation attendant upon pure imitation:

> Although imitation is one of the great instruments used by
> providence in bringing our nature towards its perfection, yet
> if men gave themselves up to imitation entirely, and each fol-
> lowed the other, and so on in an eternal circle, it is easy to
> see that there never could be any improvement amongst
> them. . . . To prevent this, God has planted in man a sense of
> ambition, and a satisfaction arising from the contemplation
> of his excelling his fellows in something deemed valuable
> amongst them. (46)

Imitation serves as a necessary glue of social behavior,
commending men to follow social fashion and proper
modes of behavior: "It is one of the strongest links of society; it is a species of mutual compliance which all men
yield to each other, without constraint to themselves, and
which is extremely flattering to all" (45). It also serves as
a characteristic of artistic merit: "Herein it is that painting and many other agreeable arts have laid one of the
principal foundations of their power" (45). But in and of
itself, pure imitation is a form of stagnant memory, a self-
referencing "eternal circle" which therefore requires
ambition's disruptive influence. As in Grosley's formula-
tions of national pride, feelings of melancholy and apprehensions of the sublime are indispensable if memory is to
realize itself in a productive capacity.

We may consider one more theorist of the aesthetics of
the state, Samuel Taylor Coleridge, whose ruminations on
the organic political body parallel Grosley and Burke's,
as well as his own theories of the imagination. His much-
celebrated distinction between the fancy and the two lev-
els of imagination also establishes a relationship between mere imitative memory and autonomous creative
production, a relationship mediated by a process of dissolution and re-contexualization. Coleridge's concept of the
fancy, like Burke's concept of imitation, "is indeed no
other than a mode of memory emancipated from the order
of time and space; and blended with, and modified by that
empirical phaenomenon of the will which we express by

the word choice."[20] Fancy is an inferior mode of creative exercise as it is incapable of producing anything truly original, having "no other counters to play with but fixities and definites" and receiving "all its materials ready made from the law of association" (305). The primary imagination, on the other end of the spectrum, is "the living power and prime agent of all human perception, and . . . a repetition in the finite mind of the eternal act of creation in the infinite I AM" (304). Between the fancy and the primary imagination lies the secondary imagination, conceived of as

> an echo of the [primary imagination], co-existing with the conscious will, yet still as identical with the primary in the kind of its agency, and differing only in degree, and in the mode of its operation. It dissolves, diffuses, dissipates, in order to re-create; or where this process is rendered impossible, yet still, at all events, it struggles to idealize and to unify. It is essentially vital, even as all objects (as objects) are essentially fixed and dead. (304)

A mode of agency which establishes unification and idealization through a process of dissolution, diffusion, and dissipation, a vital will which works upon fixed and dead objects: the makings, one might say, of a perfect museum curator. The analogies between Coleridge's secondary imagination and the representational logic of the museum emerge even more forcefully when we consider its mediating role between a memory of fixed and definite associations and an idealization of an autonomous and self-creating identity. The secondary imagination dissolves the pre-existent associations between objects and recontextualizes them in the production of unification and idealization, yet this production is always incomplete, a struggle rather than a completion, a promise of, but also a distance from, "the eternal act of creation in the infinite I AM."

Mediation in representation is matched by mediation in identification when we turn to Coleridge's comments on the State and the distinction between inorganic and organic bodies:

The difference between an inorganic and an organic body lies in this:—in the first—a sheaf of corn—the Whole is nothing more than a collection of the individual phaenomena; in the second—a man—the whole is the effect of, or result from, the parts—is in fact every thing and the parts nothing. A State is an Idea intermediate between the two—the Whole being a result from and not a mere total of, the parts—and yet not so merging the constituent parts in the result, but that the individual exists perfectly within it. Extremes meet.[21]

The State mediates between an association of parts and their absolute merger into a whole, offering itself as the idea of the whole that nonetheless maintains individual distinctions. While the ideal of the whole gains its definition through relation to the individual citizens, and, conversely, individual citizens gain identity through recourse to the ideal of the whole, neither actually exist as pure identities. Rather, they are are produced by the very idea which claims to mediate between the two: the State itself. Coleridge's marginalia to Lessing's query in his dialogue *Ernst und Falk* whether men are made for the state or the state for men asserts this same point: "Not only is the Whole greater than a Part; but when it is a Whole, and not a mere All or Aggregate, it makes each part that which it is."[22] Like Grosley's Neoplatonic civics, in which the dialectic between citizen and the "high idea of the nation" produces the very polarities whose relation is the proper location of the nation, Coleridge's formulation of the State as a mediating idea between ideals that are never fully realized offers us a powerful instance of the convergence between imaginative and civic philosophy.[23]

The maintenance of the "general complaint" by its ameliorative guidebooks may now be more clearly understood. As guides, substitutes, and revisions to, for, and of the sites of public exhibition, such narratives provide an oscillation between "a proper Idea of the Particulars" and an apprehension of the collection as a whole, thus sustaining the desire they claim to fulfill as the means of their self-production. This dynamic form may be understood as one of partial identification, a sublime experience of melancholic longing productive of a relation between the parts and the whole, with identity, poetic or social, emerging in the passage between. Such partial identification is, as Steven Knapp has persuasively argued, characteristic of eighteenth-century theories of the sublime. The empirical agency is drawn towards universal comprehension and ideals of pure reason, yet is, in Knapp's words, "condemned . . . to oscillate between sympathy and irony in relation to the self's identification with truth."[24] Such sites of public exhibition, "the Museum itself," signify beyond the sum of their exhibited objects and monuments. Gaps appear within the memorial "eternal circle": gaps between the objects and their signified origins, gaps between the particular objects and their collective identity, gaps between the spectators and the exhibitionary structures. Far from disabling the representational logic of such sites, these gaps are the disruptive means by which imitation becomes ambition, by which fancy becomes imagination, by which the spectators become a national body.

Analogously, Wordsworth's "aching and . . . barren sense / Of gay confusion" both frames and produces modes of representation which exhibit temporal and spatial distance and presence in the "wide museum" of his poetic autobiography. His rhetorical strategies in the third book of *The Prelude* correlate not only with contemporary institutions of ideological reproduction, but with rhetorical and poetic traditions whose transformations in the late eighteenth century Wordsworth's process of poetic self-identification allows us to perceive.

III

O Memory! celestial Maid!
    Who glean's't the Flowretts cropt by Time,
And, suffering not a Leaf to Fade,
    Preserv'st the Blossoms of our Prime;
Bring, bring those Moments to my Mind
When Life was new, and they were kind![25]

With this quotation from Shenstone, the Reverend Warden Butler opens his unpublished dramatic tour of the national museum, *A Pleasing Recollection, or A Walk Through the British Museum* (1767). His title's conflation of personal memory and pleasure with a peripatetic account of the national repository not only reminds us of the affective means by which exhibitions enticed individuals into participating in a public and national rite, but reminds us as well that personal memory and architectural repositories share a common and mutually-informative history in Western thought. Wordsworth's configuration of his recollecting mind as a wanderer in a "wide museum" echoes a long tradition of the representation and enactment of memory as a physical repository of objects and images, a tradition considered most extensively by Frances Yates in *The Art of Memory*. Tracing the rhetorical art from its classical origins through its medieval and Renaissance permutations, Yates's study allows us to observe the emergence of a modern subjectivity through the shifts in philosophical understanding manifested in this tradition. Wordsworth's metaphorical "wide museum" of self-recollection, which permeates the third book of *The Prelude* and links structurally and thematically to the poem as a whole, marks a transformation in this tradition beyond the theaters and treatises of the Renaissance with which Yates's study concludes.

Yates marks the tradition's movement from a rhetorical method designed to aid in the recitation of speeches to a theological device aimed at aiding the postlapsarian mind in recalling divine doctrine and on to its employment in the Renaissance as an embodiment of mystical or Hermetic truths, allowing the mind to transcend its mortal state and access the divinity. "The emotionally striking images of classical memory," Yates comments, "transformed by the devout Middle Ages into corporeal similitudes, are transformed again into magically powerful images":

> The mind and memory of man is now 'divine,' having powers of grasping the highest reality through a magically activated imagination. The Hermetic art of memory has become the instrument in the formation of a Magus, the imaginative means through which the divine microcosm can reflect the divine

macrocosm, can grasp its meaning from above, from that divine grade to which his *mens* belongs.[26]

Just as the art's movement from a medieval aid for a fallen recollecting faculty to a Renaissance tool for the collection and acquisition of divine knowledge marks a shift in understanding of the nature of the individual subject, the continual metamorphosis of the tradition after the span of Yates's study continues to correlate with a transformation in the understanding of subjective identity. The movement of collections from the curiosity cabinets and private galleries of the Renaissance to the public museums of the nineteenth and twentieth centuries is matched by a transformation of the very understanding of memory itself and its relationship to the constitution of the individual as subject. This transformation may be read through recourse to the tradition's reappearance in that apex of empirical thought, John Locke's *Essay Concerning Human Understanding*.

In the second book of his *Essay*, Locke divides the faculty of retention into two subdivisions of contemplation and memory. The first is identified as the power to keep simple ideas in view of the mind for comparison and consideration. The second is defined simply as "the power to revive again in our minds those ideas which, after imprinting, have disappeared, or have been as it were laid aside out of sight":

> This is memory, which is as it were the storehouse of our ideas. For, the narrow mind of man not being capable of having many ideas under view and consideration at once, it was necessary to have a repository, to lay up those ideas which, at another time, it might have use of. [27]

As a continuation of the traditional art of memory, Locke's "repository" allows the mind to revive ideas conceived as visual images for selective contemplation. In the broader context of Locke's philosophy, this metaphor provides an empirical model for the understanding of personal identity in which the construction of identity in general and of personal consciousness in particular are conjoined through the exhibition of ideas.

Recalling Locke's unique use of the term "ideas" as the building blocks of knowledge, mental representations of the external world which require connection by modes or relations to form a coherent knowledge, we may see that his repository is, as it were, a museum without a narrative, a collection of varied perceptions dependent upon the act of recollection to unite them into a coherent understanding. Locke more than once insists that these ideas stored in the repository of memory are to be differentiated from the ideas of current contemplation in that they bear the mark of their recollection:

> But, our *ideas* being nothing but actual perceptions in the mind, which cease to be anything when there is no perception of them; this laying up of our ideas in the repository of the memory signifies no more but this,—that the mind has a power in many cases to revive perceptions which it has once had, with this additional perception annexed to them, *that it has had them before.* (1:194, original emphasis)

Locke reiterates this point and expands upon it later in the same chapter:

> This further is to be observed, concerning ideas lodged in the memory, and upon occasion revived by the mind, that they are not only (as the word revive imports) none of them new ones, but also that the mind takes notice of them as of a former impression, and renews its acquaintance with them, as with ideas it had known before. So that though ideas formerly imprinted are not all constantly in view, yet in remembrance they are constantly known to be such as have been formerly imprinted; i.e. in view, and taken notice of before, by the understanding. (1:198)

This mark of recollection is, in essence, a mark of absence. Locke's editor and annotator Alexander Campbell Fraser recalls Hobbes's figuring of imagination and memory as a "decaying sense" and his description of "rememberance" as "nothing else but the missing of parts. To see at a great distance of place, and to remember at a great distance of time, is to have like conceptions of the thing; for there wanteth distinction of parts in both; the one conception being weak by operation at distance, the other by decay" (1:196 n. 1). Unlike the memory theaters and repositories of the older traditions of the art of memory, the Lockean repository bears on its surface the very distance and dispersal that have constituted recollected objects as such. Their further collection through relation into a coherent understanding is informed at the outset by the cognizance of their original dispersal from the contemplative mind.

The repository of the mind bears witness to the past through the mark of recollection recorded on each of its ideas while establishing knowledge through the recontextualization of these ideas into relational modes. Locke's adaptation of the repository as a metaphor for the faculty of memory internalizes the Renaissance memory theaters, allowing the human mind access to the truths of the external world, but now with an empirical rather than an ideational logic of knowledge. The mind no longer studies the images in the repository for access to a macrocosmic world of ideal truths, but instead constructs its knowledge through the act of recollection itself. The mark of recollection is thus the absence constitutive of an empirical logic of understanding, signifying the space between perception and recollection whence Locke's concept of knowledge emerges. The shift is more profound still. For the medieval and Renaissance constructions of the art of memory, the recollecting subject was separate from the act itself. While the art of memory might aid or transform the individual, it did so through the content and not the mode of its signification. Locke's internalization of not only the containment and exhibition, but also of the very constitution of knowledge, changes this relationship between subject and act. Both as a means of construing identity and difference in the world around us and as a means of establishing self-identity, memory plays both a signifying and a constitutive role.

Locke's conceptions of identity and diversity stem from a central premise that "another occasion the mind takes of comparing is the very being of things, when, considering *anything as existing at any determined time and place*, we compare it with *itself existing at another time*, and thereon form the ideas of *identity* and *diversity*" (1:439; original emphasis). But for the primary substances of which we may have direct ideas—God, finite intelligences or spirits, and bodies of particles of matter—all identities are more properly relations of these ideas, organizational modes dependent not upon the individual existence of their parts but upon the organization of those parts into a larger identity. In considering what makes an oak tree an oak, Locke explicates that the oak, "being then one plant which has such an organization of parts in one coherent body, partaking of one common life, it continues to be the same plant as long as it partakes of the same life, though that life be communicated to new particles of matter vitally united to the living plant, in a like continued organization conformable to that sort of plant" (1:443). The formulation applies equally in its converse, holding that the individual parts only maintain their identity as a part of a greater whole so long as the organization that binds them remains consistent.

In considering human identity on a purely physical level, Locke transfers this conception without addition: "This also shows wherein the identity of the same man consists; viz., in nothing but a participation of the same continued life, by constantly fleeting particles of matter, in succession vitally united to the same organized body" (1:444). In distinguishing man from other animals, however, Locke forwards the idea of personal identity as the sole domain of thinking, rational creatures. He defines a person as

> a thinking intelligent being, that has reason and reflection, and can consider itself as itself, the same thinking thing, in different times and places; which it does only by that consciousness which is inseparable from thinking, and, as it seems to me, essential to it: it being impossible for any one to perceive without perceiving that he does perceive. (1:448–49)

Locke's consideration of personal identity as based in self-reflection in time and space joins perception and memory as not merely the indicators, but also the constitutive actions of self-identity:

For, since consciousness always accompanies thinking, and it is that which makes every one to be what he calls self, and thereby distinguishes himself from all other thinking things, in this alone consists personal identity, i.e. the sameness of a rational being: and as far as this consciousness can be extended backwards to any past action or thought, so far reaches the identity of that person; it is the same self now it was then; and it is by the same self with this present one that now reflects on it, that that action was done. (1:449)

Though Locke separates his chapters on retention and on identity by 16 intermittent chapters concerning the various relational modes by which ideas are collected into knowledge, their structural interdependence must be recognized. Personal consciousness exists as the comparative and retentive faculties turned in on themselves. The memorial and foundational logics that inform the passage from memory to knowledge equally inform the passage from perception of the act of perception to the perception of a self that must perceive. Locke's internalization of the art of memory not only joins recollection and knowledge, but also, in doing so, makes the passage from perception to recollection the very site for the emergence of subjective identity. Marked as it is by distance and dispersal, the recollecting faculty constitutes a self-identity as one of mediation, bridging the informative distance between perception and recollection.

This internalization of the memory theaters and repositories and its consequential transformation of the function of self-identity in the exhibition of ideas is fundamentally a shift in representational logic. The logic of the images and signs in the Renaissance art of memory was one of transcendental idealism, the signs containing essential truths only insofar as they functioned as stable signifiers. Locke's empiricist repository changes this logic of representation from a signifying to a constitutional mode. Signs move from memorial ideas to elements of foundational knowledge through the exhibition itself, the subject emerging in just that passage. This understanding of the subject comes not as an overt element of Locke's *Essay*, but as a necessary consequence of his adaptation of the art of memory to an empiricist theory of knowledge.

What Locke's empiricist transformation of the art of memory accomplishes philosophically, Wordsworth's poetics produces as a matter of form and trope. As a museum guide, Wordsworth actively constructs knowledge through his faculties of perception and comparison. Both internal emotions and external perceptions are united through a peculiarly empirical account of poetic agency:

> for I had an eye
> Which in my strongest workings evermore
> Was looking for the shades of difference
> As they lie hid in all exterior forms,
> Near or remote, minute or vast—an eye
> Which from a stone, a tree, a withered leaf,
> To the broad ocean and the azure heavens
> Spangled with kindred multitudes of stars,
> Could find no surface where its power might sleep,
> Which spake perpetual logic to my soul,
> And by an unrelenting agency
> Did bind my feelings even as in a chain.
>
> (3.156–67)

The images in the repository serve not as signifiers of knowledge, but as immediate ideas requiring the "unrelenting agency" of the poet's eye to mediate between them, producing knowledge out of difference and relation. In such moments as he is "awakened, summoned, rouzed, constrained" to seek out the universal in the particular, to find unity in diversity, he is also struck with experiences of the sublime, "incumbances more awful, visitings / Of the upholder, of the tranquil soul, / Which underneath all passion lives secure / A steadfast life" (3.109–18). Such moments are glimpses of unity, of absolute identification, through the compared particulars of the natural world: "The great mass / Lay bedded in a quickening soul, and all / That I beheld respired with inward meaning" (3.127–29). As in the familiar master narrative of the Chain of Being, Wordsworth's perception of difference in unity and unity in difference is not a consummation of the sublime, but maintenance of mediation between part and whole through poetic vision.

It is the articulation of that vision, however, which turns the guide upon himself, seeking to apply to his own memories the logic of comparison and distinction he applied to the natural world. As the art of memory is internalized as both the form and content of poetic self-knowledge, the poet is forced to compete with the ready-made images provided in the social world:

> Hence, for these rarities elaborate
> Having no relish yet, I was content
> With the more homely produce rudely piled
> In this our coarser warehouse. At this day
> I smile in many a mountain solitude
> At passages and fragments that remain
> Of that inferior exhibition, played
> By wooden images, a theatre
> For wake or fair.
>
> (3.600–608)

The "inferior exhibition" of Cambridge is marked by a passive state of perception in which the "wooden images," rather than the poet himself, control the mediations between subject and totality. In characterizing his "loose and careless heart," Wordsworth intones that "I was the dreamer, they the dream; I roamed / Delighted through the motley spectacle: / Gowns grave or gaudy, doctors, students, streets, / Lamps, gateways, flocks of churches, courts and towers" (3.28–31). He later describes his return to sobriety after his initial infatuation with Cambridge as a return from a public spectacle: "When the first glitter of the show was passed, / And the first dazzle of the taper-light, / As if with a rebound my mind returned / Into its former self" (3.94–97). He returns to this metaphor again when recalling the same transition: "It hath been told already how my sight / Was dazzled by the novel show, and how / Erelong I did into myself return" (3.202–4), and he later reflects upon the early youthful enthusiasm of that time that "such was the tenor of the opening act / In this new life" (3.259–60). Wordsworth's consistent use of the term of spectacle, whether explicitly or as a controlling metaphor, as a figure for a state of passive perception in which the personal identity of the poet can find no room for active growth and participation, needs to be understood as a bemoaning of an insufficient mode of identification. By privileging the symbolic figure over the individual subject as the primary site of constitutive mediation, the spectacle fails to engage the imagination of the viewer. The "wooden images," in and of themselves, are insufficient representations of the world without the binding vision of the poet's mind.

Yet these "wooden images" are offered as an initial conclusion to Wordsworth's Cambridge years as his recollections seem to culminate in an extensive pageant of personified abstractions. This trope would seem to pose a direct threat to Wordsworth's poetic self-identity, offering social abstractions over and against active recollection as the mediating and cohesive bond in the poet's "wide museum." Wordsworth's familiar rejection of personification in the preface to *Lyrical Ballads* in favor of "the very language of men" and "the company of flesh and blood" is a manifestation on the level of style of his stated intention to position the poet as one who "binds together by passion and knowledge the vast empire of human society, as it is spread over the whole earth, and over all time."[28] We must therefore consider why Wordsworth would choose to employ this traditional trope in direct conflict with his formal and representational constructions of poetic identity.

IV

The fate of personification in the late eighteenth century has been the topic of many excellent studies which, while they disagree on many points, reach a general consensus which views the trope as one of mediation, both rhetorical and social. Considering the trope as a rhetorical device, Paul de Man has argued for anthropomorphic representation as "not just a trope but an identification on the level of substance," a mode of representation which "freezes the infinite chain of tropological transformations and propositions into one single assertion or essence which, as such, excludes all others."[29] Patricia Meyer Spacks notes that throughout most of the eighteenth century, personification was considered "a rhetorical figure of special emotional power," establishing a concrete link between the world of human experience and a realm of abstract ideals, fusing "the weight of generalization with the force of particularity."[30] Clifford Siskin reads the trope as "a synecdochic affirmation of community," simultaneously drawing upon the authority of a common community of language while confirming that community as a stabilizing moral presence. For the Augustan speaker, the passive construction of personification shifts the responsibility of agency from the speaker to the " 'figure' of speech" itself, whereas, Siskin argues, "overt efforts at self-definition would only tend to undermine his claim to be a representative observer" of the dramatic pageant portrayed.[31] Romantic poetry, in contrast to its eighteenth-century predecessors, seeks to forge a literary community through the act of communication itself, and thus can no longer employ the tropes of an outdated model. With the passing away of this Augustan stability, Siskin claims, personification is increasingly employed in texts which "convey a nostalgia for an irrecoverable poetic past and/or a transcendent yearning to obliterate all time in revelation."[32]

Steven Knapp offers a complementary, but more sustained account of the trope's mediating role in eighteenth-century poetics and its relation to theories of the sublime. Knapp reads eighteenth-century poetic practice as dividing the sublime experience between personified abstractions and a skeptical speaker who contemplates the personifications as allegorical surrogates. Personification undergoes less of a rejection than a transformation in the later part of the century, a transformation that does not so much reposition the trope from its mediating role as it rethinks the very nature of that mediation. Analogous to the internalization of the art of memory, personified images change from signifiers of an ideal realm to representations mediating between an incomplete subject and an anticipated merger in a totality. Personification both allows the subject access to the totality and allows him a safe distance from it by which to maintain his subjective identity.[33]

These various accounts, while concurring on the trope's mediating status, differ primarily with regard to the nature of that mediation itself. De Man's rhetorical account and Spacks and Siskin's historical narratives view the act of mediation as one which unites separate entities (past and present, particular and universal, private and social), but maintains their identities as founded in separation. Knapp's account, by relating personification to the sublime, configures mediation as the convergence and embodiment of a dialectic between polarities whose identities are understood as relational rather than essential. Both positions offer valuable insights into alternate deployments of personification and, I wish to suggest, into different rhetorical positions within the national museum. With these positions in mind, we might consider an obvious predecessor to Wordsworth's invocation of personified abstractions as embodiments of his student experiences at Cambridge, namely Thomas Gray's "Ode on a Distant Prospect of Eton College." Like the third book of *The Prelude*, Gray's ode seeks to mediate temporally between past and present and spatially between poet and society. Unlike Wordsworth's production of self-identity, Gray's ode places trope rather than poet as the agency of mediation, functioning not as reconciliation, but, rather, as a maintenance of identity-as-difference. These two poets, thus, offer two alternate models not only of lyrical recollection, but also of exhibitionary perception and aesthetic identification.

Offering one model of a museum spectator, Gray places his poetic voice in a stable prospective position, enabling him to view the past as a tableau from which he may draw his sobering lessons. Representation and estrangement are connected from the very opening lines of Gray's poem as the phrase, "Ye distant spires, ye antique towers," combines spatial and temporal distance as the site of poetic address, reminding the reader that the ode is not written about Eton College, but on the distant prospect itself.[34] The prospect serves as a topographical representation of

the temporal recollections upon which the ode is structured. From this distance, the childhood of the poet and
the more generalized childhood of the students are defined spatially and temporally as a location of innocence
and a potential source of rejuvenation:

> Ah happy hills, ah pleasing shade,
> Ah fields belov'd in vain,
> Where once my careless childhood stray'd,
> A stranger yet to pain!
> I feel the gales, that from ye blow,
> A momentary bliss bestow,
> As waving fresh their gladsome wing,
> My weary soul they seem to soothe,
> And redolent of joy and youth,
> To breathe a second spring.
>
> (11–20)

Gray's single employment of the first person voice in the
poem corresponds with the only narration of connection
in the poetic sequence, but a connection that positions
Gray as a recipient on one end of the distance separating
him from the tableau of childhood innocence he over-
looks. While the first line of this stanza, in echoing the
opening line of the poem, conflates distance and pleasure, the foreboding qualifiers of that pleasure ("fields
belov'd in vain," "careless childhood stray'd," "A
stranger yet to pain!," "momentary bliss," "seem to
soothe") suggest that the distance is not so easily bridged.
   While the ode may be characterized as a progress poem,
its representations of movement and growth are all curiously static. Gray constantly defers the act of observation
to "Father Thames," and his descriptions of the childhood observed from a distance of both time and place
take the form of emblematic images.

> Say, Father Thames, for thou hast seen
> Full many a sprightly race
> Disporting on thy margent green
> The paths of pleasure trace,
> Who foremost now delight to cleave
> With pliant arm thy glassy wave?

The captive linnet which enthrall?
What idle progeny succeed
To chase the rolling circle's speed,
Or urge the flying ball?

(21–30)

As S. H. Clark has learnedly argued, such descriptions increasingly come to resemble Lockean ideas stored in the repository of the poet's memory.[35] Like these ideas, the visions do not in and of themselves form any coherent knowledge of either childhood or the world around it, but require an act of agency to collect them into a foundational knowledge. Such agency is not to be found in the poetic voice itself, but in what M. H. Abrams some time ago identified as "the tableau-and-allegory form that Coleridge derogated as Gray's 'translations of prose thoughts into poetic language.' "[36] The speaking voice does not bridge the distance, but rather establishes it as a tension that produces increasingly iconographic representations of childhood innocence. Passive constructions and a self-effacing poetic voice conspire with the emblematic representations to produce a gap between past and present and between the poet and the social world he observes. The poem accumulates memorial images ("The tear forgot as soon as shed, / The sunshine of the breast / . . . /The thoughtless day, the easy night, / The spirits pure, the slumbers light" [43–44, 48–49]) that speak to the very distance that has produced them, but require an agency to cohere them into a relational knowledge.

Such agency is provided by the personifications that dominate the second half of the poem:

These shall the fury Passions tear,
The vultures of the mind,
Disdainful Anger, pallid Fear,
And Shame that sculks behind;
Or pineing Love shall waste their youth,
Or Jealousy with rankling tooth,
That inly gnaws the secret heart,
And Envy wan, and faded Care,
Grim-visag'd comfortless Despair,
And Sorrow's piercing dart.

> Ambition this shall tempt to rise,
> Then whirl the wretch from high,
> To bitter Scorn a sacrifice,
> And grinning Infamy.
> The stings of Falshood those shall try,
> And hard Unkindness' alter'd eye,
> That mocks the tear it forc'd to flow;
> And keen Remorse with blood defil'd,
> And moody Madness laughing wild
> Amid severest woe.
>
> Lo, in the vale of years beneath
> A griesly troop are seen,
> The painful family of Death,
> More hideous than their Queen:
> This racks the joints, this fires the veins,
> That every labouring sinew strains,
> Those in the deeper vitals rage:
> Lo, Poverty, to fill the band,
> That numbs the soul with icy hand,
> And slow-consuming Age.
>
> (61–90)

The mediation of personified abstractions affirms poetic identity, but as one end of a temporal bridge between past and present. The representational agency of personification unites the poet with his former self, but unites them as separate identities, their separation affirmed rather than effaced by the mode of representation.

As the poem concludes, the "momentary bliss" of the second stanza, bestowed upon the poet by the gales rising up from the fields of the college, turns out to be as static as the "idle progeny" which inspired it:

> To each his suff'rings: all are men,
> Condemn'd alike to groan,
> The tender for another's pain;
> Th' unfeeling for his own.
> Yet ah! why should they know their fate?
> Since sorrow never comes too late,
> And happiness too swiftly flies.
> Thought would destroy their paradise.

No more; where ignorance is bliss,
'Tis folly to be wise.

(91–100)

The mediation of personification has not altered the green as a locale of temporal innocence, impregnable to the poet's mature consciousness. But the two are fused through the social ties of the allegorical transport from innocence to experience. While the children on the green serve as memorial ideas and the subsequent drama of personified abstractions as foundational knowledge in the poet's repository of retention, the act of recollection is inscribed in the style, rather than the structure of the poem, thus deferring agency to a communal rather than a personal language.

We may now begin to understand why Wordsworth eschewed personification in favor of "the very language of men" as an insufficient means of identification. Wordsworth constructs his personifications of Cambridge life as a bridge between his personal experiences and the wider world of human affairs, noting, "that here in dwarf proportions were expressed / The limbs of the great world" (3.616–17). Though initially characterizing his sequence of personifications as both "pageant" and "spectacle," Wordsworth rejects both terms as lacking sufficient substance to convey the uniquely metonymic function of the vision which is "no mimic show / Itself a living part of a live whole, / A creek of the vast sea" (3.624–26). Yet such an insistence on absolute metonymy actually undermines the representational cohesion of the following sequence by proposing an absolute affinity between private and public that would require no agency of mediation. Indeed, Wordsworth's ambivalent posture towards personification is inscribed in the very text of its employment:

For, all degrees
And shapes of spurious fame and short-lived praise
Here sate in state, and, fed with daily alms,
Retainers won away from solid good.
And here was Labour, his own Bond-slave; Hope
That never set the pains against the prize;
Idleness, halting with his weary clog;

And poor misguided Shame, and witless Fear,
And simple Pleasure, foraging for Death;
Honour misplaced, and Dignity astray;
Feuds, factions, flatteries, Enmity and Guile,
Murmuring Submission and bald Government
(The idol weak as the idolator)
And Decency and Custom starving Truth,
And blind Authority beating with his staff
The child that might have led him; Emptiness
Followed as of good omen, and meek Worth
Left to itself unheard of and unknown.

(3.626–643)

As a narrative of institutionalized authority and its successful oppression of youthful originality and imagination, Wordsworth's sequence of personified abstractions
embodies and gives agency to the more diffuse forces narrated in the preceding lines of the book. Yet its thematic
conflation of representational error ("(The idol weak as
the idolator)") with social degeneracy ("Murmuring Submission and bald Government") undermines its very
mode of representation. Wordsworth's stated distaste for
personification was, as in both Kant and Coleridge before
him, explicitly identified with the errors of Pagan idolatry. In his 1815 "Preface," Wordsworth argues that "the
anthropomorphitism of the Pagan religion subjected the
minds of the greatest poets in those countries too much to
the bondage of definite form; from which the Hebrews
were preserved by their abhorrence of idolatry."[37] Wordsworth's thematic qualification of the very trope by which
his representation plays itself out correlates with his
framing insistence upon the pageant as symbol rather
than allegory.

To understand the importance of Wordsworth's insistence upon symbolic identification within the pageantry
of his recollections, we may recall Paul de Man's skeptical assessment of such identification and its relevance to
a rhetoric of temporality:

Whereas the symbol postulates the possibility of an identity
or identification, allegory designates primarily a distance in
relation to its own origin, and, renouncing the nostalgia and

the desire to coincide, it establishes its language in the void
of this temporal difference. In so doing, it prevents the self
from an illusory identification with the non-self, which is now
fully, though painfully, recognized as a non-self.[38]

The danger of idolatry is that it fixes the play of memory
and foundation in an embodied image. While personification may play a mediating role, it in essence freezes
that relation, allowing no central role for a constitutive
self-identity to emerge. Wordsworthian identification depends upon "an illusory identification with the non-self,"
that non-self being his own temporally dislocated experiences of childhood. One recalls the passage in the second
book of *The Prelude* in which Wordsworth claims that

> so wide appears
> The vacancy between me and those days,
> Which yet have such self-presence in my mind
> That sometimes when I think of them I seem
> Two consciousnesses—conscious of myself,
> And of some other being.
>
> (2.28–33)

Wordsworth's aim in the "Prospectus" to *The Excursion* to
"with the thing / Contemplated, describe the Mind and
Man / Contemplating"[39] enables him to configure poetic
identity as a redemptive agency for a fragmented personal and social consciousness. Such redemption draws
its power from the "wide . . . vacancy" and realizes itself
in the "wide museum." The "aching and . . . barren sense /
Of gay confusion" and the "profit . . . drawn in times to
come" are two sides of the same coin. Their interplay produces the poetic form of *The Prelude*, an always-incomplete representation of a poetic self, born out of an
always-incomplete identification. The poet's inscription
of "two consciousnesses" through the intermittent "wide
vacancy," is not achieved, as is Gray's, through personification as allegorical agency, but through a partial identification which defines both past and present selves
through a logic of mediation.
   As a rover through the "wide museum" of his own recollections, Wordsworth is thus able to supplant the personi-

fications of the previous stanza as a mediating presence
between the "passages and fragments that remain" and
the consummation of the whole into unified presence. As
a museum guide, Wordsworth can single out the individual rarities and curiosities or attempt to make one whole
of the collection, yet to fully ameliorate the "general complaint" brings the entire project to an unproductive close.
Like the earlier guidebooks, Wordsworth surveys his options. Analogous to the collection of disparate elements
from the natural world—"fishes, gems / Birds, crocodiles,
shells"—the fragmentation of lived experience necessary
for the foundation of knowledge simultaneously creates a
loss of cohesive understanding. Wordsworth has already,
in the second book of the poem, used the metaphor of the
cabinet for a privileging of the parts over the whole, viewing the separation and classification of sensations as a focusing upon the "outward shows" of life which blinds one
to the "unity of all" (2.225–27). Here again the roving
through the cabinet or wide museum is an experience of
blindness, ignorance, and separation, for "little can be
seen, / Well understood, or naturally endeared" (3.654–
55). This initial evocation of the museum's disorienting effect is followed by a crucial qualification:

> Yet still does every step bring something forth
> That quickens, pleases, stings—and here and there
> A casual rarity is singled out
> And has its brief perusal, then give way
> To others, all supplanted in their turn.
>
> (3.656–60)

Insofar as the poet may single out individual episodes of
his experience, he is able to make them serve as memorial museum pieces, engendering narratives that claim to
reproduce their lost contexts of origin. But their placement within the larger repository of the poet's recon-
structed life creates a restlessness of mind that is divided
and distracted by the enormity of the collection.

The "gaudy congress framed / Of things by nature most
unneighbourly" overwhelms the poet whose faculties are
unable to grasp the whole as a coherent unity. The "ach-

ing and . . . barren sense / Of gay confusion" which follow
are characterized as mostly lacking in "wise longings"
and "love" and the whole experience is characterized in
the final lines of the book as "submissive idleness." Presented with a collection productive of the sublime,
Wordsworth is unable to consummate the provocation
with absolute identification. The aching and confusion
fail to provoke the proper direction of longing and love
which would cause the mind to swell with inner transport
and to claim for itself the higher unity to which the sublime attests. It is precisely Wordsworth's inability to consummate the sublime experience of the "wide museum"
which allows him to sustain his autobiographical narrative and self-representation. In Lockean terms, it is his
ability to maintain a distinction between perception and
recollection that enables him to represent his poetic self
as a recuperative and mediating identity.

"Yet," Wordsworth concludes, "something to the memory sticks at last / Whence profit may be drawn in times to
come" (3.661–68). As in his more celebrated passage on
the "spots of time," Wordsworth articulates the very process by which lived experience is fragmented and reproduced as poetic form. The loss of original context central
to the representational logic of the "wide museum" provides the crucial gap between the constructed object of
study—whether that object be material or experiential—
and the forces of social practice which have produced it:
a gap enabling of both memorial and foundational representation. Mary Jacobus has spoken of the "metaphoricity
of the Wordsworthian subject" as the coincidence of the
real and the symbolic, a product of the gap between external reality and internal metaphorical signification.[40] The
Wordsworthian self is just this bridge, or repression, of
the distance between original context and museum exhibition; but insofar as it is the Wordsworthian self which
produces the idea of both origin and sign, its mediating
role is simultaneously one of constitution. The "profit . . .
drawn in times to come" is none other than the poetic self
(poet-as-prophet understood as poet-as-profit), the memorial difference left over between the event and its recol-

lection, the foundational difference left over between the object and its exhibition.

Wordsworth's art of memory is a poetic realization of the paradox attendant upon the empiricist internalization of both the form and the content of the classical rhetorical art. The process whereby the mind, in the words employed in "Tintern Abbey," "Shall be a mansion for all lovely forms," and the "memory be as a dwelling-place / For all sweet sounds and harmonies" (140–43),[41] is a process not of "naked recollection" (3.646) but one which both memorially transforms and foundationally constitutes the very identity of the self. The "abundant recompence" (89) attendant upon the passing of years, the "profit . . . drawn in times to come" is both poetic form and self. In the fifth book of *The Prelude*, Wordsworth claims that

> Visionary power
> Attends upon the motions of the winds
> Embodied in the mystery of words;
> There darkness makes abode, and all the host
> Of shadowy things do work their changes there
> As in a mansion like their proper home.
>
> (5.619–24)

Mary Jacobus cites this passage and its rhetorical affiliation with "Tintern Abbey" in her exposition as to how "the gap between word and thing, once opened, typically proves Wordsworth's richest source of meaning."[42] This representational logic, affiliated both with the empiricist internalization of the rhetorical art of memory as well as with the broader social practices of museum exhibition, is the very model for subjective identification productive of and produced by modern nationalist ideologies.

"Among the Numbers whom Curiosity prompted to get a Sight of this Collection, I was of Course one." Powlett's *General Contents of the British Museum* is more than mere enumeration, but, as its extended title proclaims, a *Directory in Viewing that Noble Cabinet*. As a literary genre, the museum guide occupies a series of conjunctive positions between the visual and the verbal, the aesthetic and the poetic, the object and the subject, the museum and the public. As these guides for the curious oscillate between "a proper Idea of the Particulars" and an apprehension of "the Museum itself," memory assumes a central and transformational presence in the institutionalization of the museum as a public resource for an ideal national unity. The museum guide stills the dizziness of the sublime and soothes the "general complaint" with an incomplete amelioration: the nation itself. Contents and directory, public and nation, converge in the walls of the British Museum, Westminster Abbey, and other consecrations to melancholy through a uniquely Romantic poetics of identification. Wordsworth's autobiographical poetics registers the representational means by which the nation manifests itself in the museum, but realizes itself only in the guide, supplement, and revision of its public exhibition.

3

Composition and Alienation:
The National Reception of the
Elgin Marbles

I

TEARS SEEM TO FOLLOW THE PROGRESS OF THE PARTHENON Marbles like keeners at a wake. Keats wrote that it was "a gentle luxury to weep" in their presence, an emotive response "that mingles Grecian grandeur with the rude / Wasting of old time" (12–13).[1] The actress Sarah Siddons was brought to view the marbles in Lord Elgin's Park Lane showcase and, according to William Hamilton, "one of the groups of female statues so rivetted [sic] and agitated the feelings of Mrs. Siddons . . . as actually to draw tears from her eyes."[2] And Edward Daniel Clarke, present at the destructive dismantling of the Parthenon, records how the Turkish Disdar, viewing the ruination, "could no longer restrain his emotions; but actually took his pipe from his mouth, and, letting fall a tear, said in a most emphatic tone of voice "τελος!"" positively declaring that nothing should induce him to consent to any further dilapidation of the building."[3] To read such effusive performances is no easy task. Lord Byron was to cite Clarke's anecdote in a footnote to *Childe Harold's Pilgrimage* as testimony to the pain felt by the sons of Athena under "the weight of Despot's chains" (2.108).[4] In turn, Clarke was to cite Siddons's effusions alongside Byron's verse in subsequent editions of his *Travels* to emphasize the barbarity of Elgin's pursuits.[5] Yet the Disdar's tearful pronouncement gestures as much towards epic fulfillment as towards tragic loss. And the tears of the actress provided Hamilton, in his promotional *Memorandum on the Earl of Elgin's Activities in Greece* (1811) with a feminine and emotive complement to the artistic testimonials of Benjamin West and Antoniô Canova in favor of the national purchase of the marbles. Even Keats's gentle tears are as ambivalent as the sonnet whose opening octave of sublime abjection they help to close. Neither critique nor panegyric, Keats's sonnet "On Seeing the Elgin Marbles" sublimates political concerns into an aesthetic response that establishes an affinity between personal despondency and historical ruination. He joins in simile "Grecian grandeur" with the aspirations of poetic vision, those "dim-conceived glories of the brain," only to register the heart's "undescribable feud" and "dizzy pain" as it vacillates between consummation and despair. But in the companion sonnet to Benjamin Robert Haydon, Keats deploys this emotive response to elevate the two artists above those who "star'd at what was most divine / With browless idiotism— o'erweening phlegm" (11–12). Felicia Hemans, in promoting the acquisition of the Elgin Marbles, echoes Keats's hierarchy of sensibility by admonishing those "souls that too deeply feel" to "envy not / The sullen calm your fate hath never known" (15–16).[6] Emotive enthusiasm opens such souls to the light of fancy and genius unknown to "that wint'ry lot" (17) unmoved by the marbles' glory. Tears, in these instances, are the currency of aesthetic purchase. The subject's longing confirms the beauty of the object of his or her desire, redeeming the temple's destruction in the subject's "tearful eyes."

Since their exportation to Britain, the Elgin Marbles have become the perennial test case in numerous yet overlapping curatorial controversies of the modern era: the claims of nation-states to the relics of their geographical and cultural past, the authority of museums as guardians of the records of civilization, the means by which antiquities may be judged and evaluated, the propriety of restoration, the methodologies of exhibition, and the aesthetic norms of academic and national art.[7] Even the denomination of the sculptures, metopes, and friezes is a point of contention. They have been known at various

times and by various parties as the Elgin Marbles, the
Athenian Marbles, or the Parthenon Marbles, depending
upon whether they are to be identified with their origin
in the Athenian Acropolis or with the man responsible
for their transport to London. But, first and foremost,
these works now form the centerpiece of the British Museum. Though originally stored in a temporary structure
attached to the side of the museum's main edifice, in 1832
they were incorporated within Robert Smirke's slowly
evolving neo-classical edifice. Here, for the better parts
of the nineteenth and twentieth centuries, they have
formed both a link and a zenith in the museum's curatorial program of cultural progress.[8] Even today, when the
museum's organization reflects a more ecumenical view
of the varied productions of antiquity, the Elgin Room
stands out as a secular shrine both to the wonders of
Athenian culture and the acquisitions of British power.

I have no wish to enter into the on-going debate regarding the proprietary rights to these works. Nor do I wish to
comment specifically on their artistic merits or archaeological significance. Rather, I wish to consider these marbles, which have generated more reactions, both prosaic
and poetic, than any of the British Museum's other holdings, as exemplary objects of national aesthetic desire. If,
as we have seen, the foundation of the British Museum
joined the private experiences of beauty and recollection
to the identification of a national body, then the actual objects of exhibition play a critical role in this grammar of
political consolidation. True to its romantic origins, it is
a grammar, I will argue, constructed upon loss and recompense, an elegiac lamentation constituting a subjective
aesthetic experience homologous with the historical fate
of the objects it comprises. In their exhibition, in their
pictorial and poetic representations, and in the debates
and promotions they have inspired, the marbles consistently figure as a supplementary sign of departed
grandeur—in Keats's famous phrase "a shadow of a magnitude." It is just that supplementary position that makes
the marbles such a consistently powerful sign for personal and communal identification. In the figurative epic
of the national museum, comprehensive in scope and tri-

umphal in presentation, loss and the sentiments it engenders afford the necessary agency of aesthetic and ideological appreciation. In considering the British Museum's acquisition of the Parthenon Marbles in the early nineteenth century we enter into the period of its definitive transformation from a noble cabinet to a public museum and the world's greatest single collection of antiquities. No other acquisition in the museum's history has had such a lasting influence on its development, nor inspired so much debate and reflection, as the Parthenon Marbles brought and sold to Britain by Thomas Bruce, Lord Elgin.

II

A notice in the *Gentleman's Magazine* of January 1817 may introduce the semantic function of the Elgin Marbles within the walls of the British Museum. As such, I quote it in full:

The publick will very shortly be gratified by free access to those famous Athenian Sculptures which were lately purchased for the Nation by the British ambassador to the porte. Two spacious rooms have been built for their exhibition on the ground floor of the British Museum, adjoining the Townley and Egyptian Galleries. In the first and smaller of these rooms will be displayed the spirited sculptures recently dug up at Phygalia, together with the casts of Athenian statuary, the originals of which still adorn Athens and its vicinity: and in the other, originals from Athens, which will henceforward be properly called the Athenian Marbles or Sculptures. On the ground floor are disposed the several statues, as the Theseus, &c.; and at the height of six feet from the floor the Friezes; while a few feet higher are the Metopes. Nothing can be more striking, more interesting, and more affecting. We are struck with them as the remains of ages so renowned, and so long passed away! We are interested with them as performances of matchless beauty, and many of them the work of Ictinus, under the superintendence of Phidias! And we are affected at that revolution of empires which has occasioned their transportation from their native city to a country which, in the age of Pericles, was esteemed the most barbarous of all countries, even if its very existence was known. They are, however, a proud trophy, because their display in the British metropolis is the result of public taste; and also a pleasing one, because they are not the price of blood, shed in wanton or ambitious wars. United to the Townley and other collections, the suite of rooms exhibits the finest display of the art of sculpture to be found in the world, and they will always do honour to the metropolis, and to the parties concerned in assembling and purchasing them. In addition to the above, and other splendid attractions, the public-spirited Trustees of the Museum have recently purchased, at the price of 1,100*l* a complete collection of British Zoology, formed by Col. Montague, of the Knowle, in Devonshire.[9]

The torturous grammar of this notice owes its passive constructions and overburdening prepositional phrases to the peculiar ideological work of its exhibitionary rhetoric. Its simultaneous celebration of public, nation, and marbles follows a circular logic of honor and legitimacy in which agency is effaced almost entirely, and the marbles themselves, ostensibly the subject of the notice, are never described. Rather, as in the very first sentence, the marbles serve only to close the circle of reference that links a gratified public to an acquisitive nation. The first-person plural pronoun which structures the evaluation of the exhibition's merit in the second half of the notice is made indefinite by its alternating position as subject and indirect object of the marbles' appreciation and honor. "We," that is, may be struck, interested, and affected by the marbles' exhibition only so far as we identify with the public taste that has warranted their removal to the British metropolis. The marbles themselves fade in their arrested functions as remains, performances, and transitive objects and in their conversion into trophies that signify nothing more than the pride and pleasure of their acquisition. The notice is less a description of an exhibition than a prescription of an exhibitionary grammar which links public and nation through "splendid attractions," sculptural or zoological.

The notice also manages to efface, through its presentation of consensus, the dominant controversies that surrounded the national acquisition of the marbles and their proper exhibitionary display. Discussions in the House of Commons in 1816 differed little from current debates, weighing the possible benefit to the arts and the need to safeguard the marbles against a profound sense of political injustice. Several members questioned Lord Elgin's authority both in removing the marbles and then in requesting economic retribution. The recent restoration of European art works from Napoleonic theft made Parliament particularly uneasy about possible comparisons. Joseph Bankes's defensive insistence that Elgin's activities "bore no resemblance to those undue and tyrannical means by which the French had obtained possession of so many treasures of art"[10] notwithstanding, many other members were unable to make such fine distinctions. As Hugh Hammersley put it, "he was not so enamoured of those headless ladies as to forget another lady, which was justice."[11] Economic prudence in the aftermath of the debt incurred in the Napoleonic wars only added to Parliament's concerns. J. C. Curwen feared "that we were fast approaching to that course of extravagance with respect to the public money, which had brought to decay the countries where these works of art were produced."[12] But such precedents could work both ways, as John Wilson Crocker demonstrated:

> It was singular that when 2500 years ago, Pericles was adorning Athens with those very works, some of which we are now about to acquire, the same cry of economy was raised against him, and the same answer that he then gave might be repeated now, that it was money spent for the use of the people, for the encouragement of arts, the increase of manufactures, the prosperity of trades, and the encouragement of industry; not merely to please the eye of the man of taste, but to create, to stimulate, to guide the exertions of the artist, the mechanic, and even the labourer, and to spread through all the branches of society a spirit of improvement, and the means of a sober and industrious affluence.[13]

Crocker's rhetoric is inflated to be sure, but it is consonant with the general tone of the promotions that surrounded the acquisition of the marbles, from their transport from Greece to their purchase for the British

Museum. The glories of the past were to be reborn in Britain through the material example of Athenian achievement, their exhibition thus serving as both a sign and a cause of British national ascendancy. Their influence would extend not only to the sculptors and painters given leave to sketch and model from the works, but to "all branches of society" as models of liberty and industry for public emulation.

Much of this rhetoric was codified and disseminated in the *Report from the Select Committee of the House of Commons on the Earl of Elgin's Collection of Sculptured Marbles* (1816), an extensive record of the political and aesthetic debates surrounding Elgin's pursuits. Arguing suggestively "that the money expended in the acquisition of any commodity is not necessarily the measure of its real value," the Committee recommended purchasing the marbles not only for their aesthetic merits, but also for their exemplary standing as products of political and economic liberty:

> Your Committee cannot dismiss this interesting subject, without submitting to the attentive reflection of the House, how highly the cultivation of the Fine Arts has contributed to the reputation, character, and dignity of every Government by which they have been encouraged, and how intimately they are connected with the advancement of every thing valuable in science, literature, and philosophy. In contemplating the importance and splendor to which so small a republic as Athens rose, by the genius and energy of her citizens, exerted in the path of such studies, it is impossible to overlook how transient the memory and fame of extended empires, and of mighty conquerors are, in comparison of those who have rendered inconsiderable states eminent, and immortalized their own names by these pursuits. But if it be true, as we learn from history and experience, that free governments afford a soil most suitable to the production of native talent, to the maturing of the powers of the human mind, and to the growth of every species of excellence, by opening to merit the prospect of reward and distinction, no country can be better adapted than our own to afford an honourable asylum to these monuments of the school of Phidias, and of the administration and homage to which they are entitled, and serve in

return as models and examples to those, who by knowing how to revere and appreciate them, may learn first to imitate, and ultimately to rival them.[14]

Parliament was hardly united behind such sentiments, voting in favor of acquisition by a margin of only two votes: 82 for, 80 against. Yet the logic of progressive cultural transmission, which simultaneously registers and effaces the historical and political distance between Periclean Athens and Regency London, has continued to prove a powerful justification for British claims to the marbles. In a 1986 polemic in *ARTNews*, John Henry Merryman put forward the argument that "even if cultural nationalism were to apply, it would not establish that the Marbles should return to Athens. They have been in England for more than a century and in that time have become a part of the British cultural heritage. The Elgin Marbles and other works in the British Museum have entered British culture."[15] Merryman's argument is not as specious as it might seem, for the program of interest and affection which the promotion in the *Gentleman's Magazine* prescribes has not only entered British culture, but, in the context of an institution of national consolidation, has helped to construct it. British culture and the Elgin Marbles are both hybrid forms, established through fraught relations with both a glorified past and an imagined community. In such manifestly nationalist promotions, the forms of the marbles prove ultimately less important than the narratives of identification they enable.

Despite its celebratory rhetoric, a profound sense of mourning informs the teleological argument of the *Gentleman's Magazine* notice. As a public articulation of the romantic sentiment of ruins, the notice displaces power with beauty and mortality with recollection. But the displacement is imperfect. Its exhibitionary prescription fuses aesthetic interest and historical consciousness in a confirmation of public, national, and cultural ascendancy and honor, but it grounds its epic apotheosis in elegiac lament. Indeed, the very elements that filled Keats with "an undescribable feud" and "a most dizzy pain" provide the dialectical paradigms of loss and recompense governing the notice's reception of Elgin's marbles. "Matchless beauty" and the "revolution of empires," or, as Keats would have it, the mingling of "Grecian grandeur with the rude / Wasting of old time" (12–13)[16] conspire to interest and affect the speculative viewer. The marbles themselves are shadow figures, fully present within the museum's walls, yet productively absent within the exhibitionary grammar of national acquisition. The viewer's sensibilities, affected by both beauty and its inevitable decay, may confirm both the glory of Periclean Athens and the cultivation of the British nation. But, insofar as they ground the grammar of exhibition in the aesthetic response of the viewing subject, they may also destabilize historical narratives of national progress.

Within the context of this sentimental promotion, Keats's response is less exemplary of political or aesthetic ambivalence and more paradigmatic of the subjective sensibilities enabling the public epic of historical progress and national acquisition:

> My spirit is too weak—mortality
>   Weighs heavily on me like unwilling sleep,
>   And each imagined pinnacle and steep
> Of godlike hardship tells me I must die
> Like a sick eagle looking at the sky.
>   Yet 'tis a gentle luxury to weep
>   That I have not the cloudy winds to keep
> Fresh for the opening of the morning's eye.
> Such dim-conceivd glories of the brain
>   Bring round the heart an undescribable feud;
> So do these wonders a most dizzy pain,
>   That mingles Grecian grandeur with the rude
> Wasting of old time—with a billowy main—
>   A sun—a shadow of a magnitude.[17]

Akin to the *Gentleman's Magazine* notice, Keats's sonnet takes for its theme the valence between symbolic union and figurative distance that reconfirms the marbles' aesthetic and historical value. Keats's poem of longing and ambivalence literally effaces the marbles themselves as objects of description, employing the space of that effacement as the constitutive root of its formal play. The caesuras of the final lines become the exhibitionary site of the marbles, standing between creative self-origination and the trace of its departure. The image of the "billowy main" seems particularly well suited both as a figure for the forms left by the presence of a creative magnitude and as an analogy to the sick eagle whose power depends upon the "cloudy winds" now absent. The complementary sonnet to Haydon, while less formally inventive, also configures both Keats and Haydon as desirous spectators, seeking sources of inspirational power in elusive objects and bemoaning their own inadequacy. Both sonnets have been well read by Grant F. Scott as exploring the range of aesthetic responses to the marbles, mediating between the denigration of their ruined state and the glorification of their artistic beauty. As Scott has noted, Keats's works seem distinguished by their reserve from the mass of poems elicited by the marbles characterized by unreserved optimism for their inspirational power.[18] But the affinities between Keats's poetry and the notice of the *Gentleman's Magazine* indicate the centrality of this vacillation between mourning and celebration to the national promotion and reception of the marbles.[19] For the sonnet's turn from elegy to alienation, from the beauties of form to the sublimity of power, establishes a motivational agency to redeem the vagaries of history in the rapture of aesthetic delight. His privileging of personal sensibility over formal idealization allows Keats a more powerful rhetorical position from which to assess the experience of seeing the Elgin Marbles. Keats's sonnet, while a masterfully concise expression of the poet's trademark melancholy, also provides an eloquent expression of the subjective response that both justified and challenged the public promotion of Elgin's efforts.

This aesthetic ambivalence between sorrow and celebration became the determinative paradigm for the early reception of the Elgin Marbles.[20] In the walls of the British Museum, the marbles both support a progressive cultural historiography culminating in British ascendancy and challenge the very foundations of that curatorial program. This challenge arises not only from the manifest evidence they provide of the transience of all human societies, but also from the aesthetic criteria their very material forms forward and subvert. By focusing, amidst the wealth of discussion surrounding their acquisition and display, upon two aesthetic debates, I wish to consider the intimate relation between personal longing and public triumph in national museum culture. I will explore the contest between Benjamin West and Benjamin Robert Haydon to make good on the promise that the exhibition of the Elgin Marbles would regenerate the public arts in Britain. I will then offer readings of the poetic reactions of Lord Byron and Felicia Hemans to Elgin's removal of the Parthenon statuary. While West and Haydon, working within and against the academic prescriptions of Sir Joshua Reynolds, are manifestly concerned with the regeneration of public historical painting and sculpture, their divergent approaches reveal two distinct understandings of the national subject and his relation to public culture. Byron and Hemans, writing to and against James Thomson's exemplary progress poem *Liberty*, offer more explicit couplings of personal lament and public proclamation, couplings that lend themselves both to political critique and national tribute. Both artistic conflicts register the mutually determining relation of ideological and aesthetic response within the context of an expanding national museum culture.

III

On February 6, 1809, the American-born painter and president of the Royal Academy Benjamin West wrote to Lord Elgin to thank him for indulging his desire to view and sketch from the Parthenon marbles and to justify his larger aesthetic practice. Repeating the commonly-expressed opinion that the exhibition of such specimens of Grecian art "has founded a new Athens for the emulation and example of the British student," West quickly foregrounds his impressions with a general statement of artistic practice:

I must premise to your Lordship, that I considered loose and
detached sketches from these reliques of little use to me or
value to the arts in general. To improve myself, therefore,
and to contribute to the improvement of others, I have deemd
it more important to select and combine whatever was most
excellent from them into subject and composition.[21]

West follows this apology with a detailed account of the
various scenes from Greek mythology composed from the
Parthenon fragments and his own imagination. The battle
of the Centaurs, the triumph of Theseus and Hercules
over the Amazons, Theseus's slaying of the Minotaur,
Neptune and his company, and Alexander with his horse
Bucephalus emerge consecutively from the fragments
and reliefs exhibited at Elgin's Park Lane showcase.[22]
"Your Lordship may perhaps be inclined to think with
me," West continues, "that a point, and, if I may so express
it, a kind of climax, is thus given to those works, by the
union of those detached figures, with the incorporation of
the parts of individual grandeur, and abstracted excellence of Phidias." Claiming the example of Raphael and
other Italian masters, West rhetorically queries, "is it not,
moreover, this combination of parts which comes the
nearest to perfection in refined and ideal art? For, thus
combining what is excellent in art with what possesses
character in nature, the most distinguished works have
been produced, in painting, poetry, and sculpture."[23]

West's letter to Elgin exemplifies the normative aesthetic of academic painting that was to serve the cause of
nationalizing the marbles. But the young painter Benjamin Robert Haydon had also been admitted to sketch the
marbles in their Park Lane showcase, and more than artistic rivalry informs Haydon's account of West's initial efforts:

While I was drawing there, West came in, and seeing me, said
with surprise, "Hah, hah, Mr. Haydon, you are admitted, are
you? I hope you and I can keep a secret." The very day after,
he came down with large canvasses, and without at all entering into the principles of these divine things, hastily made
compositions from Greek history, putting in the Theseus, the
Ilyssus, and others of the figures, and restoring defective

parts—that is, he did that which he could do easily, and
which he did not need to learn how to do, and avoided doing
that which he could only do with difficulty, and which he was
in great need of learning how to do.[24]

At odds with the Royal Academy, Haydon could not help
but see West as the embodiment of all he disdained in
modern artistic practice. His autobiography contrasts his
own conception of the unification of the ideal and the natural with the Academy's insistence on the Platonic beau-
ideal through a personalized conflict of the two artists in
Elgin's Park Lane exhibition:

> My early attempt to unite Nature with the ideal form of the
> antique was now proved correct by the perfection of that
> union in these faultless productions. The advantage to me
> was immense. No other artist drew there at all for some
> months, and then only West came, but he did not draw the
> marbles, and study their hidden beauties. He merely made a
> set of rattling compositions, taking the attitudes as models
> for his own inventions. This was not doing what I had done,
> investigating their principles deeply and studiously. West de-
> rived little benefit from this method, while in every figure
> I drew the principle was imbibed and inhaled forever.
> (1:107–8)

A comparison of the two artists' sketches bears out Haydon's claims, revealing the younger artist to have at-
tended much more closely to the subtleties of the forms.
But it is difficult to pin too much on either West or Haydon's pronouncements. Their language is impossibly
vague and both were committed to historical painting to
serve as a model for a public and national taste. Furthermore, both describe a union of the natural and the ideal
as the proper goal for the artist. The difference in their
approaches lies primarily in the model of subjectivity
that they suggest; models inextricably bound up with the
representation of the marbles as aesthetic objects. West
develops affinities using recognizable typologies, placing
the forms of the Parthenon marbles within allegorical
compositions of figurative images bound up in narrative
and temporality. Haydon's insistence on form over com-

Benjamin West, "Sketches of the Parthenon Metopes." The Pierpont Morgan Library, New York. 1970. 11:135.

Benjamin Robert Haydon, "Head of horse from the Parthenon pediment"
© Copyright The British Museum.

position paired with his insistence on the simultaneity of
the natural and the ideal establishes the possibility of
identification through a communion of subject and object. His rhetoric of depth, of "hidden beauties of form"
to be "imbibed and inhaled," pursues an artistic goal as
inspirational as West's compositional union of "individual grandeur" and "abstracted excellence." The true
public art, in Haydon's view, is one that appeals primarily
to aesthetic appreciation and not rhetorical demonstra-
tion. More than a personal artistic rivalry, the conflict of
approaches between West and Haydon suggests two models of aesthetic and ideological incorporation, both of
which would service the evaluation and exhibition of the
Elgin Marbles within the walls of the British Museum.

　　West's stylistic ambitions for a "refined and ideal art"
and his choice of mythological subjects conform to the
grand style of historical painting favored by the Royal
Academy. Informed by a strain of Platonic and rhetorical
criticism stemming from Leon Battista Alberti's fifteenth-

century writings on painting, the academic style favored works of *istoria*, didactic and narrative scenes from classical or biblical history that allegorically exemplified universal ethical codes. As John Barrell has demonstrated, this style was patterned by an evolving strain of civic humanism that sought to address, confirm, and thereby establish a national public through the cultivation of taste.[25] West's privileging of "subject and composition" over "loose and detached sketches" exemplifies the rhetorical norms of this style, which followed the prescriptions for public oration both to instruct and to persuade its audience to exercise their civic duties. Such ambitions dictated both the content and the style of academic art. Its subjects were to be historical or mythological in the epic fashion, namely public heroes performing great and noble actions. Equally important, its style was to elevate it above mere mechanical mimesis towards a communication of the ideal, aligning the private taste for beauty with the public pursuit of virtue.[26] As West's predecessor Sir Joshua Reynolds noted in his famous series of discourses:

> It has been often observed, that the good and virtuous man alone can acquire this true or just relish even of works of art. This opinion will not appear entirely without foundation, when we consider that the same habit of mind which is acquired by our search after truth in the more serious duties of life, is only transferred to the pursuit of lighter amusements. The same disposition, the same desire to find something steady, substantial, and durable, on which the mind can lean as it were, and rest with safety, actuates us in both cases. The subject only is changed. We pursue the same method in our search after the idea of beauty and perfection in each; of virtue, by looking forwards beyond ourselves to society, and to the whole; of arts, by extending our views in the same manner to all ages and all times.[27]

By instructing its audience in the grounds of abstraction and idealization, in finding the universal in the particular, public art simultaneously instructs its audience in the grounds of republican citizenship, looking past individual interest to the welfare of the community. Seeking to temper the self-interest foundational to a modern mercantile society with the cultivation of virtue in politics and the arts, Reynolds advocated the elevation of the mind above "the gratification of the senses" towards "the idea of general beauty, and the contemplation of general truth. . . . Whatever abstracts the thoughts from sensual gratifications, whatever teaches us to look for happiness within ourselves, must advance in some measure the dignity of our nature."[28] Paradoxically, such Platonic standards seem to efface the very objects they are meant to appraise. By converting paintings into signs, Reynolds's rhetorical aesthetic privileges historical narrative and civic virtue above the visual immediacy of the works themselves. Likewise, as in the discourse surrounding the British Museum, such an advocacy of universal virtue stumbled on the actual public attending the exhibitions of the Royal Academy. In rhetoric by now familiar, Reynolds noted that the Academy's exhibitions "while they produce such admirable effects by nourishing emulation and calling out genius, have also a mischievous tendency, by seducing the Painter to an ambition of pleasing indiscriminately the mixed multitude of people who resort to them."[29] The academic tradition, in both style and subject, offers a self-consciously public model of aesthetic production and reception, but one whose pronounced idealism proves unable to accommodate the seductive immediacy of the works themselves or the actual public in all its multitudinous diversity.

West's own quest to combine "what is excellent in art with what possesses character in nature" in the production of "refined and ideal art" carries on this tradition, with an even greater emphasis on painting's rhetorical function.[30] "Accustom yourselves to draw all the deviations of the [human] figure," he advised his students, "till you are as much acquainted with them as with the alphabet of your own language, and can make them with as much facility as your letters; for they are indeed the letters and alphabet of your profession, whether it be painting or sculpture."[31] Having mastered their alphabet, the students may progress to a proper grammar of forms "arising from the philosophical consideration of the subject intended to be represented." The end of this grammar is not a fixation on the objects of representation, but an aesthetic reflection upon the public and civic ideals they exemplify:

> When the student has settled in his own mind the general and primary characteristics, in either sex, of the human figure, the next step will enable him to reduce the particular character of his subject into its proper class, whether it rank under the sublime or the beautiful, the heroic or the graceful, the masculine or the feminine, or in any of its other softer or more spirited distinctions. For the course of his studies will have made him acquainted with the moral operations of character, as they are expressed upon the external form; and the habit of discrimination, thus acquired, will have taught him the action or attitude by which all moral movements of character are usually accompanied.[32]

Hence derives the benefit to Britain of the example of the Elgin Marbles. As West would emphasize in his discourse of 1811, the marbles "are the union of Athenian genius and philosophy" and illustrate "the mental impression which is so essentially to be given to works of refined art." "It is," he insists, "the mental power displayed in the Elgin marbles that I wish the juvenile artist to notice."[33] West's own selections and combinations of the excellence displayed in the London metropolis restore the fragmented clauses of the Athenian forms within grammatical compositions of heroic action.[34] West was later, in his testimony before the House of Commons, to claim the marbles as models for his late self-denominated "epic" paintings, *Christ Healing the Sick* and *Christ Rejected*, the latter of which Sir George Beaumont praised for its "comprehensiveness and completeness." The catalogue prepared for this monumental work used similarly epic descriptions, claiming, "The delineation of nearly the whole scale of human passions, from the basest to those which partake most of the divine nature, has thus been necessarily attempted."[35] Like the epic, historical painting in the grand style could engage the noble passions and inspire its audience with displays of public virtue. Defining his sense of epic painting to Farington in 1807 in

Benjamin West. "Christ Healing the Sick" (1815). Courtesy of the Historic Collections of Pennsylvania Hospital, Philadelphia.

regards to his painting of *The Death of Lord Nelson* of the year before, West commented that

> to move the mind there should be a spectacle presented to raise & warm the mind, & all shd. be proportioned to the highest idea conceived of the Hero. No Boy, sd. West, wd. be animated by a representation of Nelson dying like an ordinary man, His feelings must be roused & His mind inflamed by a scene great & extraordinary. A mere matter of fact will never produce this effect.[36]

In his initial compositions, West attempts to restore the forms of the Parthenon within the mythological system that inspired their creation. Casting the forms and principles of the Elgin Marbles into such an epic context elevates the mind of the viewer towards the "highest idea conceived of the Hero." In his latter epic masterworks, West transposes the forms of pagan antiquity into the heroic actions of the Christian passion. Here, in a justification derided by Hazlitt as beyond presumptuous, West aims "to excite feelings in the spectator similar to those produced by a perusal of the Sacred Texts, which so pa-

Benjamin West. "Christ Rejected" (1814). Courtesy of the Pennsylvania Academy of the Fine Arts, Philadelphia. Gift of Mrs. Sarah Harrison (The Joseph Harrison, Jr. Collection).

thetically describe these awful events."[37] In aligning the verbal power of the scriptures with the visual composition of his own painting, West seeks their rhetorical power to excite the passions and move the spectator towards awe and emulation. In both his pagan and his Christian paintings, West attempts a public epic vision that will both unite and confirm his audience as members of a republic of virtue and taste.

West's aesthetic practice is rhetorical in another sense, for his letters to Lord Elgin were not solely private correspondences. They appeared in William Hamilton's promotional *Memorandum of the Earl of Elgin's Pursuits in Greece* (1811) amidst various accounts of the marbles' acquisition and attestations to their aesthetic merit. Seeking to advance the nationalization of the marbles, the *Memorandum* retells the familiar story of Elgin's competition with France and diplomatic efforts with the Turkish

government for the sketching and subsequent removal of
the marbles. It calls forward the testimonies of West and
Canova alongside the effusive response of Sarah Siddons.
It then offers two suggestions regarding their exhibition.
The first, that casts be made for a historically accurate
presentation "in an elevation, and in a situation similar
to that which they actually had occupied" while the originals are presented "in a view to the more easy inspection
and study of them." The second, that the marbles be employed in conjunction with British athletes as models for
artistic study:

> Under similar advantages, and with an enlightened and en-
> couraging protection bestowed on genius and the arts, it may
> not be too sanguine to indulge a hope, that, prodigal as na-
> ture is in the perfections of the human figure in this country,
> animating as are the instances of patriotism, heroic actions,
> and private virtues deserving commemoration, sculpture
> may soon be raised in England to rival the ablest productions
> of the best times of Greece.[38]

The same epic and rhetorical conception of public art
promoted by West and the Royal Academy informs the curatorial method of these sanguine suggestions. The marbles must be cast within a composition—either in an
imaginative recreation of their original setting or in tandem with living athletes—in order to manifest their value
for the arts and the nation. Fusing the forms of Periclean
Athens with the "heroic actions" and "private virtues" of
British culture, the modern sculptor may restore the arts
in their public function. Within this context, West's pictorial practice serves as an aesthetic counterpart in the
larger project of incorporating the statues into national
culture. As he hopes in his letter, the marbles "will not
only afford to the British people, the frequent opportunity of contemplating their excellencies; but will be the
means of enlightening the public mind, and correcting
the national taste, to a true estimation of what is really
valuable and dignified in art."[39] The relation of Britain to
Greece as heir apparent is reproduced in microcosm by
West's conceit regarding "the means you [Elgin] have af-

forded me of adding my name to that of Phidias, by arranging his figures in my own compositions."[40] If the original epic structure of the Parthenon has been dismantled, it may be restored in the nationalist saga of British artistic accomplishment. "We feel rejoiced," he proclaims to the Academy, "that the exertions recently made by a noble personage to enrich our studies in [architecture and sculpture] are such, that we may say, London has become the Athens for study."[41]

Despite such aspirations, neither Siddons's tears nor West's compositions were greeted with universal approbation. An anonymous review of the *Memorandum* published in the *British Review and London Critical Journal* (1811) dismissed Siddons's performance as mere "stage-effect" and attacked West's efforts on almost every front. "The president also hopes that these specimens of the arts brought from Greece 'will be the means of enlightening the public mind, and correcting the national taste to a true estimation of what is really valuable and dignified in art.' That this hope will not be gratified, we suspect; and one reason for our suspicion is the use that Mr. West has made of them."[42] Considering the employment of classical mythology a mere servile imitation of a previous age, thoroughly banned from painting's sister art of poetry, the reviewer chastises West's continued use of these subjects:

> Yet now we have Mr. West prospectively announcing the improvement of English taste in his art, and giving, as specimens to ameliorate the national feeling, paintings of Neptune, and Theseus, and Hercules, and Amazons, and monsters, and 'chimeras dire.' This is to imitate the ancients; making their footsteps the measure of our motions. Such subjects are unsuited to us, either as poets or painters. What was historical to them, is worse than mythological to us. . . . The obtruding monsters of Pagan antiquity must be extirpated from the domain of the arts, before our artists can fulfil [sic] the destination of their genius. (46)

Though reflecting in part the classic debate between the ancients and the moderns, the reviewer's attack upon the degradation from history to mythology should be recog-

nized more specifically as an attack on the rhetorical aesthetic promoted by West's compositions. For it is not the
subject matters per se to which the reviewer objects, but
their ossification over so many years. "It is observable,"
the reviewer notes, "that allegories have frequently lost
their aerial character, and have after a period of proba-
tion been naturalized into the world of realities" (52). The
resurrection of such ancient allegories is inherently re-
gressive in attending to subject over form. Compositions
that once had a power of semantic play have now become
reified into dead metaphors, incapable of reviving the
mind or instilling a powerful sense of common taste in the
public eye. For the reviewer, the power of public art
comes not in its representation of fixed compositions but
in its exhibition of objects still capable of eliciting response through their mimetic accomplishment. "Ancient
statuary should be studied," the reviewer concedes, "as
the rules of science exemplified; but the paramount
study, the matter of the ancients and moderns, is the living world" (57). Without the ability to provoke aesthetic
appreciation through formal mastery, any composition
will remain lifeless and inert. This initial attack is merely
the opening salvo in an extensive denigration of West's
subjects and style, a denigration that continually praises
the Greeks at the expense of the moderns. The static nature of the poses, the exhibition of grief, the overcrowd-
ing of the scenes, and the representation of catastrophes;
each find their turn as emblems of all that is wrong in
modern painting, with West's portrayals of Christ used as
the primary source of examples.

Just as West's aesthetic apology appears within a
broader contextual agenda, so too do the reviewer's attacks. While the reviewer is sympathetic to Elgin's victo-
ries over French competition and "the iconoclastic fury
of the Mahometans," he questions the advantage of nationalizing the acquisitions. Resisting the *Memorandum*'s
agenda of situating the fragments as elements of a national culture, he attacks the notion of exhibitionary reconstruction, noting "that neither casts, nor even the
originals in their unconnected state, could afford to an
artist an adequate conception of the combinations or

general effect of Grecian, or, indeed, of any other buildings" (41). Furthermore he questions, as had so many others of the time, the wisdom of using public funds for such expenditure. Sounding views still current today, the reviewer notes that any reimbursement for Lord Elgin's expenditures "should be performed by his opulent countrymen, who delight in contemplating works of art, or who apply them to add loveliness to luxury" (42). By relegating aesthetic appreciation to a private sector of the population, the reviewer fuses an aesthetic critique of West's practice of allegorical composition with a social and political critique of Elgin's attempts to seek national retribution for what the reviewer terms his "industry from ruined Greece" (42). Both West's compositions and Elgin's pursuits seek to recast the fragments within an epic context, whether that be the "comprehensiveness and completeness" of national art or the animating patriotism commemorated and encouraged in the exhibitionary apparatus of the British Museum. Such approaches ring hollow to the reviewer not only as misguided appropriations of public funds, but also as representational strategies which draw our attention away from the beauties of the natural world.

IV

In his denigration of the academic tradition of public art and his opposition to the national purchase of the Elgin Marbles, the reviewer offers a solely negative critique, forwarding no alternative vision of exhibitionary practice other than relegating the marbles to private delight and opulent ornamentation. Yet it was possible to critique West's rhetorical academic style while maintaining a commitment to public art and national exhibition. Haydon's marginalia in his own copy of Hamilton's *Memorandum* provides a critique both more sympathetic to the project of nationalization and more specific in its chastisement of West's pronouncements. In response to West's denigration of "loose and detached sketches," Haydon writes,

I must be allowed to premise that loose & detached & accurate studies from things as they are—are the only methods to accumulate materials for producing things as they ought to be and hasty, careless compositions are at all times of little use to the Artist himself, 'or value to the Arts in general.' . . . Let Mr. West point out all the hidden beauties of form in these divine productions in his own compositions from them. I defy him or an angel from Heaven to do it, for this simple reason, because they are not there. Of what assistance then can such a method of study be to him or any body. He came down with immense canvasses, rattled in the whole collection in a week, with his usual rapid and superficial hand, and then infers that loose, detached drawings, executed with patient attention, and highly and daily contemplations and investigation, are of less use to the Artist or value to the Arts in general, than his senseless, useless, thoughtless, superficial compositions.[43]

Given the acerbic *ad hominem* nature of this attack, it is easy to miss the shared ambitions of the two artists. While Haydon attacks West's methods, he is sympathetic to his goal of an improvement in public arts. In contrast to the article in the *British Review*, Haydon eagerly promotes the nationalization of the marbles as models for artistic emulation. But unlike West, Haydon views their power as antithetical and disruptive to the normative aesthetic of the Royal Academy. In a letter to his father (21 December 1808) from this same period, Haydon argues that the Elgin marbles "will produce a revolution in the art of this country":

The academic style, thank God, is done for—and done for, forever. No more 'sign-painting' now, if the artists can only appreciate what a treasure we have got. But I fear them; I fear the low taste of the patrons. Art is looked upon as nothing but a sort of gilding for their drawing rooms and chimney pieces. They have no conception of the public function.[44]

Rejecting both West's allegorical grand style and his detractor's dismissal of public art, Haydon offers a vision of historical painting at once public and subjective. Locating taste less in the composition of "sign painting" and more in the power of immediate forms, Haydon would seem to offer a more democratic, because more accessible vision of public art. Yet his critique of the Platonic beau ideal favored by the Academy reveals a more conflicted stance:

> You say after all beauty is the thing. No, it is not the chief thing; intellect, the feelings of the heart, are the chief things. The more beautiful the garb that expression is dressed in, the better, but if you dress expression so beautifully as to overwhelm it, the object is not attained.
> Beauty of form is but the vehicle of conveying Ideas, but truth of conveyance is the first object. If the vehicle attract on its own score, what it is intended to convey is lost, and the mind drawn to an object foreign. So with colour, light & shadow, and the means of the Art, for beauty is but a means.[45]

In Haydon's view, truth and beauty have parted company, but that division becomes the site for private subjective identification even as art achieves its "public function." The power of art manifests itself not in the idea signified by art as "sign-painting," but in the "truth of conveyance" of the sign or expression itself. Individual genius and public taste are united, as the representational form becomes the manifestation of aesthetic value, offering the public eye a peculiar aesthetics of interiority. Moving from "things as they are" to "things as they ought to be," Haydon's artistic practice moves inductively from the natural to the ideal, producing a relational gap within which a model of aesthetic subjectivity might emerge. Though the Elgin Marbles are said to have achieved this perfect integration of the natural and the ideal, only through re-experiencing that passage may the "hidden beauties" of the marbles be revealed and the "principle . . . imbibed and inhaled forever."

If Haydon's academic pronouncements are hopelessly muddled, we might do well to consider the context. Whereas West's artistic statements are made as a public figure and readily published as authoritative claims for the national interest, Haydon's remarks appear either as private correspondence and marginalia, or in the self-absorbed rhetoric of his autobiography. This latter work has been well characterized by Roger J. Porter as a *bildungs-*

roman in which Haydon casts himself as a noble hero
overcoming personal obstacles and societal indifference.[46] Certainly, wherever we look in the autobiography
we find confirmation of Leigh Hunt's characterization of
Haydon as "one who turned disappointment itself into a
kind of self-glory."[47] Throughout his tortured narrative,
Haydon pursues vindication for his beliefs and nostalgic
amelioration for his latter sufferings. The account of his
exposure to the marbles, in what has become a staple example of Romantic prose, provides a perfect instance, offering Haydon's own tormented self as an agency of
originality to mediate and fuse the polarized realms of
nature and ideal. In the sixth chapter, Haydon returns
from the funeral of his mother to "London, dear old London" and recounts his struggles over the painting of the
Death of Dentatus, his first major work. His problem is not
one of composition, but one of form. "I felt that the figure
of Dentatus must be heroic," he records, "and the finest
specimen of the species I could invent. But how could I
produce a figure that should be the finest of its species?"
Rejecting both the mannerisms of academic generaliza-
tions and the meanness of natural form, Haydon rhetorically asks, "How was I to build a heroic form, like life, yet
above life?"[48] When a visiting artist views his sketches
and asks, "Where did you copy that?" Haydon feels certain that he is approaching his goal, replying, "I imagined
it, with nature before me" (1:82). By embracing both nature and imagination, Haydon constructs a creative subjectivity that simultaneously mediates and maintains the
distance between the real and the ideal. But Haydon configures this artistic identity as one of unrealized potential, in need of a proper model or guide.

Placed within this context, the Elgin Marbles make
their narrative entrance as Wilkie calls upon the despairing artist to drag him off to Park Lane. But just as he enters the exhibition with an affectation of "the utmost
nonchalance," the narrative breaks, at the moment of revelation, to reflect for two pages upon the youthful antics
of Haydon and his fellow students. Haydon paints a picture of studious commitment and sincere discussion in-
terrupted periodically with forays to sites of popular

entertainment, events narrated with no small amount of class consciousness as the rowdy students single each other out for playful jests among the predominantly working-class audience:

> As soon as we had finished [working at the Academy], out we went, and in passing a penny show in the piazza, we fired up and determined to go in. We entered, and slunk away in a corner; while waiting for the commencement of the show, in came all our student friends, one after the other. We shouted out at each one as he arrived, and then popped our heads down in our corner again, much to the indignation of the chimney sweeps and vegetable boys who composed the audience, but at last we were discovered, and then we all joined in applauding the entertainment of 'Pull Devil, Pull Baker,' and at the end raised such a storm of applause, clapping our hands, stamping our feet, and shouting with all the power of a dozen pair of lungs, that, to save our heads from the fury of the sweeps, we had to run down stairs as if the devil indeed was trying to catch us. After this boisterous amusement, we retired to my rooms and drank tea, talking away on art, stating principles, arguing long and fiercely, and at midnight separating, to rest, rise, and work again until the hour of dinner brought us once more together, again to draw, argue or laugh. (1:83–84)

The purpose of this narrative interruption becomes clear once Haydon resumes the narrative of his initial exposure to the marbles. Park Lane stands in stark contrast to the light-hearted and lower-class amusements of the penny show, the solemnity and awe of the marbles' exhibition standing in relief to the competitive jesting outside. Indeed, his initial approach to the marbles' exhibition has all of the reverence of an approach to the infant Jesus in the manger: "To Park Lane then we went and after passing through the hall, and thence into an open yard, entered a damp dirty pent-house, where lay the marbles, ranged within sight and reach" (1:84).

Haydon's following description is as fragmentary in its style as the marbles are in their exhibition, allowing his subjective perception to serve as a simultaneous representation and guide:

The first thing I fixed my eyes on was the wrist of a figure in one of the female groups, in which were visible, though in a feminine form, the radius and ulna. I was astonished, for I had never seen them hinted at in any female wrist in the antique. I darted my eye to the elbow, and saw the outer condyle visibly affecting the shape as in nature. I saw that the arm was in repose and the soft parts in relaxation. The combination of nature and idea which I had felt was so much wanting for high art was here displayed to mid-day conviction. My heart beat! If I had seen nothing else, I had beheld sufficient to keep me to nature for the rest of my life. But when I turned to the Theseus, and saw that every form was altered by action or repose—when I saw that the two sides of his back varied, one side stretched from the shoulder blade being pulled forward, and the other side compressed from the shoulder blade being pushed close to the spine, as he rested on his elbow, with the belly flat because the bowels fell into the pelvis as he sat—and when, turning to the Ilyssus, I saw the belly protruded, from the figure lying on its side—and again, when in the figure of the fighting metope I saw the muscle shown under the one armpit in that instantaneous action of darting out, and left out in the other armpits because not wanted—when I saw, in fact, the most heroic style of art, combined with all the essential detail of actual life, the thing was done at once and forever. (1:84–85)

This account, simultaneously fragmentary and comprehensive, lays claim to the very characteristics attributed to West's epic forms: "the most heroic style of art, combined with all the essential detail of actual life." In his narrative account, Haydon brings about the very point and climax that West had spoken of "by the union of those detached figures," but through autobiographical narrative rather than allegorical composition. The play between fragments and comprehensiveness that characterizes Haydon's descriptive account establishes his imaginative power in just that passage between the forms exhibited and the natural immediacy they are paradoxically claimed to reproduce.

The immediacy of this initial exposure, never again repeated in his autobiographical accounts, serves as a justification for all of his subjective endeavors, positioning

Haydon and England as the teleological benefactors of Elgin's pursuits:

> Here were principles which the common sense of the English people would understand; here were principles which I had struggled for in my first picture, with timidity and apprehension; here were the principles which the great Greeks in their finest time established, and here was I, the most prominent historical student, perfectly qualified to appreciate all this by my own determined mode of study under the influence of my old friend the watch-maker (Reynolds, of Plymouth)— here was the hint at the skin perfectly comprehended by knowing well what was underneath it!
>
> Oh, how I inwardly thanked God that I was prepared to understand all this! Now I was rewarded for all the petty harassings I had suffered. Now was I mad for buying Albinus without a penny to pay for it? Now was I mad for lying on the floor hours together, copying its figures? I felt the future, I foretold that they would prove themselves the finest things on earth, that they would overturn the false beau-ideal, where nature was nothing, and would establish the true beau-ideal, of which nature alone is the basis.
>
> I shall never forget the horses' heads—the feet in the metopes! I felt as if a divine truth had blazed inwardly upon my mind, and I knew that they would at last rouse the art of Europe from its slumber in the darkness. (1:85)

As Jacob Rothenberg has demonstrated through recourse to Haydon's diaries, his initial enthusiasm is a retrospective myth, an autobiographical product of a much longer period of consideration. His claim, "I do not say this now, when all the world acknowledges it, but I said it then, when no one would believe me" (1:85–86), contains a germ of truth insofar as Haydon had firmly sided with the marbles by the time Parliament began its hearings on their purchase for the British Museum, but it is exaggerated here for a purpose. In pitting himself against West and the rules of the Academy, Haydon substitutes original insight for academic tradition just as he privileges an individual response to pure form over allegorical composition as the proper manifestation of value in aesthetic exercise. The narrative function of this initial exposure to the marbles serves as both a personal and a national point of refer-

ence. In the passage between the fragmented images and
the anticipation of exhibitionary totality, between "things
as they are" and "things as they ought to be," both personal and national consciousness are posited and redeemed.

Archibald Archer's 1819 oil painting of the Temporary
Elgin Room at the British Museum reconciles West and
Haydon within an epic and triumphal vision for the Elgin
Marbles. Among the many luminaries portrayed amidst
the marbles, Benjamin West, in his role as President of
the Royal Academy, shares the central position with Joseph Planta, Principal Librarian of the British Museum.
Their position underscores the allegiance of the two institutions in the preservation and emulation of the wonders of antiquity and establishes an affinity between the
rhetorical aesthetic of the Royal Academy and the programmatic exhibitions of the British Museum. Yet occupy-
ing an equally important, if less apparent, position,

Archibald Archer, "The Temporary Elgin Room" (1819). © Copyright
The British Museum.

Haydon stands to the side, gazing at the marbles in a fit of private rhapsody. Though isolated from the group of dilettantes and antiquarians, Haydon's presence in the painting is critical. He affords Archer the emblem of melancholic rapture and aesthetic transport justifying the more accomplished stance of West and Planta. Archer's painting captures perfectly the essential relation between both of these stances, triumph and loss, public academician and private genius, informing the national reception of the Elgin Marbles.

V

Historical painting offered both West and Haydon a means of simultaneously signaling and enacting the progressive historiography justifying the acquisition of the Parthenon Marbles. In their visions of historical *translatio*, Periclean Athens and republican Rome serve as cultural ancestors to modern Britain, embodying a genius of artistic accomplishment rooted in commercial and political liberty. Paradoxically, this genius is mobile, moving perpetually westward and north. Yet where Haydon located this mobility in the sensibilities of an aesthetic subject, West projected it onto the act of composition, an allegorical gesture of abstraction rooted less in place than in *polis*, less a product of native traditions than of republican ideals. This model of historical painting had its verbal counterpart in the eighteenth-century progress poem. Grounded in the experience of the Grand Tour, the ideology of civic republicanism, and the doctrine of historical progress, works such as Joseph Addison's *Letter from Italy* (1703), Thomas Gray's *The Progress of Poesy* (1757), and Oliver Goldsmith's *The Traveller* (1764) offered a doctrinal and descriptive poetry that subordinated individual achievement to historical order. Akin to historical painting's deployment of allegorical rhetoric, such poetic visions leaned heavily upon personification, as the figures of Liberty, Honor, and Genius moved from one geographical habitation to another in the progressive course of human history. By abstracting political and aes-

thetic ideals from their historical context, such progress
poems were able to portray a rebirth of Athenian glory in
modern Britain. By converting the temporal cycle of political rise and decline into a linear narrative of progressive
anticipation, these works could position Britain at the
center of cultural history.[49]

James Thomson's five-book blank verse *Liberty* (1735–36)
exemplifies both the panoramic comprehensiveness and
didactic bombast of the genre. Based upon his tour of the
continent in 1730–31, Thomson's poem frames his experiences within the standard devices of the progressive vision, moving from historical ruin to political rebirth.
Thomson's poetic persona, a lonely wanderer situated
among the ruins of Rome, receives a vision from the goddess Liberty, "whose vital radiance calls / From the brute
mass of man an ordered world" (4.11–12).[50] At his request,
the goddess relates her origins and progress through classical times, the Middle Ages, and the Renaissance, land-
ing, predictably, in modern Britain. Such sentiments
were already trite and programmatic in 1735, and Thomson's poem does very little to rejuvenate them. His Miltonic edifice merely re-exhibits the standard scenes of
the Grand Tour within a progressive curatorial panorama, offering institutional codification rather than poetic engagement. *Liberty* is a famously unreadable poem,
having frustrated even Samuel Johnson, and was commer-
cially unsuccessful, as the diminishing numbers of each
book's publication attest. Yet it tellingly provided the
model for the two most extensive treatments of the Elgin
Marbles in English verse, Lord Byron's *Childe Harold's Pilgrimage* and Felicia Hemans's *Modern Greece*. Byron organized the details of his travels both within and against
Thomson's traditional topographical progress poem[51] and
Hemans begins modern Greece with an epigraph from the
second part of *Liberty*:

> O Greece! thou sapient nurse of finer arts
> Which to bright Science blooming Fancy bore!
> Be this thy praise, that thou, and thou alone,
> In these hast led the way, in these excelled,
> Crowned with the laurel of assenting Time.
>
> (2.252–56)

Each poet found a means of reviving the progress poem's basic structure and themes, producing infinitely superior works. Much of this accomplishment results from the dismantling of allegorical personification, as each poet emphasizes Thomson's figure of the solitary wanderer over the vision of Liberty as the mouthpiece for his or her aesthetic and historical ruminations. Yet their aesthetic achievement is inextricable from their ideological power, even though these two poems offer politically opposed stances on the question of Elgin's activities. For they share, along with Haydon and Keats, an emphasis on subjective response over allegorical arrangement that places their visions firmly within a modern museum aesthetic. That this aesthetic is no less ideological for being personal and idiosyncratic provides another telling insight into the multifarious production of national culture. Despite their opposing political stances, both Byron and Hemans occupy figuratively Haydon's position within Archer's portrait of the Elgin Room. Their melancholic longing and inspired raptures establish the terms by which the removal of the marbles would be contested and received.

Although Byron's famous stanzas on Lord Elgin occur at the beginning of the second canto, it is surely the fourth canto of *Childe Harold's Pilgrimage* that first comes to mind when we think of the aesthetics of the modern museum. Its abundant descriptions of art and architecture are unparalleled in the poet's *oeuvre* and its paratactic arrangement of visual scenes most nearly approximates the sublime confusion we have identified as the central stimulus to the imaginative faculty in the museum tour. Though Byron quips that "I have been accustom'd to entwine / My thoughts with Nature rather in the fields, / Than Art in galleries" (4.545–47), the fourth canto is a veritable gallery walk, moving from the Venus de Medici in Florence's Uffizi to the architectural panorama of St. Peter's, the Dying Gladiator in the Capitoline Museum, and the Laocoön and Apollo Belvedere in the Vatican. Thomson had surveyed most of these same pieces as they composed the essential itinerary for any young gentleman's tour of Italy. But in Byron's poem, these pieces disrupt rather than uphold a comprehensive and progressive vision. As Bruce Haley, commenting on the canto's "sculptural aesthetic" has observed, "the dominant image is the emergent, self-sufficient art object, the sculptural or architectural form, whose essence is antipicturesque—antithetical to the non-emergent, compositional nature of the picture."[52] Such sequential ordering parallels and reinforces the poet's own narrative of alienation, casting him as a "ruin amidst ruins" (4.219) in the "marble wilderness" (4.710) of Venice, Florence, and, most prominently, Rome. Byron refers to Italy in his dedicatory letter to Hobhouse as a "labyrinth of external objects," too heterogeneous and expansive to admit of exhaustive elucidation, even in what he considered "the longest, the most thoughtful and comprehensive of my compositions."[53] Unlike Thomson, Byron offers no faith in historical progress to survey and unify this labyrinth as a picturesque panorama of Liberty. Rather, having collapsed the distinction between Harold and the poet, Byron presents "the author speaking in his own person" as the only unifying presence in the poem. The result is a simultaneous narrowing and expansion of the poetic vision, as multitudes of isolated objects are joined through the longings of a single poetic persona.

Stephen Larabee rightly noted, as have many critics after him, that Byron's general allegiance to the Platonic beau-ideal over-determines his responses to these famous works.[54] In the "form and face" of the Venus de Medici we "behold / What mind can make, when Nature's self would fail" (4.438–39) and in the "delicate form" of the Apollo Belvedere "are exprest / All that ideal beauty ever bless'd / The mind within its most unearthly mood" (4.1450–55). Yet Byron fuses this aesthetic idealism with a profound recognition of the mind's earthly limitations, positioning such works less as consummations than as sublime objects of desire:

Of its own beauty is the mind diseased,
And fevers into false creation:—where
Where are the forms the sculptor's soul hath seized?
In him alone. Can Nature show so fair?

Where are the charms and virtues which we dare
Conceive in boyhood and pursue as men,
The unreach'd Paradise of our despair,
Which o'er-informs the pencil and the pen,
And overpowers the page where it would bloom again?
                                                    (4.1090–98)

In this famous stanza, Byron unites a praise of imaginative abstraction with a despairing portrait of artistic struggle. The mind's own beauty compels it towards idealization and inevitable disappointment as "we see too sure / Nor worth nor beauty dwells from out the mind's / Ideal shape of such" (4.1101–3). This is the "hard decree" of consciousness, the "uneradicable taint of sin . . . which throb through / The immedicable soul, with heart-aches ever new" (4.1127–34). The distance between the ideal and the natural becomes the site for Byron's pronounced subjectivity, binding these fragmented descriptions together through his own insatiable desire. The poet's final farewell to "the Pilgrim of my song" in stanzas 164 to 174 reinforces his speaking position even as it aligns the "immedicable soul" with the "immedicable wound" of the Italian nation's departed grandeur, a "gulf . . . thick with phantoms" (4.1498–1500). Alienation, both personal and national, emerges as the only consistent trope uniting Byron's survey of departed glory.

Like his fourth canto, though with fewer moments of sublime rapture, Byron's second canto differs from Thomson in its rejection of the ideology of historical progress and its embrace of personal alienation as the proper ground for social and aesthetic pronouncements.[55] Indeed, the second canto's entire scene at the ruined Parthenon is one extended drama of performative melancholy. Standing amidst the ruins, "a nation's sepulchre" (2.21), Byron laments the passing of ages and faiths and bemoans the vanity of human endeavors. Athena is invoked only to be dispatched, powerless against "the dread sceptre and dominion dire / Of men who never felt the sacred glow / That thoughts of thee and thine on polish'd breasts bestow" (2.7–9). Her former sovereignty over those "men of might" and "grand of soul," "First in the

race that led to Glory's goal," is now reduced to "A school-
boy's tale, the wonder of an hour!" (2.11–15). Byron's narrative voice is left vacillating between the ideals of the
past and the degradations of the present, reduced along
with all humanity to a "Poor child of Doubt and Death,
whose hope is built on reeds" (2.27). He even plays Hamlet
as he "Remove[s] yon skull from out the scatter'd heaps"
and asks "Is that a temple where a God may dwell? / Why
ev'n the worm at last disdains her shatter'd cell!"
(2.44–45):

> Look on its broken arch, its ruin'd wall,
> Its chambers desolate, and portals foul:
> Yes, this was once Ambition's airy hall,
> The dome of Thought, the palace of the Soul:
> Behold through each lack-lustre, eyeless hole,
> The gay recess of Wisdom and of Wit
> And Passion's host, that never brook'd control:
> Can all saint, sage, or sophist ever writ,
> People this lonely tower, this tenement refit?
>
> (2.46–54)

The architectural language, anticipating the impressions
of the ruined Parthenon, establishes the affinities between personal and cultural mortality that guide so much
of the poem's meditations. But in and of itself, this stanza
is a standard *memento mori*, fully grounded in the melancholic tradition. Throughout these opening stanzas, Byron's narrator moves programmatically through the
classic poses and reflections of the melancholic, even situating himself amidst the ruins of the temple of Jupiter,
whom he identifies as a "son of Saturn" (2.84).

The general tone of these stanzas expands the melancholic stance traditionally employed at the beginning of
ruin pieces, topographical verse, and progress poems,
emphasizing the poet's own emotional responses over historical or philosophical order. Yet Byron's specific invocation of Athena as a goddess of vanquished glory
enables the more pointed critique of the stanzas on Elgin's role in her destruction. Here Byron gives full vent to
his splenetic contempt of Elgin's desecration:

> But who, of all the plunderers of yon fane
> On high, where Pallas linger'd, loth to flee

The latest relic of her ancient reign;
The last, the worst, dull spoiler, who was he?
Blush, Caledonia! Such thy son could be!
England! I joy no child he was of thine:
Thy free-born men should spare what once was free;
Yet they could violate each saddening shrine,
And bear these altars o'er the long-reluctant brine.

But most the modern Pict's ignoble boast,
To rive what Goth, and Turk, and Time hath spared:
Cold as the crags upon his native coast,
His mind as barren and his heart as hard,
Is he whose head conceived, whose hand prepared,
Aught to displace Athena's poor remains:
Her sons too weak the sacred shrine to guard,
Yet felt some portion of their mother's pains,
And never knew, till then, the weight of Despot's chains.

(2.91–108)

Byron's *ad hominem* attacks are vicious to be sure, but
they form an integral part of his larger argument. Elgin's
barren mind and hardened heart "violate each saddening
shrine" specifically because they are impervious to the
melancholy seductions of the scene. As Byron notes, "we
can all feel, or imagine, the regret with which the ruins of
cities once the capitals of empires, are beheld: the reflections suggested by such objects are too trite to require
recapitulation."[56] Too trite, that is, for all but such a man
as Elgin whose actions mark him as lacking in sensibility
or imagination. For Byron, the debate over the marbles
has nothing to do with political authority or economic
value. It has nothing to do even with aesthetic merit—
neither the Parthenon nor the marbles themselves are
ever described in his work. Rather, it is a contest of tem-
peraments, the melancholic over the phlegmatic, and the
"gloomy wanderer" over the "dull spoiler." It is here that
Byron quotes in a footnote Edward Daniel Clarke's account of the Disdar's tearful pronouncement of "τελος!"
commenting that Athena's sons, though "too weak the
sacred shrine to guard, / Yet felt some portion of their
mother's pains." Byron capitalizes upon such tragic sentiments in his emotive narrative of mournful reflection and

moral condemnation. As a master of sensitive lamentation, Byron stands apart from not only Elgin, but the immediate residents of Athens: "Yet these proud pillars
claim no passing sigh; / Unmoved the Moslem sits, the
light Greek carols by" (2.90). Within this context of sentimental distinction, Lord Elgin figures as an extreme example of the indifference ruining these remains:

Cold is the heart, fair Greece! That looks on thee,
Nor feels as lovers o'er the dust they loved;
Dull is the eye that will not weep to see
Thy walls defaced, thy mouldering shrines removed
By British hands, which it had best behoved
To guard those relics ne'er to be restored.
Curst be the hour when from their isle they roved,
And once again thy hapless bosom gored,
And snatchd thy shrinking Gods to northern climes abhorr'd!
(2.126–35)

The mournful lover achieves moral authority over the
cold rapist through his performance of anguish. The teleology of British acquisition is reversed, signaling an end
of days rather than a rebirth of glory. Yet Byron is not ab-
dicating nationalist pride. He is careful to distinguish
Elgin as Scottish, not English. More importantly, his stanzas offer a model of nationalism based not in civic republicanism and Whiggish progressivism, but in a native
pride joined to place and tradition. As Bernard Beatty
has rightly emphasized, Byron's poetic fame from these
cantos was as international as domestic, owing in no
small part to the model of alienation and aspiration he offered Europe's burgeoning nationalist movements.[57] In
emphasizing loss over *telos*, Byron offers a sentimental
model for the nascent Greek nationalism his verses inspire even as they bemoan its absence.

Melancholic sorrow turns to spirited rage in Byron's
other famed attack on Elgin, *The Curse of Minerva* (1811).
Again we find the poet amidst the ruins at sunset, distinguished through his sensitivity: "All, tinged with varied
hues, arrest the eye; / And dull were his that pass'd them
heedless by" (47–48).[58] Here Byron is closer to Thomson's
poetics, if not his vision, as the spirit of Pallas Athena ap-

pears to curse both Elgin and the British empire. Both a mocking satire of exhibitionary reception and a classic vision of the cyclical passing of empires, *The Curse of Minerva* is more prophetic oratory than elegiac dirge, more Juvenallian satire than Saturnalian longing. Scotland, as Elgin's native land, is mocked as "a barren soil, where nature's germs, confined / To stern sterility, can stint the mind" (133–34), and West and Hamilton's programs for exhibition and emulation are mercilessly ridiculed:

> Meantime, the flattering, feeble dotard West,
> Europe's worst dauber, and poor Britain's best,
> With palsied hand shall turn each model o'er,
> And own himself an infant of fourscore.
> Be all the bruisers cull'd from all St. Giles',
> That art and nature may compare their styles;
> While brawny brutes in stupid wonder stare,
> And marvel at his lordship's "stone shop" there.
> Round the throng'd gate shall sauntering coxcombs creep,
> To lounge and lucubrate, to prate and peep;
> While many a languid maid, with longing sigh,
> On giant statues casts the curious eye;
> The room with transient glance appears to skim
> Yet marks the mighty back and length of limb;
> Mourns o'er the difference of *now* and *then*;
> Exclaims, "These Greeks indeed were proper men!"
> Draws slight comparisons of *these* with *those*,
> And envies Lais all her Attic beaux.
> When shall a modern maid have swains like these!
> Alas! Sir Harry is no Hercules!
> And last of all, amidst the gaping crew,
> Some calm spectator, as he takes his view,
> In silent indignation mix'd with grief,
> Admires the plunder, but abhors the thief.
>
> (175–98)

The sexual mockery of the British spectators seems a mirror image of the seductive charms of the ruins themselves. Far from imparting the glory of Grecian art to the British Isles, the removal and exhibition of the marbles merely accentuates the historical, cultural, and physical gap between the two cultures. Yet across this gap, Britain may perceive in Athens's fate a premonition of her own decline. Reversing Thomson's faith in progress, Byron foresees the inevitable disintegration of Britain's imperial holdings and concludes that "The law of heaven and earth is life for life, / And she who raised, in vain regrets, the strife" (311–12). Hence the disruptive logic of ruins is brought round to the sensitive traveler and his own cultural origins.

Byron's poetic contributions to the Elgin Marbles debate evidence the two genres of discourse—tragedy and irony—employed in chipping away at the achieved epic form of exhibitionary rhetoric promoting the marbles' national reception. Both insist upon the discordance between past and present, whether through sympathetic mourning or uncharitable satire, which belies the epic claims to teleological comprehension. But as we have seen, elegiac lament is not intrinsically incompatible with narratives or exhibitions of nationalist appropriation. Hamilton's *Memorandum* presents Sarah Siddons's tears alongside Benjamin West's epic apologia as complementary testimonials to the marbles' aesthetic merit and value for the nation. Haydon's autobiography positions the aesthetic union of nature and ideal as an epiphany by which his own artistic longing and the cultural desires of his nation may be both posited and redeemed. And Keats's sonnet constructs the power of the marbles as residing in the "dizzy pain" produced between "a sick eagle looking at the sky" and "a shadow of a magnitude." If Byron's "gloomy wanderer" proves an eloquent critic of Elgin's endeavors, such a pose may potentially serve as an equally compelling advocate.

VI

Such is the nature of the poetic apologia produced by Felicia Hemans at the conclusion of the debate concerning the marbles' nationalization. The continuum between political ideology and poetic articulation is nowhere more evident than in Hemans's *Modern Greece*, a 101-stanza panegyric to the glory of ancient Greece and its rebirth in modern Britain.[59] Printed in 1817 by John Murray, who had just published the *Report of the Select Committee*, *Modern Greece* offers a poetic and emotive articulation of the committee's conclusions, citing several passages of testimony by Haydon, West, Lawrence, Westmacott, and Flaxman in its extensive endnotes. Though borrowing many formal and rhetorical elements from Byron, Hemans's work is much closer ideologically to Thomson's *Liberty*, promoting a progressive historiography that feeds directly into a nationalist panegyric. Fusing travel narrative, patriotic hymn, and personal tribute, *Modern Greece* builds upon the imagery and themes of Hemans's earlier work to articulate a teleological vision of British cultural supremacy. Its opening stanza sets the tone for the entire poem:

> Oh! who hath trod thy consecrated clime,
> Fair land of Phidias! theme of lofty strains!
> And traced each scene, that, midst the wrecks of time,
> The print of Glory's parting step retains;
> Nor for awhile, in high-wrought dreams, forgot,
> Musing on years gone by in brightness there,
> The hopes, the fears, the sorrows of his lot,
> The hues his fate hath worn, or yet may wear;
> As when from mountain-heights, his ardent eye
> Of sea and heaven hath track'd the blue infinity?
>
> (1–10)

Cultural memory here serves the interest of personal amnesia, releasing the melancholic wanderer from the pains of circumstance by tracing the departed glory of the past. Like Thomson, Hemans grounds her vision of historical redemption in a lonely wanderer amidst the ruins of antiquity, sensitive to the instructive lessons of the past.

Yet in response to the popularity of Byron's own melancholic travelogue, Hemans attends much more than Thomson to the sensibilities of her poetic persona, offered in contradistinction to those cut off from such noble feelings of the heart:

> Is there who views with cold unaltered mien,
> His frozen heart with proud indifference fraught,
> Each sacred haunt, each unforgotten scene,

Where Freedom triumph'd, or where Wisdom taught?
Souls that too deeply feel, oh, envy not
The sullen calm your fate hath never known:
Through the dull twilight of that wint'ry lot
Genius ne'er pierced, nor Fancy's sunbeam shone,
Nor those high thoughts, that, hailing Glory's trace,
Glow with the generous flames of every age and race.

But blest the wanderer, whose enthusiast mind
Each muse of ancient days hath deep imbued
With lofty lore; and all his thoughts refined
In the calm school of silent solitude;
Pour'd on his ear, midst groves and glens retired,
The mighty strains of each illustrious clime,
All that hath lived, while empires have expired,
To float for ever on the winds of Time;
And on his soul indelibly pourtray'd
Fair visionary forms, to fill each classic shade.

Is not his mind, to meaner thoughts unknown,
A sanctuary of beauty and of light?
There he may dwell, in regions all his own,
A world of dreams, where all is pure and bright.
For him the scenes of old renown possess
Romantic charms, all veil'd from other eyes;
There every form of nature's loveliness
Wakes in his breast a thousand sympathies;
As music's voice, in some lone mountain-dell,
From rocks and caves around calls forth each echo's swell.

(11–40)

The poetry echoes *Childe Harold* both formally and thematically, but in a different key. Adding an additional line to Byron's Spenserian stanzas and basing her evocations of Greece on various travelers' accounts rather than her own experience, Hemans presents us with the ideal proponent for Elgin's endeavors. Once again, we have a "sad wanderer" as Hemans later calls him, set amidst ruins and groves fit for enthusiastic contemplation. And once again we have the phlegmatic foil, "with cold unaltered mien," a "frozen heart," and "proud indifference." All the scorn Byron heaped upon Lord Elgin is here reserved for a purely speculative nemesis whose "sullen calm" makes "the dull twilight of [his] wint'ry lot" impervious to Genius and Fancy. By contrast, the "enthusiast mind," though racked by longing, perceives the "fair visionary forms" that dominate the Grecian landscape. He is positioned in "the calm school of silent solitude / . . . midst groves and glens retired," a prerequisite to the figurative sounding of the land and arts, released upon "the winds of Time" by the expiration of their original culture. The forms "fill each classic shade" and "wake[ ] in his breast" and thereby assume their power over and against shade and slumber just as the music in the final image depends upon space and distance for its "echo's swell." The beauties of nature, the ocean, and the sunset, which occupy the immediately subsequent stanzas, inspire his poetic soul even as the ruins of Greece and the savagery of its inhabitants recall the lowly state of humanity.

But this blessed wanderer is no Byronic figure, despite the formal and symbolic echoes of *Childe Harold*. His mind is "a sanctuary of beauty and of light / . . . /A world of dreams, where all is pure and bright," and, like Thomson's allegory of Liberty, he is able to subjectively heal the wounds of time as he traces with fancy and devotion the mark of Glory's departing step. Arriving in Athens to gaze upon the Parthenon, Hemans imaginatively declares "Oh! Let us gaze on thee, and fondly deem / The past awhile restored, the present but a dream" (698–99):

> Still be that cloud withdrawn—oh! Mark on high,
> Crowning yon hill, with temples richly graced,
> That fane, august in perfect symmetry,
> The purest model of Athenian taste.
> Fair Parthenon! Thy Doric pillars rise
> In simple dignity, thy marble's hue
> Unsullied shines, relieved by brilliant skies,
> That round thee spread their deep ethereal blue;
> And art o'er all thy light proportions throws
> The harmony of grace, the beauty of repose.
>
> And lovely o'er thee sleeps the sunny glow,
> When morn and eve in tranquil splendour reign,
> And on thy sculptures, as they smile, bestow
> Hues that the pencil emulates in vain.

Then the fair forms by Phidias wrought, unfold
Each latent grace, developing in light,
Catch from soft clouds of purple and of gold,
Each tint that passes, tremulously bright;
And seem indeed whate'er devotion deems,
While so suffused with heaven, so mingling with its beams.

(731–50)

Landscape and architecture here produce an indivisible symmetry, harmony, and beauty. Yet, as she paints the picture of the marbles' situation in the Acropolis, Hemans comes to understand that the pieces have literally lost their aesthetic value without an appreciative populace:

Oh! live there those who view with scornful eyes
All that attests the brightness of thy prime?
Yes; they who dwell beneath thy lovely skies,
And breathe th'inspiring ether of thy clime!
Their path is o'er the mightiest of the dead,
Their homes are midst the works of noblest arts;
Yet all around their gaze, beneath their tread,
Not one proud thrill of loftier thought imparts.
Such are the conquerors of Minerva's land,
Where Genius first reveal'd the triumphs of his hand!

For them in vain the glowing light may smile
O'er the pale marble, colouring's warmth to shed,
And in chaste beauty many a sculptured pile
Still o'er the dust of heroes lift its head.
No patriot feeling binds them to the soil,
Whose tombs and shrines their fathers have not rear'd,
Their glance is cold indifference, and their toil
But to destroy what ages have revered,
As if exulting sternly to erase
Whate'er might prove *that* land had nurs'd a nobler race.

(851–70)

Despite their imaginative restoration, the marbles are reduced to "a sculptured pile," their seductive power as objects of desire unrealized as "chaste beauty," incapable of imparting a "proud thrill" to those who gaze upon them. Within this paradigm of sensitive evaluation, the removal of the marbles is an easily justified enterprise:

And who may grieve that, rescued from their hands,
Spoilers of excellence and foes to art,
Thy relics, Athens! borne to other lands,
Claim homage still to thee from every heart?
Though now no more th'exploring stranger's sight,
Fix'd in deep reverence on Minerva's fane,
Shall hail, beneath their native heaven of light,
All that remain' of forms adored in vain;
A few short years—and, vanish'd from the scene,
To blend with classic dust their proudest lot had been.

. . . .

Lone are thy pillars now—each passing gale
Sighs o'er them as a spirit's voice, which moan'd
That loneliness, and told the plaintive tale
Of the bright synod once above them throned.
Mourn, graceful ruin! on thy sacred hill,
Thy gods, thy rites, a kindred fate have shared:
Yet art thou honour'd in each fragment still,
That wasting years and barbarous hands had spared;
Each hallow'd stone, from rapine's fury borne,
Shall wake bright dreams of thee in ages yet unborn.
(861–70, 881–90)

In the peculiar logic of the exhibition, Greece's glory is attested to all the more in its absence. In a paradox telling of the sexual ambivalence underlying the political legitimation of acquisition, the "chaste beauty" has been saved from "rapine's fury" through consummating its power in its acquisition.

Like Thomson, Hemans presents a republican vision of national culture, a culture not founded in land or in heritage, but in abstracted principles of freedom and glory. If Byron's Hellenism revives nationalist sentiment through personal alienation, Hemans's poem, ironically given its title, serves to fully bury any aspirations for Greek liberation and renaissance. Though Greece may fill the soul with beauty, its beauty is as the flower over the ruin, masking the death of its cultural achievements:

For all the loveliness, and light, and bloom,
That yet are thine, surviving many a storm,
Are but as heaven's warm radiance on the tomb,
The rose's blush that masks the canker worm:
(81–84)

And though she evokes Byron's famous exile, Hemans
uses the sensitive traveler both as a register of loss and a
promise of redemption. Grecian glory is simultaneously
evoked and reduced to a "trace," "soft as a vision of re-
membered joy":

> And he who comes, the pilgrim of a day,
> A passing wanderer o'er each Attic hill,
> Sighs as his footsteps turn from thy decay,
> To laughing climes, where all is splendour still;
> And views with fond regret thy lessening shore,
> As he would watch a star that sets to rise no more.
>
> (191–200)

Hemans's insistence upon Greece's decay is, of course,
necessary to the more immediate purpose of this elegy;
namely, the transfer of Greece's remains to those more
able to appreciate them and revive the spirit of the past.
The glory of the British nation is manifested and con-
firmed in the exhibition of the Parthenon marbles:

> Yes; in those fragments, though by time defaced,
> And rude insensate conquerors, yet remains
> All that may charm th'enlighten'd eye of taste,
> On shores where still inspiring freedom reigns.
> As vital fragrance breathes from every part
> Of the crush'd myrtle, or the bruised rose,
> E'en thus th'essential energy of art,
> There in each wreck imperishably glows!
> The soul of Athens lives in every line,
> Pervading brightly still the ruins of her shrine.
>
> (901–10)

As the seduction is consummated, political and aesthetic
values are conflated, as liberty and beauty are reborn in
their reception by a free and noble nation. The "vital fra-
grance" emanating from "the crush'd myrtle, or the
bruised rose," testifies to the disruptive and even violent
consummation which has released "th'essential energy of
art" onto the fertile soil of the exhibition. Hemans here
cites Haydon's observation that "in the most broken fragment the same great principle of life can be proved to

exist, as in the most perfect figure."[60] But it is the marbles'
fragmentary condition itself, both material and contextual, which allows for the ideological and aesthetic capi-
talization of their political and cultural value.

Having converted the marbles into signs of an imagined
past and desired present, Hemans turns to their aesthetic
status as museum objects, seeking to represent in language the beauty of their form:

> Mark—on the storied frieze the graceful train,
> The holy festival's triumphal throng,
> In fair procession, to Minerva's fane,
> With many a sacred symbol move along.
> There every shade of bright existence trace,
> The fire of youth, the dignity of age;
> The matron's calm austerity of grace,
> The ardent warrior, the benignant sage;
> The nymph's light symmetry, the chief's proud mien,
> Each ray of beauty caught and mingled in the scene.
>
> Art unobtrusive there ennobles form,
> Each pure chaste outline exquisitely flows;
> There e'en the steed, with bold expression warm,
> Is clothed with majesty, with being glows.
> One mighty mind hath harmonized the whole;
> Those varied groups the same bright impress bear;
> One beam and essence of exalting soul
> Lives in the grand, the delicate, the fair;
> And well that pageant of the glorious dead
> Blends us with nobler days, and loftier spirits fled.
>
> (911–30)

The only two stanzas in the poem that actually attempt to
describe the marbles themselves position their representation between the two poles enabling of such autonomous appreciation: the original sculptor and the museum
visitor. The opening imperative constructs the trajectory
of perception that circles back upon itself by the end of
the next stanza. On the other end is the "mighty mind" of
the sculptor whose "bright impress" is said to harmonize
the collection of figures. The representation that connects the two functions as an ameliorative bridge which
"blends us with nobler days, and loftier spirits fled." He-

mans's only descriptive passage paradoxically effaces the very temporal and spatial dislocation that she has emphasized throughout the poem. The melancholy of the wanderer is healed in the aesthetic faith of the museum spectator.

Historical reconciliation is matched by aesthetic harmony, for Hemans's description presents the sculptures as yet another type of fusion, lying between the natural and the ideal. Here she cites two other authorities from the Committee's report, Antonio Canova and Benjamin West. Canova wrote that "every thing here breathes life, with a veracity, with an exquisite knowledge of art, but without the least ostentation or parade of it, which is concealed by consummate and masterly skill."[61] Benjamin West observed of the equestrian scenes "in observing them we are insensibly carried on with the impression, that they and their horses actually existed, as we see them, at the instant when they were converted into marble."[62] In Hemans's poetic enunciation, such academic aesthetic pronouncements allow her to produce a pageant of social types united by their wedding of nature and ideal. Youth and age, the matron, warrior, and sage, the nymph and the chief; all are clothed with aesthetic majesty. What was a representation of social difference and stratification becomes a testament to the "beam and essence of exalting soul" which unifies and equalizes "the grand, the delicate, the fair." Just as the representation of the marbles' positioning as museum objects unifies past and present in aesthetic contemplation, the representation of the marbles' own contents subsumes the social order portrayed under the magnitude of its aesthetic achievement.

The marbles thus both strike and interest Hemans for their embodiment of glories past and the power of aesthetic beauty. But as museum pieces they also affect her with the revolution of empires that has brought them to her view. The abstractions of Genius, Hope, Thought, and Excellence once again emerge as she concludes her poem, a rhetorical prerequisite for the rebirth of Athenian Glory:

And who can tell how pure, how bright a flame,
Caught from these models, may illume the west?
What British Angelo may rise to fame,
On the free isle what beams of art may rest?
Deem not, O England! that by climes confined,
Genius and taste diffuse a partial ray;
Deem not th'eternal energies of mind
Sway'd by that sun whose doom is but decay!
Shall thought be foster'd but by skies serene?
No! thou hast power to be what Athens e'er hath been.
                                                (931–40)

Again Hemans is citing the testimony of others, this time
Benjamin West's public correspondence with Lord Elgin
from Hamilton's *Memorandum*. "Let us suppose a young
man at this time in London," West wrote, "endowed with
powers such as enabled Michael Angelo to advance the
arts, as he did, by the aid of one mutilated specimen of
Grecian excellence in sculpture; to what an eminence
might not such a genius carry art, by the opportunity of
studying those sculptures in the aggregate, which
adorned the temple of Minerva at Athens?"[63] Yet the aspiration to Athenian glory through the contemplation of its
ruins leads not only to the common recognition of Britain's own transience, but the understanding that only in
its decay will its value become apparent:

Yet rise, O Land in all but Art alone,
Bid the sole wreath that is not thine be won!
Fame dwells around thee—Genius is thine own;
Call his rich blooms to life—be Thou their Sun!
So, should dark ages o'er thy glory sweep,
Should thine e'er be as now are Grecian plains,
Nations unborn shall track thine own blue deep,
To hail thy shore, to worship thy remains;
Thy mighty monuments with reverence trace,
And cry, "This ancient soil hath nurs'd a glorious race!"
                                                (1001–10)

Again, we have Byron in a different key, as Minerva's
curse becomes her blessing. The elegiac logic of Hemans's evaluation of the Elgin Marbles spreads to the
epic hopes she shares with many of her contemporaries,

deferring the value of British art to its prospective view-
ers in a future age. Loss and redemption join in the progress of civilization displayed in the British Museum. Like
Athens, Britain's glory will emerge only in the print of its
parting step, consummating its beauty only in its exhibition.

4

Ekphrasis and Empire:
Wordsworth's Egyptian Maid

I

IN THE PREFACE TO HIS POEM, "THE EGYPTIAN MAID; OR, THE Romance of the Water Lily," Wordsworth notes that its central image of the "Lotus, with the bust of the Goddess appearing to rise out of the full-blown flower, was suggested by the beautiful work of ancient art, once included among the Townley Marbles, and now in the British Museum."[1] Although this Roman bust was one of Charles Townley's favorite pieces, the identity of the represented figure has never been determined definitively. While the British Museum often refers to it as "Clytie," the girl transformed into a flower because of her love for Helios, Townley's manuscripts vacillate between Greek and Egyptian interpretations, variously identifying the piece as "Bust like Agrippina ending in a sunflower" or "Isis in the flower of the Lotus." The image is now commonly believed to portray not a mythological figure but a Roman matron, possibly Antonia, the daughter of Mark Antony and mother of the Emperor Claudius.[2]

André Malraux long ago identified such indeterminacy as the aesthetic root of modern museums which "have tended to estrange the works they bring together from their original functions and to transform even portraits into 'pictures.' "[3] In Wordsworth's hands, this transformation assumes dizzying proportions. The first 354 lines of "The Egyptian Maid" narrate a religiously allegorical tale of an Egyptian maiden's arrival upon the shores of Arthurian Britain. Here she meets a near-fatal catastro-

163

British Museum Catalogue Sculpture 1874. © Copyright The British Museum.

phe at the hands of a jealous and suspicious Merlin who causes a tempest to rise up and destroy her vessel. The ship, a "winged Shape so fair" (13) has at its prow the bust of the maiden emerging from the lotus flower. Nina, the lady of the lake, who helps him to rescue the unconscious maiden and bring her to King Arthur's court, reproves Merlin for his actions. She reveals that, due to Arthur's freeing the Egyptian lands from foreign invaders, heaven has ordained one among the knights to be her husband. All of the knights approach the sleeping maiden to touch her hand and are successively turned away until Sir Galahad succeeds and the two are joined in marriage as an angelic carol concludes the poem.

Wordsworth's transformation of the decidedly Roman image into an Egyptian emblem within a medievalist allegory of British military prowess participates in numerous overlapping generic, institutional, and ideological norms. As a work of ekphrastic poetry, it narrates allegorically the verbal representation of a visual object. Deploying a gendered poetics of desire and fear in a project of spiritual idealization, its representational maneuvers mirror the curatorial systems of acquisition and exhibition that surrounded Townley's piece, both in his private collection and in the national museum. As an Orientalist fantasy, the poem describes a process of simultaneous differentiation and incorporation of the foreign within the imperial body. And as a medievalist romance, it invents an idealized past in which social and religious antagonisms are subsumed within a paternalistic feudal order. While exemplifying Wordsworth's personal poetic development in his later years towards doctrinal and political conservatism, "The Egyptian Maid" offers a narrative correlative to the systems of imperial and domestic administration promoted by the British Museum. As we follow the Roman bust's passage from its indeterminate origins into Townley's private collection and its subsequent re-absorption into the national museum and inscription within Wordsworth's poetic and political projects, we witness a sequence of aesthetic and ideological galleries in which a manifestly foreign, material, and feminized object is exhibited within an imperial drama of erotic desire and memorial haunting.

Though written in 1828, "The Egyptian Maid" first appeared in Wordsworth's 1835 volume *Yarrow Revisited and Other Poems*, a collection of nostalgic and laudatory verse that, coinciding with his dramatic rise in popularity, would become his biggest selling single-volume title to date.[4] The volume is a figurative pageant of medievalist paternalism and imperialist acquisition, and, not coincidentally I will suggest, contains five of the 24 ekphrastic poems in the poet's total body of work. These poems play out the common generic elements of erotic desire and abject fear, not in the service of personal catharsis and aesthetic apotheosis, but as a means of national and imperial consolidation. The volume's publication was followed the next year by the *Report from the Select Committee (of the House of Commons) on the Condition, Management, and Affairs of the British Museum together with the Minutes of Evidence, Appendix, and Index for 1835–36*. This two-volume magnum opus comprises over 1,200 pages of testimony, documents, and tables that seek to regulate the museum's administration and to deploy the aesthetic antiquarianism it promotes as a tool of public moral improvement. Both Wordsworth's volume and the Committee's report may be read, according to their different generic protocols, as part of a broader debate as to how best to realize the potential resources of Britain's imperial holdings, historical traditions, and social and religious institutions in consolidating and promoting a national culture.

Richard Altick has argued that the Parliamentary hearings, which accompanied similar inquiries into Westminster Abbey and St. Paul's Cathedral, were motivated, on the one hand, by an attack on the conservative management of the national institutions, and, on the other hand, by a fear of public uprisings.[5] The same may be argued for Wordsworth's volume of poems. Its nostalgic and patriotic verses are accompanied by a postscript essay "Of Legislation for the Poor, the Working Classes, and the Clergy," in which the poet argues the Tory position for an *in loco parentis* role for the state and upper classes of society. Wordsworth mounts this argument in direct opposition to both the severities of the Poor Law Amendment Act and to the revolutionary rhetoric of the rising Chartist movement. Both Wordsworth's volume of poetry and the published hearings of the Parliamentary committee promote moral improvement in place of economic reform and invest the nation as a normative category with a power to incorporate, and thereby contain, both domestic and foreign cultures. National institutions such as the British Museum are no longer to be viewed primarily as enclaves for an educated elite, but as tools for the fashioning and reformation of a national public culture. Yet the model of culture promoted by both the British Museum and *Yarrow Revisited* is haunted by visions of the past and of the foreign it wishes to simultaneously differentiate from and consolidate within an imagined national tradition.

II

In casting a self-evidently Roman statue as an emblem of Egyptian culture, Wordsworth poetically mimics the fraught juxtaposition of Egyptian and Roman antiquities in the Townley Gallery of the British Museum. Completed in 1808, the new gallery formed a northwest extension of Montagu House and exhibited the museum's Egyptian antiquities and Townley's collection in subsequent galleries until 1846, when Robert Smirke's new edifice supplanted the old structure.[6] This arrangement joined collections formed of radically different acquisitions. While the museum had always held a number of Egyptian relics, including approximately 150 in Sir Hans Sloane's collection alone, its holdings experienced an enormous influx beginning in 1802 with the bounty from Napoleon's failed Egyptian campaign. Additional relics, most famously the bust of Ramses II presented to the museum in 1817 by Henry Salt, the British Consul-General in Cairo, and Jean Louis Burckhardt, the Swiss Orientalist, forced the construction of a new Egyptian Sculpture Gallery between the main edifice of Montagu House and the Townley Gallery. Charles Townley had helped to plan the new wing in its early stages, but following his death in 1805 and the donation of his collection of mostly Roman antiquities, the galleries assumed a pragmatically hybrid arrangement.

Charles Townley himself was something of a hybrid figure, reflecting the European cosmopolitanism of his aristocratic peers. His family traced their lineage to the time of the Conquest and had been landed at Towneley in Lancashire since the twelfth century. But as a Roman Catholic, Townley was educated at Douai and followed his education with the obligatory Grand Tour of the Continent where he resided for a majority of his young adulthood, forming friendships with such fellow aspiring dilettantes as Sir William Hamilton and Pierre d'Hancarville. It was in Italy that he began his collecting pursuits in 1768, and, by 1772, Townley had already crated and shipped back many busts, reliefs, and sarcophagi when he arrived in Naples and purchased the anonymous Roman bust. By the end of 1777, Townley had returned to London where his personally designed exhibits in his private residence proved highly popular among students and dilettantes.[7] In his autobiographical portrait of Townley from 1811, John Nichols praises Townley's private exhibitions in terms revelatory of the classical aspirations of eighteenth-century antiquarians:

> ... purchasing a house in Park-street, Westminster, he there exhibited his stores of Greek and Roman art, with an arrangement classically correct, and with accompaniments so admirably selected, that the interior of a Roman villa might be inspected in our own metropolis. It was, in a superior degree, gratifying to learned eyes, to contemplate a scene realized from the descriptions of Cicero, and Pliny Junior. But the urbanity and intelligence of their owner held forth equal attraction. He allowed a most liberal access to all those who were known in the literary circles as men of taste or as antiquaries, and never disappointed the curiosity of others, less versed in the history, but no less susceptible of pleasure from the effect produced by the assemblage of objects of genuine beauty. It was delightful to see him frequently joining himself to these visitants; and when he found them desirous of more information than the Catalogue contained, freely entering into conversation, and, with a gracefulness of manner pe-

culiarly his own, giving a short dissertation upon any piece of sculpture under consideration. With delicacy and good sense, he always proportioned his own display of erudition to the measure of that which he found his inquirers to possess.[8]

Nichols's portrait displays all the hallmarks of the private collector in his element. Composition and erudition unite in the harmonious experience of the virtuoso and his collection. "Liberal access," whether for intellectual gratification or pleasurable curiosity, is assured to all who display sufficient taste for the beauties of the pieces. In reassembling the fragments in a manner evoking the villas of classical Rome, Townley imaginatively bridges the historical and cultural rifts between British antiquarians and Roman philosophers. "Like the elegant Virtuoso of antiquity," Nichols recalls, "Mr. Townley enriched the passing conversation, naturally dictated by the surrounding objects, by profound knowledge in the arts of design, and enlivened it by pleasantry and anecdote."[9]

As indicated by Nichols's account, the logic of Townley's exhibitions tended less towards archaeological reconstruction and more towards the mythopoeic elaboration favored by his colleagues d'Hancarville and Richard Payne Knight. The overt eroticism of such works as d'Hancarville's *Recherches sur l'origine l'esprit et les progres des arts de la Grece* (1785) and Knight's scandalous *Discourse on the Worship of Priapus* (1786) influenced Townley's own thinking, notably causing him to refer to one Egyptian figure of a man on a crocodile as the "Genius of Production."[10] A less erudite eroticism may have led him to favor the bust of the anonymous woman whose naked presence is both revealed and concealed by her lineaments and the petals of the lotus flower. Indeed, the seductive power of this piece is attested to by a commonly repeated story. During the Gordon Riots of 1780 that threatened both Townley's gallery and the British Museum, Townley grabbed only the bust as he fled his house, declaring, "I must take care of my wife."[11] Though Townley constantly modified his exhibitions to alter the focus of the viewing experience for his distinguished guests, the bust in the lotus flower was usually positioned as the central focal point, as in Johann Zoffany's portrait of *Charles Townley's Library*. Zoffany's portrait of Townley's library, cluttered with marbles to the point of chaos, the significance and function of each individual piece lost amid the larger image of acquisition and control, places Townley and his guests as the naturalized heirs to Western civilization and power.[12] Though the bust occupies a central position in the painting's composition, none of the four men present actually gaze at the image. Zoffany transfers the role of voyeur to the imagined spectator who is invited through the compositional logic to assume the aristocratic role of Townley and his peers. The bust obtains both presence and absence in the voyeuristic circulation of Zoffany's painting, standing out among the marbles to the viewer yet absent to the gaze of the antiquarians. Zoffany's painting thus mirrors in its composition the formal characteristics of male desire promoted by Townley and his fellow dilettantes and embodied by the indeterminate image itself.

Once transferred to the public domain, this fusion of liberal access, performative erudition, and erotic desire comes under a national rubric. As Ian Jenkins has noted, no other significant group of sculptures in the British Museum was ever a private *collection* before its absorption into the national repository. The Townley Gallery echoed its collection's unique source, many of its rooms quoting the style of private galleries in both their architecture and exhibitionary design, including the use of top lighting, circulatory vestibules, and the picturesque arrangement of sculptures witnessed in Zoffany's portrait.[13] Writing in 1811, John Nichols praises this transfer, noting that

> The British Museum, by a happy coincidence, now contains [the joint acquisitions of Townley and Sir William Hamilton]; and under the same roof are deposited a collection which reflects the highest honour on our Nation, and which may claim, in certain instances, a proud rivalship with, if not a superiority over, the Musée Napoleon.[14]

The pride of the antiquarian becomes the honor of the nation that in turn becomes appreciative of its "national ob-

Charles Townley and his Friends in the Townley Gallery, 33 Park Street, Westminster, 1781–83 (oil on canvas) by Johann Zoffany (1733–1810). Towneley Hall Art Gallery and Museum, Burnley, Lancashire / Bridgeman Art Library.

ligations to Mr. Townley, as having introduced a knowledge and love of the art of sculptural design, by rendering so many fine examples the property of the publick [sic]."[15] The placement of Townley's marbles in the national repository allows all members of the public to vicariously experience the privileges of the aristocracy:

> . . . . many lovers and judges of the art of sculpture are not sufficiently opulent to make, as Mr. Townley did, accompanied by d'Hancarville, a tour into countries remotely distant from each other, for the sole purpose of seeing various collections; and therefore, for that reason at least, the concentration of these curiosities in the metropolis may be considered, among national advantages, as tending to the improvement of Artists, and the dissemination of classical principles.[16]

The exhibition of Townley's collection condenses and disseminates the Grand Tour to the national public, allowing any member to potentially place himself (and the gendered bias is intentional) in the position of the antiquarians gathered in Zoffany's painting. Although his classical antiquities were typically cast as emblems of ideal beauty, their obvious physicality spoke just as much to sensual delight. In the context of a national museum, erotic pleasure joined less easily with instructing an increasingly diverse public in the archaeological erudition and aesthetic judgments of a reflective connoisseur. The very novelty and sensuality attractive to such connoisseurs as Townley and his circle could prove menacingly seductive within the walls of the British Museum. But, an equally menacing power could be found in the adjoining galleries.

While the Egyptian antiquities were usually cast as the precursor of Grecian culture, their material form and historical associations haunted and challenged the aesthetic values and narrative models promoted by the museum's librarians and trustees. A *Gentleman's Magazine* review of the Townley Gallery from 1810 complained, "that the Egyptian Collection, consisting chiefly of large stone coffins, and massive uncouth figures, ought never to have been placed on an upper story, and among the elegant

Greek and Roman sculptures." The reviewer recommends of the Egyptian sculptures that "their nature being chiefly sepulchral, it would be much more in character to see them in the solemn recess of a Catacomb, which in this instance should be fitted up in the Egyptian style."[17] In the reviewer's suggested curatorial design, elegant grace is literally elevated above corpulent mass, the life of civilization above death-shrouded barbarity.

The reviewer's theatrical bent is of a piece with the fashionable Egyptomania that followed in Western Europe following the military exploits of Napoleon and the archaeological adventures of Giovanni Battista Belzoni. In dramatic productions, landscape architecture, poetry, and the decorative arts, the influence of Egypt during the Regency period would seem to present less of a threat than a craze. From obelisks and pyramids in the gardens of country estates to the Egyptian wares of Wedgwood and Bentley and the decorative Egyptian designs of Piranesi, eighteenth century Britain was certainly already intrigued by the beauty and mystery of an idealized ancient Egypt. But Napoleon's 1798 campaign spurred a new and qualitatively different fascination with Egypt that joined a sense of global military competition with an apprehension of the monumental grandeur of this "antique land." Given the military inability of the French revolutionary forces to launch an attack on England, Napoleon, in 1798, attempted a conquest of Egypt as a means of destroying the British control of India. The occupation was a dismal failure and, in 1801, British and Turkish forces drove out the French occupation. Although the British remained in Egypt for only one more year, evacuating in 1802 as part of the treaty of the Peace of Amiens, the military occupations, as well as laying the foundations of nineteenth-century Orientalist discourse, set the stage for a greatly expanded European presence in the area. Under the leadership of Mohammed Ali, Egypt began to emerge as a significant economic power in the Western cotton and industrial markets. A series of British and French interventions in the region aimed at preserving a balance of power between the Turkish and Egyptian forces finally

led to a European takeover subsequent to the defeat of
Ali in 1841.[18]

The literature of Napoleon's campaign, both the Insti-
tut d'Egypte's monumental *Description de l'Egypte* (published 1809–28) and the more popular *Voyage dans la Basse
et la Haute Egypte* of Vivant Denon (published in London
1802) fused military ambitions and archaeological exoti-
cism. They spurred a popular imagination that could now
observe physical fragments in the British Museum and its
more populist counterpart, William Bullock's newly created Egyptian Hall in Piccadilly. Though Leigh Hunt dismissed the architecture of the latter as an "uncouth
anomaly,"[19] it was emblematic of a European imagination
that constructed the Orient, in the words of Edward Said,
as a source for "sensuality, promise, terror, sublimity,
idyllic pleasure, [and] intense energy."[20] This Egyptian
craze was often characterized by rhetoric of natural su-
pernaturalism, an effort to naturalize in the terms of Oc-
cident and Orient the older religious terms of Christian
and Pagan. In addition to Egypt's appeal for the popular
culture, the high culture of the countries of Western Europe viewed Egypt as a critical locale for the arts and sciences as well as for political control due to its role as the
cradle of Western civilization. The country acquiring
Egypt, intellectually, culturally, and /or politically could
be viewed as the historical heir to a preeminent place in
global power.[21]

The perceived distance between the forms of ancient
Egypt and classical civilizations, coupled with the manifestly foreign nature of contemporary Egyptian society,
made Egypt as frightening as it was alluring. Timothy
Mitchell has demonstrated how by the Victorian period
exhibitionary models of representation increasingly
came to be used to both evoke and deflect the reality of
Egyptian culture in a fashion that always gave epistemological supremacy to Western Europe. Such representational strategies mirrored in the domestic sphere the
models of colonial administration being applied in Egypt
itself.[22] In the popular realm of fashionable taste from
theatrical spectacles to ornamental jewelry, the reac-

tions to Egyptian forms tended to be less sober-minded. Robert Southey noted in 1807 that

> At present, as the soldiers from Egypt have brought home with them broken limbs and ophthalmia, they carry an arm in a sling, or walk the streets with a green shade over the eyes. Every thing now must be Egyptian: the ladies wear crocodile ornaments, and you sit upon a sphinx in a room hung round with mummies, and the long black lean-armed long-nosed hieroglypical men, who are enough to make the children afraid to go to bed.[23]

Southey's fusion of military acquisitions and fashion, feminine ornaments and infantile horror perfectly exemplifies the fraught imagination of Egyptian culture during this period. Egypt is at one and the same time an object of representational desire and a menacing figure of grotesque monstrosity. Its commodified reproduction at home speaks both to novel delight and to sublime foreboding. This very ambivalence between desire and fear constructs in the cultural imagination both a proliferation of representations and a dizzying loss of distinction between the domestic and foreign.

This popular imagination receives institutional sanction in the volumes on the British Museum's Egyptian Antiquities published in 1832 by *The Library of Entertaining Knowledge*. These volumes seek to incorporate Egypt's will to power under modern Europe's art of knowledge as they move from the Grecian to the Egyptian galleries. "Passing from the contemplation of the almost faultless representations of the human form in marble, the triumph of Grecian art," notes the author, the visitor "comes to figures more remarkable, at first sight, for their singular forms and colossal size, than for their beauty." Aesthetic contrast soon gives way, however, to an archaeological fantasia:

> Though the contrast between what he has just left, and the new scene to which he is introduced, creates at first no pleasing impression, feelings of curiosity and admiration soon arise from a more careful examination of what is around him. The colossal dimensions in which some figures are exhibited, the hardness of the materials employed, and the strange

combinations of the human and the animal form, all unite in
exciting an intense desire to know in what country, and in
what age of the world, such marvelous specimens of human
art were produced. When he is told that these are but a few
samples of the wonderful works that still exist in Egypt; that
other European capitals—Rome, Turin, Paris, and Berlin—
have their galleries enriched from the same source, or their
public places ornamented by them; that the antient tombs
and temples of that country still furnish inexhaustible materials to enrich our Museums and gratify the curiosity of the
antiquary,—he will at once perceive that a mere knowledge
of the names assigned to these pieces of stone would convey
no information at all, and that any description of them must
be unintelligible, if it does not connect them with the country
from which they came, and the monuments of which they are
but a part.[24]

The aesthetic logic of this description moves from discomfort through curiosity to sublime admiration. The
magnitude and strangeness of the Egyptian artifacts not
only provokes the spectator's desire for knowledge, but
also fills him or her with the wonder of excavation and exhibition. Egypt is converted from a strange and distant
culture into a source of gratification, enrichment, and ornamentation for the museums of the modern European
capitals. The description thus evokes sublimity only to
deflate it into novelty as admiration turns into gratification. It deflects the power of Egyptian forms towards the
beauty of the public museum, constituting the British
subject as the natural beneficiary of the ruins of antiquity. Though the juxtapositions of the Townley Gallery
might prove disturbing to some, they enabled a mapping
of cultural progress and decline in which the power of
Egypt and the seductions of Rome were contained within
a curatorial program of aesthetic idealization and progressive accumulation and display.

III

This exhibitionary drama of aesthetic deflection and
national affirmation finds a particularly telling articula-

tion in the 1826 *Guide to the Beauties of the British Museum. Being a Critical and Descriptive Account of the Principal works of Art contained in the Gallery of Antiquities of the Above National Collection.* Reflecting the expanded ambitions for the national museum as an institution of public improvement and national consolidation, the *Guide* fuses drama and reverie to cast the visitor as a performative subject in both the museum's idealization of form and its narrative promotion of national ascendancy. Staking its claim to the supplementary role established over sixty years earlier by the museum's earliest guides, the *Guide to the Beauties of the British Museum* positions itself as "a useful companion and an agreeable remembrancer."[25] Helping visitors to discriminate amidst "the multiplicity of objects of which this grand national Gallery consists," the Guide addresses "that numerous class of persons who have no time to seek out for themselves the peculiar beauties of this extensive collection," but "who yet are both able and willing to enjoy those beauties the moment they are made apparent to them." Such visitors, "for want of some Guide of the kind now offered to them, are but too apt to pass a whole morning amidst the almost unrivalled riches of this spot, and to leave it without having gained any distinct or permanent impressions of what has been presented to them; and are merely able to reply to their own question of 'What have we been seeing?' by the answer, 'The British Museum' " (iii).

Yet the *Guide* is a far more sophisticated supplement than its eighteenth-century counterparts, offering a companion which not only reproduces the aesthetic and archaeological commonplaces of its time, but which sublimates the relation between visitor and guide in a productive narrative of national authority and imperial administration. Tensions between specular seduction and intellectual gratification, transparently performed as social drama in earlier guidebooks, are now replayed as elements of disinterested aesthetic appreciation, casting subjective judgment as the mark of domestic national consolidation and global historical progression. In this context, the *Guide* offers the public an exemplary account of the Roman bust:

> A Bust of a youthful Female, which rises out of, and is termi-
> nated by, the leaves of the lotus flower. This bust is one of the
> most charming works in the whole collection. Nothing can
> surpass the natural grace, sweetness, and intellectual beauty
> of its expression; and it has the rare advantage of being as
> perfect as when it came from the sculptor's hand: or rather it
> is more so, since it has received those softening and height-
> ening touches which no hand but that of Time can give. (25)

The *Guide*'s romantic and gendered terminology recasts
the play of desire and power found in Townley's private
collection as the grace, sweetness, and beauty of the
youthful image, qualities which are only softened and
heightened through the passage of time, privileging its
belated exhibition over its original production. Display-
ing a Keatsian bent towards idealization, the *Guide* transforms a manifestly physical and alluring object into an
emblem of intellectual beauty.

Indeed, the author of the *Guide* displays a consistent
fear of the physical and material, certainly an ironic position for a museum guide. In his prefatory remarks on the
superiority of sculpture among the imitative arts, the
author distinguishes it from the deceptive nature of
painting, which gains its affective power insofar as it "resembles and reminds you of what it is not." "In a marble
statue," by contrast, "there is no deception. It is hard,
cold, and lifeless; and it looks to be no other. And yet, the
more you endeavour to impress upon yourself that it is a
dead image of stone, the more it affects you as a thing of
life" (4). Sculpture's very physicality converts it into a
more potent sign by allowing the subject sufficient protection from its material form and the subsequent ability
to exercise his imagination:

> . . . it is to its freedom from deception, arising from its ab-
> sence of colour, that Sculpture owes its chief power of affect-
> ing us. By means of that negative quality, its other positive
> qualities are enabled to appeal to the imagination, without
> communing too intimately with the senses by the way; and
> their effect, therefore, becomes more purely intellectual,
> and consequently more permanent and complete. (4)

Sculpture's very incongruity with reality lends it an affective power, as its mimetic failure becomes its aesthetic victory. The passage of time, which has stripped statuary of their color, detaches them from the world of the senses and becomes the "negative quality" by which their positive qualities of beauty may appeal to the mind of the spectator. This paradoxical formulation marks sculpture as exterior to the regular play of the senses even as it emphasizes the grace, sweetness, and beauty of the form, betraying an aesthetic ambivalence between sensual gratification and mental idealization. Such Platonic criteria for the appreciation of classical statuary dates back at least to Winckelmann who had insisted that art "should afford more food for thought than material for the eye."[26] His formula for "the universal and predominant characteristic of the Greek masterpieces," was "a noble simplicity and tranquil grandeur" that, "however strong their passions," reveal like the depths of the sea in a storm, "a great and dignified soul."[27] In the setting of the national museum, this power of revelation is transferred to the viewing subject himself, marking in the aesthetic domain the authority of the British subject over the objects he observes.

In the body of its narrative, the *Guide* makes good on these premises, consistently praising "the air of purity and grandeur which pervades" the classical forms of Greece and Rome. Even when confronted with the Statue of Venus, the *Guide* is careful to avoid the physicality of the form in favor of the purity of the spirit. "The Greeks," he tells us, "were in fact a people so wholly intellectual, that their idea of voluptuousness itself was an imagination rather than a sentiment." Hence, "the naked female statues of the Greeks, with all their resplendent beauty, do not appeal to the mere bodily passions with half the mischievous eloquence that any given 'Portrait of a Lady' does, on the chaste walls of our Royal Academy, and from the pencil of some grave R. A."[28] Analogously, the *Guide* excuses the "spirited Statue of a Faun" as "redolent of wine and the woods, without having any thing about it in the slightest degree conventional." Taking his aestheticism to an absurd extreme, he claims, "it has an ideal grossness and sensuality belonging to it, unmixed with any thing that can be called low or vulgar" (17). Throughout his survey of the Greek and Roman antiquities, the *Guide* avoids confronting the gross, voluptuous materiality of the objects, offering a transcendent and spiritual beauty as their true point of value.

The tension between materiality and contemplation informing its assessment of Greek and Roman statuary takes on a different dynamic in the second section of the *Guide* as we enter the Egyptian Galleries. The exhibition of a virtuoso's collection of Roman antiquities alongside Egyptian artifacts acquired through military and archaeological exploits creates a series of overlapping tensions both aesthetic and ideological. "The wonders which modern discovery has placed before us, in connection with the Arts of Egypt," explains the *Guide*, "exercise an almost painful and oppressive effect on the imagination, when we permit it to be directed fully and exclusively towards them" (26–27). The ideal beauty signified by the forms of classical antiquity is now offset by the awe and terror evoked by Egyptian relics. If the classical antiquities threatened the museum spectator with a seductive beauty, the Egyptian antiquities offer the sublime terror of unmediated power. The artifacts of Egypt "aggrandize, to a vast extent, our notions of the physical power of the race of beings to which we belong, without in a proportionate degree, or indeed without in any degree, elevating our conception of the intellectual power which is allied to it" (27). The physical power of Egyptian culture is contained by debasing it as inferior to the intellectual power of the age that re-exhibits these monuments. But though this distinction maintains a progressive historiography culminating in British domination, the physical might of the Egyptian age still produces "a feeling of awe-stricken amazement" in an age unable to reproduce such edifices:

I do not mean that the *art* of constructing them is lost, if we had the necessary materials; but that no single *will* could now so influence and direct the wills of others, as to achieve the works in question. And yet who shall deny that in point of *knowledge*, the present day surpasses that of any other which has preceded it? What becomes of the maxim, then, that "Knowledge is Power?" (27)

"Leaving this question for the philosopher to solve," the *Guide* seems initially unable to resolve the tension created out of its construction of Egypt as a source of power to be subsumed into the exhibitionary knowledge of modern Britain. The power represented by Egyptian antiquities is one "which nothing but a new Deluge can ever restore to the world—if we should not rather say, inflict upon it" (28).

When it turns to a consideration of the general characteristics of Egyptian sculpture, the *Guide* manages to resolve aesthetically what it was unable to resolve historically. Defending the Egyptian sculpture against those who would term it "rude," the *Guide* views its intent as wholly different from Greek and Roman art. Holding that "it is only in a state of society verging towards over-refinement, that men set up graven images to one another," the *Guide* reasons that the Egyptians "had, in fact, too little reverence and respect for themselves to think of perpetuating their mere outward and visible forms. They had high abstract notions of their power, as a race of people; and well they might, considering the stupendous evidences of that power which were constantly before their eyes!" (28). Hence to judge Egyptian art by the standards of Greece and Rome is erroneous as it misses the different objective of art in these distinct cultures. While the latter is assessed according to its mimetic conformity with the human form, the former is to be judged purely as expressions of the imagination:

The forms of Egyptian sculpture are, in their general character, like those which we see in feverish dreams, and which haunt us in that nervous affection called the night-mare; and these latter are obviously founded on something that we have previously seen, though more unlike anything belonging to the real world than we could possibly imagine in our waking hours. In a word, Egyptian sculpture, properly so called, like the annals of the country which produced it, and the associations which we are accustomed to connect with those annals and that country, more resembles "a phantasma and a dream," than a reality. (29)

"In Egypt," the *Guide* concludes, "sculpture was not an 'imitative art.'" If the Grecian and Roman Marbles departed from mimesis in elevating the viewer towards intellectual beauty, the latter does so only to haunt him with nightmarish apparitions of the sublime. The alterity the *Guide* perceives as constitutive of sculpture's aesthetic play may allow for the exercise of imaginative idealization. But it may also suggest an irreconcilable distinction between the acquisitive subject and the objects of his observation. If the forms of statuary may not be brought at least partially within the fold of the subject's imagination, they threaten to disrupt his aesthetic complacency and sense of harmonious proportion.

By displacing this power into the realm of dreams and phantasms, the *Guide* is able to ease though not efface the historical tensions that "exercise an almost painful and oppressive effect on the imagination." In the nightmare we find precisely the exercise of physical power without the restraints of the intellect that the *Guide* witnesses in the Egyptian artifacts. The culture that produced them may analogously lay claim to human power without threatening the cultural superiority of later Western civilizations. Looking back in awe upon its achievements allows the contemporary British subject to simultaneously lay claim to and distinguish himself from the power of Egyptian antiquity. These premises of haunting recollections inform all of the *Guide*'s evaluations of particular pieces. The "shadowy character" of Egyptian art is exemplified in a relief of figures "linked together hand in hand, as if engaged in dancing." The uniformity of the figures combined with their indistinct relief against the granite block reveal its function as a cultic evocation of mystery.

> The desired impression seems to have been that of shadowy forms, passing by us as if in a dream;—scarcely seen, and not to be remembered as visible objects; but only to be felt, as we feel the impression of a dream long after we have forgotten all the detail of its forms and circumstances. (31)

Such a dream world is simultaneously perceived and effaced; leaving only an impression that keeps the objects at a comfortable remove. Similarly, the famed head of Memnon "is like a beautiful mask. . . . We do not feel the least degree of human sympathy with this face, because there is nothing individualized about it; the impression is therefore merely shadowy—like that of an outline" (32). The consistent logic here evokes power and denies sympathy, enabling a simultaneous recognition of difference and identity. Taken together, the classical and Egyptian antiquities present a dilemma to the British subject. Even as their physicality attests to the beauty and power of previous civilizations, the subject must incorporate them within a progressive logic of history that positions the present culture as the rightful heir to these forms and the cultures that produced them. Both aesthetic and cultural consummation must remain ever-elusive goals whose promise both enables and threatens the acquisitive practices of British museum culture.

The Elgin Marbles seem to resolve this dilemma. Having specifically asked the visitor to pass over these galleries during the initial round of classical antiquities, the *Guide* returns to them to complete the triptych arrangement of its tour. Here the *Guide* reverses his strategies of privileging the verbal over the visual. He admits, "he very much doubts whether any thing can be said of them, that shall increase the impression they are calculated to convey to those who are susceptible of that impression, or create any impression in regard to them which they cannot create for themselves." He will, therefore, "merely place the reader before the most striking and remarkable of these objects, and then let them, as it were, speak for themselves; for it is as objects of immediate sight that these fragments are chiefly valuable" (36). This deference to the Elgin Marbles' physical self-evidence derives from the view that they have achieved what the other specimens of antiquities merely signify, namely, the union of the material and the ideal, the word made flesh. "Every portion of them, even the least excellent, is instinct with spirit and vitality; and the whole produce an effect superior to any thing else of the kind that we possess" (38).

The pure aesthetic accomplishment of the marbles not only frees them from the framing devices of the museum guide, but also justifies their more material liberation from the framing devices of the Parthenon. "It is true," the *Guide* admits, "there are some noble and inspiring associations connected with them, which have little to do with their intrinsic merits. But it is these latter that we are considering because it is on these that their chief, not to say their sole interest and value depend" (37). Mythological, historical, and cultural context is purely secondary to the marbles' aesthetic accomplishment. Analogously, "if the sculptures from the Parthenon had possessed a less superlative degree of excellence than they do, it would have been a shame and a sacrilege to have brought them away from that hallowed spot" (37). The *Guide* is not above understanding claims to architectural and geographical integrity, as he voices his objections to the removal of the Caryatis figure from the Araechtheon due to the purpose it still served as an object of affection for the local inhabitants. But the Parthenon Marbles present a qualitatively different case due to their aesthetic achievement. As it is, however, England gains a model for artistic emulation and Athens maintains the rich associations of its glorious past. "In short, England is infinitely richer than before she possessed them, and Athens is no poorer than before she lost them" (37).

Such willingness to bypass the Marbles' *in situ* function allows for a particularly idealizing aesthetic vision. In gazing upon the Theseus, the *Guide* quickly passes over its architectural and cultural history. Instead, he commands the spectator to "contemplate this statue from any point of view he pleases, and then let him say if it be possible to stand before it, or even to think of it afterwards, without a sentiment of mingled surprise and delight, with which no other external object whatever is capable of inspiring him." Mingling the sublime and the beautiful, the Theseus, unlike the metaphorical objects already surveyed, achieves a symbolic communion that transcends time and place. "There is an easy yet dignified elevation of character, which seems as it were to emanate from this noble work as a whole, added to an absolute truth, purity, and simplicity in all the various details, which perhaps do not belong to any other statue known to be in existence" (39).

Yet even at this moment of aesthetic apotheosis, the material rears its head. Noting that the Theseus formed part of the pediment iconography of the Parthenon, the *Guide* follows the natural line of curiosity and asks, "Of what, then, must have consisted the interior ornaments of the sacred places of such a temple?" The answer, far from elevating the viewer's mind towards ever-new heights, drags him back down into the corporeal. Having achieved the "extreme verge" of accomplishment, art inevitably descended. "The mere skill of the Greek sculptors at the period in question, was so fertile in its efforts, and, at the same time, reached to such absolute perfection, that mere skill was not sufficient to satisfy the appetites to which it was destined to administer. Accordingly, we find that the statue of the Goddess of the Parthenon, which was placed in the interior of the Temple, was composed of ivory and gold!" (40). The psychosexual dynamics of this passage from the lofty masculine forms of the pediment to the degenerate feminine materiality of the interior are not hard to read. "From this period the Arts of Greece began to degenerate; for the taste which is not satisfied with absolute and intrinsic beauty of effect, unless it be allied to rarity and costliness of material, is not a taste that can support Art at the highest point of its perfection; that is to say, at the highest point where it reaches, without passing beyond, the purity and truth of that Nature on which it is founded" (40–41).

The *Guide*'s narrative thus finds its apotheosis in the symbolic communion of the Elgin Marbles. Fusing spirit and form, truth and beauty, the Marbles achieve the power and grace towards which all the other objects in the museum point. In all the previous galleries of the British Museum, the *Guide* consistently converts objects into signs, pointing either towards ideal beauty, as is the case of the classical relics, or towards sublime power, as is the case of the Egyptian antiquities. In both instances, the materiality of the objects is transformed or passed through in the interest of rhetorical reflection. Converting them to signs not only denies them their physical presence, but also diminishes any sense of their intrinsic power, allowing the viewing subject a potent agency in the aesthetic encounter. Under the *Guide*'s tutelage, the spectator engages in a fantasy of spiritual consummation that redeems not only the alterity of the object but also the act of acquisition. In a circular logic of desire and legitimation by now familiar, the cultural and historical distance between Britain and the ruins of antiquity enables the spiritual identification that in turn justifies their acquisition.

IV

Wordsworth's "Egyptian Maid," also seeks to join the power of Egypt and the beauties of Greece and Rome within the structures of national acquisition. But, where the *Guide to the Beauties of the British Museum* contains the power of Egyptian imagery within rhetoric of debasement and repudiation, Wordsworth eroticizes its alterity by subsuming it within a decidedly Roman image. As a narrative recasting of a sculptural representation of an indeterminate female persona, Wordsworth's poem dramatizes the gendered play of desire and fear common to nineteenth-century ekphrastic verse within an allegory of imperial acquisition.

Generally defined as the verbal representation of visual representation, ekphrasis, as Grant F. Scott has noted, is the museum genre *par excellence*.[29] Recent critical studies of ekphrasis by Scott, W. J. T. Mitchell, Murray Krieger, Wendy Steiner, and James A. W. Heffernan have all concurred with Lessing's division in *Laocoön* between the verbal and visual arts as qualitatively distinct modes of representation engaged in perpetual competition.[30] Ekphrasis is both thematically and generically a struggle with alterity, evoking in language an object of visual depiction even as it maintains that object as distinctly foreign from the poetic subject. The identity between mediums that ekphrasis seeks in its representational maneuvers threatens to undermine the authority of the speaking subject in favor of the commanding visual object. This conflict is typically marked by a gendered competition between masculine will and feminine matter that achieves a fraught consummation in the poetic act. Ekphrasis pits the actively verbal against the passively visual, the masculine voice against the feminine silence, the spiritually transcendent against the materially seductive, yet it seeks to reconcile these hierarchical differences within an ideology of representational communion.

This reconciliation takes a descriptive form that usually moves past mere parataxis in its enumeration of the object's component elements towards a narrative structure that places the object within a context of poetic meaning. In earlier cultural periods, when ekphrasis tended to form part of a larger verbal structure, the genre of this narrative was typically epic and its trajectory towards an affirmation of community. The paradigmatic example here is Homer's description of the shield of Achilles, which forms a microcosmic image of the epic worldview dramatized throughout *The Iliad.* Beginning in the eighteenth century, however, ekphrasis follows the alienation of the artistic object from an *in situ* cultural function to an isolated museum artifact. Hence it is only in the era of the modern museum that poets produce a plethora of self-contained ekphrastic pieces. The attempted reconciliation between the verbal and the visual now assumes a more confessional model, narrating the subject's own aesthetic responses to an object presented sometimes as a metonymic trace of a vanished culture and other times as an ontologically self-sufficient expression of metaphysical order. The materially foreign object itself, though it serves as the inspiration for the ekphrastic meditation, threatens at every stage to supplant the speaking subject who deploys narratives of historical speculation and aesthetic appreciation to assert his or her (usually his) epistemological priority. Combining a desire for representational union with a fear of subjective dissolution, modern ekphrasis reveals not only the isolation of the aesthetic object, but also the alienation of the contemplative subject.

Keats's "Ode on a Grecian Urn," is the quintessential

piece of alienated Romantic ekphrasis, converting historical belatedness into aesthetic idealization. Both James
A. W. Heffernan and Grant F. Scott, who have offered extended but divergent readings of the Ode within its generic traditions, concur that its famous conclusion is at
best a compromise between verbal and visual representation, maintaining the tension between still beauty and
active truth. Typical to its period and genre, the Ode constructs a sequence of oppositions between the masculine
speaker and the feminized object in order to establish an
idealized space for poetic reflection. Mingling memory
and desire, Keats transforms the "still unravish'd bride of
quietness" into a "Sylvan historian" (1–3)[31] through his
own vain inquiries into the origins of its representational
imagery, predicating his perception of truth and beauty
upon the very wasting of generations such ideals are said
to transcend. Due to its non-linguistic materiality, the urn
both beckons and repels the poetic speaker, and his questions to the silent object do not so much engage with its
storied face as deflect the debilitating power of this "fos-
ter-child of silence and slow time, / . . . who canst thus
express / A flowery tale more sweetly than our rhyme" (2–
4). Keats's poetry transforms the displacements of history
that have constituted the urn as culturally as well as se-
mantically foreign into the grounds for an erotic inquiry
that paints a picture of "mad pursuit" and "wild ecstasy."
Despite its overt sensuality, Keats's conversion of historical alienation into aesthetic rapture is fundamentally a
gesture of idealization, in which a manifestly material object bearing copious traces of historical specificity is
transformed into a sign of spiritual transcendence:

> Heard melodies are sweet, but those unheard
>   Are sweeter; therefore, ye soft pipes, play on;
> Not to the sensual ear, but, more endear'd,
>   Pipe to the spirit ditties of no tone:
>
> (11–14)

The poet's subsequent reading of the urn's "leaf-fring'd
legend" fuses *eros* and *thanatos*, pursuit and stasis, and
prolongs desire by insisting on its perpetual deflection.

By idealizing the urn's imagery, Keats creates a space for his own narrative queries and aesthetic reflections, asserting the supremacy of the poetic word over the "silent form." This idealization not only staves off the material presence of the urn by transforming it into a catalyst for subjective meditation, but also directly serves Keats's elusive goal of cultural consummation. Keats employs his final proclamation of moral truth and beauty not only to stabilize the vicissitudes of history, but also to forge an identification of the poet and the urn that simultaneously transcends and re-inscribes their mutually defining alterity. Converting historical rupture into cultural continuity, Keats unites eternity and mortality in a "Cold Pastoral" that may momentarily "tease us out of thought" (44). But the final epigrammatic conclusion merely divides the temporally bound poet and the ostensibly eternal urn even as it posits their reconciliation.

Where Keats offers a confessional ode of aesthetic transport, Wordsworth provides a narrative romance of seduction, idealization, and incorporation. In his own ekphrastic pieces, which multiplied exponentially as the poet matured, Wordsworth consistently uses the tension between desire and fear to construct an idealized space of Platonic beauty that informs even as it transcends the material world. As James A. W. Heffernan has noted, Wordsworth's corpus as a whole includes at least twenty-four ekphrastic pieces, most famously his "Elegiac Stanzas, Suggested by a Picture of Peele Castle, in a Storm, Painted by Sir George Beaumont" (composed 1805; published 1807). Heffernan reads Wordsworth's general attitude towards poetry's sister art as a paragonal struggle between "the iconophilic desire to gaze and the iconoclastic urge to violate" and reads the "Elegiac Stanzas" as an enactment of the movement from the former to the latter.[32] This passage from identification to repudiation allows Wordsworth to construct an idealized space out of the act of verbal reconstruction itself, creating through elegy the "Elysian quiet" denied to him by Beaumont's painting. The verbal medium offers a space of spiritual calm both enabled and yet threatened by the visual representation. A similar, but more manifestly narrative ma-

neuver characterizes his "Lines, Suggested by a Portrait
from the Pencil of F. Stone" and its accompanying "The
Foregoing Subject Resumed" which occupy the penulti-
mate position in the order of *Yarrow Revisited and Other
Poems*.[33] These poems warrant a brief digression for the
insight they provide into the gendered and cultural values Wordsworth invests in the genre during this stage of
his career. Wordsworth here offers support to W. J. T.
Mitchell's suggestion that ekphrasis adopts as one of its
principle themes the very ambivalence that constitutes it
as a genre, resolving in argument what remains sus-
pended in form. Wordsworth vacillates in these two
poems between spiritual idealization and material seduction, both fearing and eroticizing the portrait of the
demure yet tantalizing female form. Cast as private meditations, these poems offer a generic and ideological correlative to Wordsworth's nationalist romance of "The
Egyptian Maid."

Frank Stone's pencil drawing of Rotha Quillinan from
1833 provides the most likely subject of Wordsworth's
poem, though it differs in crucial details from the verbal
sketch Wordsworth provides.[34] The portrait's deflected
gaze and use of lineaments to frame the female form reso-
nate visually with Townley's Roman bust. Wordsworth's
poems expand the correlation by interpreting both images as figures of immortal beauty, both tantalizing and
dangerous. Yet Wordsworth's meditations on Stone's portrait would seem solely personal, an attempt, as Matthew
Brennan suggests, to find in art the purity of imaginative
vision that remains so elusive in the temporal world.[35]
The first of the two poems on Stone's sketch offers an extended apostrophe to the portrait in which Wordsworth
wavers between the incompatible desires for representational presence and for aesthetic and moral idealization.
Wordsworth situates himself in a passively receptive
mood as he contemplates the portrait of a young maid:

> Beguiled into forgetfulness of care
> Due to the day's unfinished task; of pen
> Or book regardless, and of that fair scene
> In Nature's prodigality displayed

F. Stone's 1833 sketch of Rotha Quillinan. Dove Cottage, The Wordsworth Trust.

> Before my window, oftentimes and long
> I gaze upon a Portrait whose mild gleam
> Of beauty never ceases to enrich
> The common light; whose stillness charms the air
> Or seems to charm it, into like repose;
> Whose silence, for the pleasure of the ear,
> Surpasses sweetest music.
>
> (1–11)

Wordsworth allies the portrait's distracting and seductive beauty with its stillness and silence, its muteness enabling the poet's own imaginative voicing. Situated in his room between verbal representation and immediate nature, the portrait assumes an almost bewitching power, though its actual mimetic content is initially unarticulated. When the form is evoked, its terms are manifestly sculptural and symbolic:

> There she sits
> With emblematic purity attired
> In a white vest, white as her marble neck
> Is, and the pillar of the throat would be
> But for the shadow by the drooping chin
> Cast into that recess—. . . .
>
> (11–16)

Both the statuesque description and the emblematic association with purity negate the physical presence afforded by the painting, converting the image into a sign that allows for ekphrastic self-reflection. In true Platonic fashion, Wordsworth figures the skill of representation as twice removed from the ideal form as he analogously associates it with the shepherd's gazing on the reflection of the morning sun on surrounding mountains. This double remove suggests a triple remove for the ekphrastic poet, yet this distance only provokes a greater desire for communion. Turning to the reader, Wordsworth commands us to

> Look at her, who'er
> Thou be that, kindling with a poet's soul,
> Hast loved the painter's true Promethean craft

Intensely—from Imagination take
The treasure,—what mine eyes behold see thou,
Even though the Atlantic ocean roll between.

(22–27)

Invoking pictorial mimesis as Promethean transgression, Wordsworth aspires to a sympathetic relationship between poet and reader to bridge the acknowledged gap between verbal and visual representation. The actual terms of his extended description move instinctively towards emblematic interpretation:

A silver line, that runs from brow to crown
And in the middle parts the braided hair,
Just serves to show how delicate a soil
The golden harvest grows in; and those eyes,
Soft and capacious as a cloudless sky
Whose azure depth their colour emulates,
Must needs be conversant with upward looks,
Prayer's voiceless service; but now, seeking nought
And shunning nought, their own peculiar life
Of motion they renounce, and with the head
Partake its inclination towards earth
In humble grace, and quiet pensiveness
Caught at the point where it stops short of sadness.

(28–40)

Wordsworth evokes each physical feature of the portrait only to transform it into a sign of spiritual purity. The painting's stillness and silence are pregnant with meaning for the poet whose gaze speaks for the voiceless image. Ironically, his emphasis on interpretation in place of description hinders the very verbal transparency he claims to desire. But it also affords both poet and reader a power over the absorptive influence of the image, appropriating the power of interpretation in a paradoxically iconophobic gesture.

Akin to the contorted conduct of the *Guide to the Beauties of the British Museum*, this tension between means and ends arises because Wordsworth's narrative voice is simultaneously seduced by the portrait's evocation and committed to maintaining its distant purity:

Offspring of soul-bewitching Art, make me
Thy confidant! say, whence derived that air
Of calm abstraction? Can the ruling thought
Be with some lover far away, or one
Crossed by misfortune, or of doubted faith?
Inapt conjecture! Childhood here, a moon
Crescent in simple loveliness serene,
Has but approached the gates of womanhood,
Not entered them; her heart is yet unpierced
By the blind Archer-god; her fancy free:
The fount of feeling, if unsought elsewhere,
Will not be found.

(41–52)

In his effort to maintain the portrait as both virgin and beauty, Wordsworth articulates both his longing and its chaste reproof. Grant F. Scott has argued that the ekphrastic sub-genre of the portrait poem is constructed out of the masculine voice's fear of seduction and emasculation by the power of the feminine image.[36] Wordsworth's contribution to the genre adopts a different yet complementary strategy, deploying idealization to deflect the lust engaged by the seductive image. This typical casting of the female as either ideal spirit or seductive matter draws him back to the "emblematic purity" invoked earlier as a means of consummating his desire for full representational presence without sullying the maiden's innocence:

The floweret, held
In scarcely conscious fingers, was, she knows
(Her Father told her so) in youth's gay dawn
Her Mother's favourite; and the orphan Girl,
In her own dawn—a dawn less gay and bright,
Loves it, while there in solitary peace
She sits, for that departed Mother's sake.
—Not from a source less sacred is derived
(Surely I do not err) that pensive air
Of calm abstraction through the face diffused
And the whole person.

(63–73)

Both the maiden and the flower represent a sentimental purity that their own form seductively compromises. The

parenthetical remarks belie the confidence with which
Wordsworth seeks to represent the maiden's virtue of
mind and body, revealing the tension between material
form and mental idealization motivating the extended description. This representational ambivalence becomes
increasingly manifest as the stanza and the first half of
the poem's argument conclude:

> Words have something told
> More than the pencil can, and verily
> More than is needed, but the precious Art
> Forgives their interference—Art divine,
> That both creates and fixes, in despite
> Of Death and Time, the marvels it hath wrought.
>
> (73–78)

Wordsworth here simultaneously applauds and deni-
grates ekphrasis as both superior and inferior to pictorial
representation. As an instance of pure form, it transcends
"Death and Time," but is thereby isolated from true communication, a created yet static marvel. The poet's description of the portrait is less an attempt at mimetic
union and more an attempt to hold temporality and form
in productive yet ambivalent relation. This attempt foregrounds the poet himself in fraught dialogue with purity
and grace, the actual portrait receding ever further from
full presence.

In the second half of its argument, the poem further
contemplates the divide between verbal and visual representation, but now in a wider social context. Wordsworth
begins the long second stanza with an explicit praise of
the pictorial arts as lasting memorials in a world of transience and decay:

> Is not then the Art
> Godlike, a humble branch of the divine,
> In visible quest of immortality,
> Stretched forth with trembling hope?
>
> (88–91)

From this elevation of the portrait's capability to en-
shrine the maiden's virginity of spirit and body, it is no

great leap to manifestly religious art, the subject of the
rest of the stanza. Wordsworth evokes pilgrims who, "In
every realm, / From high Gibraltar to Siberian plains, / . . .
would echo this appeal" (91–94), particularly an imagined
monk in the Escurial monastery whom Wordsworth imagines gazing upon Wilkie's portrait of the Last Supper.
Thinking of his deceased and scattered brethren, the
monk meditates upon the portrait of the gathered apos-
tles to the point of exchanging representation for reality:
"They are in truth the Substance, we the Shadows" (117).
Transforming ekphrastic desire into religious quest,
Wordsworth takes the privileging of pictorial representation to its logical conclusion, undermining not only verbal
representation, but also the epistemological privileging
of subject over object that underlies it. Such monastic ekphrasis exemplifies at once the ideal of full communion
and its distance from the world of time and chance.
Wordsworth does not end the poem with this religious apotheosis, but returns to the portrait and his own more
worldly meditations:

> So spake the mild Jeronymite, his griefs
> Melting away within him like a dream
> Ere he had ceased to gaze, perhaps to speak:
> And I, grown old, but in a happier land,
> Domestic Portrait! have to verse consigned
> In thy calm presence those heart-moving words:
> Words that can soothe, more than they agitate;
> Whose spirit, like the angel that went down
> Into Bethesda's pool, with healing virtue
> Informs the fountain in the human breast
> Which by the visitation was disturbed.
> —But why this stealing tear? Companion mute,
> On thee I look, not sorrowing; fare thee well,
> My Song's Inspirer, once again farewell!

(118–31)

The verbal act is simultaneously agitating and soothing, a
disturbing visitation and a healing virtue, and hence re-
stores the poet to the position of power by relegating the
portrait to an inspiring image. The poetic art fulfills the

pictorial marvel's restorative purpose. Ultimately both
Wilkie's painting and Stone's portrait are consigned to
the role of informative absences, their removal or departure necessary for the verse's conclusion. The mute inspiration for Wordsworth's lines remains distant as a
requisite condition of her emblematic purity and the
poet's sense of self-integrity.

Wordsworth extends the meditation in his "The Foregoing Subject Resumed" in which "the Painter's skill, /
Humbling the body, to exalt the soul" (3–4) presents a religious vision of immorality to inform the poet's mortal
meditations. The portrait of the girl, now consigned to
memory, continues to provoke "thoughts that haunt [the
poet] still" (13) and provide "a . . . salutary sense of awe"
(24). In the logic of Wordsworth's verse, portraiture and
painting constitute an ideal realm of timeless purity, yet
lend meaning through their representation in verse to the
world of temporal flux and decay. Wordsworth's ekphrasis
thus seeks to incorporate the power of the idealized
image while maintaining its difference as a prerequisite
for the constitution of meaning. The perpetual valence
between verbal and visual, between mortal and divine,
becomes the enabling characteristic of Wordsworth's ekphrastic representation.[37]

What is cast as a personal and interior struggle between seduction and idealization in these two poems is
allegorized in "The Egyptian Maid" as a national struggle for self-definition and imperial acquisition. James
Douglas Merriman reads the sequence of the narrative
as representative of Wordsworth's own poetic career: the
pagan youthfulness of the maiden corresponding to the
poet's own youthful construction of a doctrinally-free
imaginative power in combat with the cold rationalism of
Enlightenment thought. The maiden's marriage and incorporation into a Christianized Arthurian court corresponds as well to the poet's subsequent enclosure of
imaginative power within more specifically Christian
doctrine.[38] However, Wordsworth's acceptance of a "British theme . . . / Within the groves of Chivalry"[39] places
these personal tensions within the broader cultural discourses of Orientalist imperialism and medieval pater-

nalism. Paralleling his deployment of the verbal and visual mediums in his ekphrastic meditations, Wordsworth here uses the opposition of Anglican spirituality and Oriental idolatry to create a safe haven for his poetic vision. Representing simultaneously the cradle of civilization and an important colonial acquisition, Egypt is both invoked as a land of mysterious power and personified as a virginal maid encased within a seductive idol. The challenge for Arthurian Britain is to simultaneously subdue its power and incorporate it as a rejuvenating presence within the imperial body. In his ekphrastic meditation on Stone's portrait, Wordsworth deflects the seductive power of the painted image by converting it into a sculptured emblem of purity and grace. In "The Egyptian Maid," the allure of the Roman bust is repudiated as idolatrous in favor of the maiden it signifies, a maiden who may be re-inscribed within the confines of Anglican piety. Ekphrasis and empire join rhetorically and ideologically in this romance of colonial conquest and medieval chivalry.

Adopting a public neo-Spenserian tone, Wordsworth constructs the entire narrative of his poem around dichotomies of Western Christianity and Oriental Paganism, secular reason and religious vision, masculine spectators and feminine objects. King Arthur and his knights, in keeping with the tradition of the legends, are paragons of Christian virtue. Sir Galahad, the most chaste of all of the knights, is the natural bridegroom to the heavenly maiden. Merlin stands outside of the court, defined as a "Mechanist, whose skill / Shames the degenerate grasp of modern science" and further condemned for "practicing occult and perilous lore" (19–22). He thereby becomes a figure for not only mechanistic rationalism, but for occult practices of a black science. Nina, the lady of the lake, assumes the role of a heavenly messenger, but the most enigmatic of the figures are the Egyptian maiden herself and the vessel of the Water Lily.

The maiden is concealed during the original confrontation with Merlin who does not know of her presence in the boat bearing the image of Townley's marble at its prow:

> While Merlin paced the Cornish sands,
> Forth-looking toward the rocks of Scilly,
> The pleased Enchanter was aware
>   Of a bright Ship that seemed to hang in air,
>   Yet was she the work of mortal hands,
> And took from men her name—THE WATER LILY.
>
> (1–6)

Yet the image of the ship itself is sufficient to simultaneously seduce and threaten. Merlin's reactions to the ship's image vacillate between erotic desire and competitive fear:

> Upon this winged Shape so fair
> Sage Merlin gazed with admiration:
> Her lineaments, thought he, surpass
> Aught that was ever shown in magic glass;
> Was ever built with patient care;
> Or, at a touch, produced by happiest transformation.
> . . . .
> Provoked to envious spleen, he cast
> An altered look upon the advancing Stranger
> Whom he had hailed with joy, and cried,
> "My Art shall help to tame her pride—"
> Anon the breeze became a blast,
> And the waves rose, and the sky portended danger.
>
> (13–18; 25–30)

Merlin's initial encounter shifts between "admiration" and "envious spleen" producing an "altered look upon the advancing Stranger" that contains in microcosm the tensions between eroticization and debasement that the rest of the poem's narrative will seek to resolve.

The Egyptian maiden is sheltered and clothed by the vessel of the Water Lily, an object gendered as female and closely identified with the Moon. Her "spread sail and streaming pendant," along with her glorious "lineaments" cause Merlin's admiration and subsequent envy. In the following storm, the poem frames the confrontation in specifically gendered and highly eroticized language:

> Behold, how wantonly she laves
> Her sides, the Wizard's craft confounding;

> Like something out of Ocean sprung
> To be for ever fresh and young,
> Breasts the sea-flashes and huge waves
> Top-gallant high, rebounding and rebounding!
>
> But Ocean under magic heaves,
> And cannot spare the Thing he cherished:
> Ah! what avails that she was fair,
> Luminous, blithe, and debonair?
> The storm has stripped her of her leaves;
> The Lily floats no longer!—she hath perished.
>
> (43–54)

The eroticized feminine other confronts the mechanistic, masculine Britain and falls under the power of his craft. "Stripped of her leaves," her power proves as fleeting as the youth she attempts to arrest. Yet, as the narrative explicitly implores, we are meant to side with the fallen ship over the degenerate practitioner of "occult and perilous lore":

> Grieve for her, she deserves no less;
> So like, yet so unlike, a living Creature!
> No heart had she, no busy brain;
> Though loved, she could not love again;
> Though pitied, *feel* her own distress;
> Nor aught that troubles us, the fools of Nature.
>
> Yet is there cause for gushing tears;
> So richy was this Galley laden,
> A fairer than herself she bore,
> And, in her struggles, cast ashore;
> A lovely One, who nothing hears
> Of wind or wave—a meek and guileless Maiden.
>
> (55–65)

Wordsworth's representation of the bust as a location of idealized innocence produces a radically ambivalent desire. These lines construct the figure as unattainable, simultaneously similar and different from the desiring spectator. In that space of tantalizing distance, Wordsworth may interpolate through sympathetic imagination a masculine subject defined through its relation to an unfeeling feminine other. Only at this stage of the narrative does Wordsworth reveal the similarly detached contents of the vessel: "A lovely One, who nothing hears / Of wind or wave—a meek and guileless Maiden" (65–66). This description is a sharp contrast to depictions of Egyptian art as a sublime and masculine force which "exercise[s] an almost painful and oppressive effect on the imagination."[40] By constructing an image of the Orient both fantastic and vulnerable, specifically feminine in gender, and recessed within the form of the vessel, Wordsworth creates an image that can be controlled, not only physically by the craft of the Occidental mechanist, but ideologically by the poet-narrator. Wordsworth represses the persona of the maiden and imposes an interpretation upon the image to reconstitute the Arthurian legends he has more directly, and therefore less malleably, inherited.

Nina, as a heavenly messenger, later described as a "gentle Sorceress, and benign, / Who ne'er embittered any good man's chalice" (95–96) corrects a repentant Merlin's errors by revealing the potential rejuvenation the Water Lily offers:

> "On Christian service this frail Bark
> Sailed" (hear me, Merlin!) "under high protection,
> Though on her prow a sign of heathen power
> Was carved—a Goddess with a Lily flower,
> The old Egyptian's emblematic mark
> Of joy immortal and of pure affection.
>
> (73–78)

This emblematic encapsulation of the image of the woman and the lotus interprets its meaning within the standard Orientalist parameters, constructing the East as a source of pure emotional revitalization. But Wordsworth exhibits this "sign of heathen power" as specifically other and therefore must subsume it into a "Christian service" to incorporate and control its force. Nina's encounter with the image of the bust is marked by a desire similar, though less dramatic, to that of Merlin:

> Soon did the gentle Nina reach
> That Isle without a house or haven;

> Landing, she found not what she sought,
> Nor saw of wreck or ruin aught
> But a carved Lotus cast upon the beach
> By the fierce waves, a flower in marble graven.
>
> Sad relique, but how fair the while!
> For gently each from each retreating
> With backward curve, the leaves revealed
> The bosom half, and half concealed,
> Of a Divinity, that seemd to smile
> On Nina, as she passed, with hopeful greeting.
>
> (121–32)

The bust functions here as a seductress, beckoning Nina away from the true source of her quest. The "hopeful greeting" produced by the half-revealed bosom again figures the Pagan Orient as a promiscuous object of desire. But Nina specifically passes over the image of the lotus goddess lying on the beach to rescue and restore the maiden who also has been cast ashore:

> No quest was hers of vague desire,
> Of tortured hope and purpose shaken;
> Following the margin of a bay,
> She spied the lonely Cast-away,
> Unmarred, unstripped of her attire,
> But with closed eyes,—of breath and bloom forsaken.
>
> Then Nina, stooping down, embraced,
> With tenderness and mild emotion,
> The Damsel, in that trance embound;
> And, while she raised her from the ground,
> And in the pearly shallop placed,
> Sleep fell upon the air, and stilled the ocean.
>
> The turmoil hushed, celestial springs
> Of music opened, and there came a blending
> Of fragrance, underived form earth,
> With gleams that owed not to the sun their birth,
> And that soft rustling of invisible wings
> Which Angels make, on works of love descending.
>
> And Nina heard a sweeter voice
> Than if the Goddess of the flower had spoken:

"Thou hast achieved, fair Dame! what none
Less pure in spirit could have done;
Go, in thy enterprise rejoice!
Air, earth, sea, sky, and heaven, success betoken."

(133–56)

Nina's "tenderness and mild emotion" stand in contrast to the seductive "vague desire" elicited by the bust's image, just as the maiden's "Unmarred, unstripped" condition differs from the Lotus figure's promiscuous and partially-revealed form. The voice of Angels' wings is unlike any voice the Goddess may have used. Nina and Merlin place the maiden into an angelically blessed "ebon car" pulled by "two mute Swans," who later signify the maiden's proper suitor as they "clap their wings; / And their necks play, involved in rings, / Like sinless snakes in Eden's happy land" (321–23). By recessing the maiden in a holier, and thereby more powerful vessel, Nina and Merlin subsume the ineffectual imaginative force of the Pagan world under the power of Christian spirituality. Only through the maiden's joining with the heavenly-ordained bridegroom of Sir Galahad may her life be revived and her imaginative power re-contained within a doctrinally Christian framework.

By the end of the poem, Merlin's erotic admiration is repudiated as idolatrous and his envious spleen, though wicked in and of itself, is redeemed as serving the nobler cause of bringing the maiden within the Arthurian court. For though the vessel in which the maiden arrives "seemed to hang in air," it is merely the "work of mortal hands." Its fatal flaw, as revealed by the angels in their final chorus, is that its splendor is the work of idolaters:

A Ship to Christ devoted
From the Land of Nile did go;
Alas! the bright Ship floated,
An Idol at her prow.

By magic domination,
The Heaven-permitted vent
Of purblind mortal passion,
Was wrought her punishment.

> The Flower, the Form within it,
> What served they in her need?
> Her port she could not win it,
> Nor from mishap be freed.

(359–70)

The vessel's power over Merlin emerges as ineffectual, the Pagan imagination represented through Townley's marble uninformed by Christian spirituality. Wordsworth is thus able to work through both the erotic desire and abject fear provoked by the Egyptian forms towards an idealized vision that sees through the forms to the virginal maid that lies within. By condemning both rationalist science and pagan idolatry, Wordsworth locates his own vision in a strongly Christianized England, embracing the spiritual over the rational without falling into the errors of false worship.

Lest we misunderstand this gesture of incorporation, Wordsworth bends the Arthurian legends even further in explaining the origins of the maiden's journey. Upon viewing the unconscious Egyptian maid, King Arthur bemoans her tragic fate and registers a guilty feeling of responsibility:

> "Alas! and I have caused this woe;
> For, when my prowess from invading Neighbours
> Had freed his Realm, he plighted word
> That he would turn to Christ our Lord,
> And his dear Daughter on a Knight bestow
> Whom I should choose for love and matchless labours.
>
> "Her birth was heathen; but a fence
> Of holy Angels round her hovered:
> A Lady added to my court
> So fair, of such divine report
> And worship, seemed a recompense
> For fifty kingdoms by my sword recovered.

(223–34)

Wordsworth's invention of Arthur as a benevolent mercenary, freeing the Egyptian lands from foreign invaders, not only distorts the traditional constructions of the Arthurian legends, but registers the peculiar relationship between Britain and Egypt during the first half of the nineteenth century. Casting Arthur against Napoleon recasts the global military and economic interests of Britain and France as nothing short of a holy mission. Indeed, the spiritual incorporation of the maiden is here explicitly deployed as a justification for foreign military intervention.

As David Spurr has argued, the paradoxical nature of imperial rhetoric is to insist simultaneously upon radical difference in the construction of colonial authority and upon essential identity as a philosophical prerequisite for a civilizing agenda. Maintaining the colonized as foreign for purposes of self-definition is always accompanied by seeking an identity that in turn threatens to destabilize imperial authority. Both the desire and the fear definitive of a modern alienated subjectivity are deflected in this discourse onto the colonized object itself. Hence, as Spurr puts it, "the desire to emphasize racial and cultural difference as a means of establishing superiority takes place alongside the desire to efface difference and to gather the colonized into the fold of an all-embracing civilization."[41] Particularly during periods of stress in the social and cultural order, the need for positive self-definition assumes an urgency that reveals the ambivalence towards perceived alien presence within the imperial body. In a paradoxical union of debasement and eroticisation, the foreign is subsequently degraded as a protection from a colonized alterity that is desired even as it is repudiated. The simultaneous desire for and fear of representational union that we witness in Wordsworthian ekphrasis offer in microcosm broader tensions informing the mediation of colonized societies within the culture of imperial conquest.

Wordsworth's nationalist allegory demonstrates the ideological power of ekphrasis as a genre of substitution and idealization. Haunted by an antagonistic struggle between representational mediums, ekphrasis paradoxically gains a power to deflect political and social tensions into the realm of aesthetic response. Here, the fears and desires of an individual or collectivity may be transposed onto objects of exhibition, newly arranged to comfort and confirm a sense of personal or national integrity. As a genre manifestly concerned with distinction and incorporation, ekphrasis joins the aesthetics of the museum to the ideologies of empire. It also joins the alienated stance of romantic poetry to a collective affirmation of national community. Both Wordsworth's "Lines on a Portrait by F. Stone" and his "Egyptian Maid" incorporate through idealization foreign and material objects of desire. But whereas the former situates this incorporation within a drama of artistic doubt, affirmation, and restoration, the latter allegorically links aesthetic ambivalence with imperial consolidation. This powerful poetic union of self and nation transfers the aesthetic ideology of the British Museum to the sensibilities of the reading and viewing public.

"The Egyptian Maid; or, The Romance of the Water Lily" thus stands in exhibition in numerous yet simultaneous galleries. Most immediately, that of a volume, *Yarrow Revisited and Other Poems*, whose works appropriate cultural objects and historical sites as constructed repositories of poetic imagination; whose postscript politically contextualizes the works within a nationalist and religious conservatism; and whose final pages advertise new works from the publisher falling into three categories: collections of British poetry, works on natural history, and tales of voyages and travels in foreign lands. The entries in this final category (*Travel in Ethiopia, English in India and Other Sketches,* and *Egypt and Mohammed Ali; or Travels in the Valley of the Nile,* among others) clearly indicate the rising Orientalist interests of the English reading public. Coterminous with this gallery are those of a poet reframing earlier imaginative impulses within the boundaries of religious and nationalist identity; of a culture seeking to re-exhibit itself in terms of its medieval past and its opposition to an Oriental other; of a discourse attempting to both embrace and control the acquired and constructed rejuvenating forces of the East. Wordsworth appropriates an already appropriated image whose origi-

nal signification is lost in the passages of time and place
for the purpose not of finally understanding the sources
of its appearance, but for creating a Pagan, Oriental, feminine other to redefine his own creative self and the spirit
and soul of his nation.

5

Babel's Curse and the Museum's Burden: Shelley, Rossetti, and the Exhibition of Alterity

> for it may be assumed as a maxim that no nation or re-
> ligion can supersede any other without incorporating
> into itself a portion of that which it supersedes.
> —Percy Bysshe Shelley, *A Defence of Poetry*

> When tradition, thus adorned and exaggerated, has
> surrounded the founders of families and states with so
> much adventitious power and magnificence, there is
> no praise which a living poet can, without fear of being
> kicked for clumsy flattery, address to a living chief,
> that will not still leave the impression that the latter is
> not so great a man as his ancestors.
> —Thomas Love Peacock, *The Four Ages of Poetry*

I

WHEN DOES A CURSE BECOME A BURDEN?
Speaking of the vanity of translation, Percy Bysshe
Shelley argues in *A Defence of Poetry* that "it were as wise
to cast a violet into a crucible that you might discover the
formal principle of its colour and odour, as seek to trans-
fuse from one language into another the creations of a
poet. The plant must spring again from its seed or it will
bear no flower—and, this is the burthen of the curse of
Babel."[1] Shelley's articulation of the legacy of Babel im-
plies a constructive yet unstable relation between the
curse and the burden, between the multiplicity of tongues
and the necessity of translation, between the inadequacy
and the imperative of metaphor. The curse of Babel

208

marks a fissure between a unified humanity and a self-perpetuating condition of linguistic and cultural difference. The burden of this curse brings us into history and forces us to choose between nostalgia for a lost identity, passive acceptance of insurmountable difference, or an always partial and insufficient attempt to translate one culture's system of understanding into our own. Shelley's organic metaphor posits a self-generating essence of poetic expression in contrast to the always-differentiating origin of translation. But in Shelley's account of the development and progress of cultures, poetry's metaphoric power engages in a perpetual transfer of imperfect meanings that bridge past, present, and future from germination through growth and fruition. The poet "not only beholds intensely the present as it is, and discovers those laws according to which present things ought to be ordered, but he beholds the future in the present, and his thoughts are the germs of the flower and the fruit of latest time" (483). Poetry "is at the same time the root and blossom of all other systems of thought" (503). It comprises both perception and production in an on-going dialectic of aesthetic reception and re-creation whose "power arises from within, like the colour of a flower which fades and changes as it is developed" (504). Only through its powers of metaphor or *translatio* may "poetry defeat[] the curse which binds us to be subjected to the accident of surrounding impressions" (505). The epistemological curse of Babel that severs organic communication, separating the plant from its seed, emerges in Shelley's poetics as the historical burden at the root of the flower of belated signification.[2]

This movement from curse to burden finds a naive expression in the opening pages of W. H. Boulton's *The Romance of the British Museum* (1930). Opposite the title page offering the volume as "The Story of its Origins, Growth and Purpose and Some of its Contents," the frontispiece reproduces an image of "The Building of the Tower of Babel" from a Book of Hours, about A.D. 1423, executed in France for John Duke of Bedford and now contained by the museum as Add.MSS.18850. One may speculate endlessly why Boulton chose this frontispiece, but the juxta-

ADD 18850, Building the Tower of Babel. By permission of the British Library.

position of the Tower of Babel with the British Museum
exemplifies perfectly the transformation of Babel's curse
into the museum's burden in the institution's construction of romance. Sir Frederic Kenyon, Director and
Principal Librarian to the British Museum, 1909–30, elu-
cidates the essence of this romance in his forwarding remarks to Boulton's volume:

> The visitor to the Museum, if he is to get value for his visit,
> should come with his mind prepared. To wander through the
> Museum, with no comprehension of the meaning of the ob-
> jects exhibited, may indeed provoke a passing sense of won-
> der, but is more likely to produce boredom and repulsion.
> The wider the knowledge of the visitor, and the more culti-
> vated his taste for art, the more he is able to see what place
> the several objects hold in the long history of human civiliza-
> tion. The Museum is a picture-book of the history of man; and
> to study it is to enlarge one's comprehension of what man has
> done and what man can do. Everywhere the spade of the ex-
> plorer is revealing fresh chapters of man's past. The royal
> graves of Ur, the palaces of Minoru, Crete, the treasures of
> the tomb of Tutankhamen, the pottery, porcelain and paint-
> ing of China, the art of the "barbarous" races of Central and
> Eastern Europe, all these are but a few of the additions
> which have come during the last generation to supplement
> what we had already of the art of Greece and Rome, of Egypt
> and Assyria. The universe of man, like the universe of nature,
> extends its boundaries daily before our eyes; and it is in our
> museums that the story is displayed for the visitor to see.[3]

Archaeological knowledge and aesthetic taste merge in
Kenyon's curatorial romance to produce an inclusive narrative of progressive history and extensive boundaries.
The advancing cultivation of the visitor and the ongoing
revelations of the explorer's spade meet in the museum's
picture book of the ever-expanding universe of man. Past
accomplishments and future possibilities thereby manifest in the proper arrangement and appreciation of objects, converting metonymic traces of vanished cultures
into metaphoric pictures of universal humanity. Yet the
curse of Babel that underlies the story of "origins, growth
and purpose" is a burden from this romance's very opening pages.

Both Shelley's poetic manifesto and Boulton's exhibitionary catalogue conflate disruption and unification in a vision simultaneously romantic and ironic. If romance posits a transcendence of historical vicissitudes in the establishment of a permanent and self-sufficient realm of knowledge and communion, irony reveals the insurmountable distance between fractured difference and unified identity. The central genius of Romantic art has long been understood as the fusion of these two tropes into an aesthetic vision both deconstructive and recuperative,[4] but in the history of the British Museum they have most often been viewed as irreconcilable curatorial options. When the Department of Antiquities emerged in 1807 under the direction of Taylor Combe from the already impossible Department of Natural and Artificial Productions, it consisted primarily of Greek and Roman statuary. But beginning in the 1820s, under the direction of Edward Hawkins, the museum received a series of major acquisitions from Egypt and Assyria that in the 1850s brought to head long-standing tensions between aesthetic formalism and archaeological historicism in the arrangement and reception of antiquities. The contiguous exhibition of Greek and Roman sculptures alongside those from Egypt and Assyria that Kenyon views as natural threatened at the time to collapse the distinction between ideal form and historical curiosity. Their juxtaposition would either elevate the achievement of the Oriental cultures, or, as was more commonly feared, reduce the accomplishments of Greece and Rome to mere relics, no more or less historically contingent than sarcophagi and winged bulls. In 1860, reflecting in part a failure of conceptual integration, the Department was itself divided into three new Departments: Oriental Antiquities, Greek and Roman Antiquities, and Coins and Medals.[5]

This chapter offers a meditation on this division insofar as it speaks to the unstable relation between the curse of alterity and the burden of exhibition in Romantic museum discourse. Particularly, I consider the provocation posed by the influx of Assyrian statuary at mid-century to the British Museum's display of progressive historiography and exposition of the Greek ideal in the service of national education and improvement. Austen Henry Layard's archaeological defense that promoted the statuary to the British public and Dante Gabriel Rossetti's poetic critique of its display each capitalized upon the precarious foundations of nationalist cultural historiography. Offering teleological romance on the one hand and cyclical irony on the other, Layard and Rossetti derived opposing yet complementary imaginative responses to the burden of history. However, a reading of Shelley's characteristic romantic irony in his own meditations on ruins and progress offers a means of reconciling historical difference and aesthetic identity readily adaptable to the practice of a national museum. Read against the backdrop of the public debates over the integrity of the museum's holdings in the 1850s, these works offer a range of curatorial options for translating Babel's curse into the museum's burden.

II

Emerging from the exhibitions inside the national repository to the larger spectacle of urban London, Dante Gabriel Rossetti seizes upon the "burthen of the curse of Babel" as a site of institutional deconstruction in his poem "The Burden of Nineveh," which begins by conflating the Tower and the Museum:

> I have no taste for polyglot:
> At the Museum 'twas my lot,
> Just once, to jot and blot and rot
> In Babel for I know not what.
>   I went at two, I left at three.
> Round those still floors I tramp'd to win
> By the great porch the dirt and din;
> And as I made the last door spin
> And issued, they were hoisting in
>   A winged beast from Nineveh.

(1–10)[6]

Rossetti's poem "The Burden of Nineveh" first appeared in the August 1856 edition of the *Oxford and Cambridge*

Magazine and later, in a substantially revised version, in his *Poems* of 1870. Its original twenty-one stanzas record the poet's imagined impressions of the Assyrian statuary brought to the museum in the late 1840s and early 1850s by Austen Henry Layard, whose own highly-popular excavation narrative *Nineveh and its Remains* (1849) served as an explicit sub-text for Rossetti's satirical commentary. The poet's characterization of the national repository as a Babel of polyglot images, however, is all his own. Rossetti places as an epigraph a dictionary definition: "Burden. Heavy calamity; the chorus of a song." Both definitions serve his purpose. For while the repetition of the name of Nineveh functions as a refrain to end each stanza of the poem, his sustained observations on the Nineven beast's travels through time and place make explicit the cultural, historical, and semiotic disruption at the root of the museum's song of national romance.

The winged bull, as Carl Woodring has noted, was the most popularly recognized piece of Layard's excavations. Its image adorned the covers of both his 1849 narrative and the cheaper edition, *A Popular Account of Discoveries at Nineveh* (1851), as well as appearing in many of the peri-

RECEPTION OF NINEVEH SCULPTURES AT THE BRITISH MUSEUM.

Reception of the Nineveh sculptures at the British Museum. *Illustrated London News,* **February 28, 1852, 184.**

odical accounts of his efforts.[7] The frontispiece to the second volume of *Nineveh and its Remains* provides an even more striking image, "Procession of the Bull Beneath the Mound of Nimroud." The engraving shows the 300 Arabs in Layard's service dragging the bull on carts, with Layard himself in military gear in a dramatic equestrian pose. C. J. Gadd has remarked that "the closest parallel for the frontispiece of Layard's second volume is the scene depicted on slabs of Sennacherib's palace at Nineveh, showing these same huge stones being hauled into their place by the enslaved enemies of the Assyrians; the wheels of the cart and some details of costume are almost the only difference in twenty-six centuries."[8] Layard offers similar reflections himself as he surveys the proceedings of his cargo down the Tigris river:

> I watched the rafts until they disappeared behind a projecting bank forming a distant reach of the river. I could not forbear musing upon the strange destiny of their burdens; which, after adorning the palaces of the Assyrian kings, the objects of the wonder, and may be the worship, of thousands, had been buried unknown for centuries beneath a soil trodden by Persians under Cyrus, by Greeks under Alexander, and by Arabs under the first descendants of their prophet. They were now to visit India, to cross the most distant seas of the southern hemisphere, and to be finally placed in a British Museum. Who can venture to foretell how their strange career will end?[9]

Procession of the Bull Beneath the Mound of Nimroud. Austen Henry Layard, *Nineveh and its Remains*. London, 1849.

Kuyunjik relief depicting Assyrians moving a bull colossus. Austen Henry Layard, *Discoveries in the Ruins of Nineveh and Babylon*. London, 1853.

The Nineven winged bull's transformation from statuary to burden marks the recurrent image of its removal and transportation as the most potent site of meaning. As a burden, the winged bull becomes a literally floating signifier of indeterminate origin and destiny. The material and historical connections between power and signification made apparent in its articulation as burden destabilize all semiotic connections between its form and content. It is, however, a burden to be borne, for the ironic destabilization of cultural signification brought about by the burden of Nineveh is precisely what enables Layard, and Rossetti after him, to watch its progress and muse upon its destiny.

In Layard's narrative, the winged bull's status as a floating burden lends itself to a systematic establishment of a self-affirming and self-generative cultural history. Layard records the wondering of the Arab Sheik Abd-ur-rahman who aids him in his excavations and offers the English explorer a peculiarly naive wisdom:

> Wonderful! wonderful! There is surely no God but God, and Mohammed is his Prophet. . . . In the name of the Most High,

tell me, O Bey, what you are going to do with those stones. So
many thousands of purses spent upon such things! Can it be,
as you say, that your people learn wisdom from them; or is it,
as his reverence the Cadi declares, that they are to go to the
palace of your Queen, who, with the rest of the unbelievers,
worships these idols? (2:70–71)

The Sheik's query perceptively contrasts the accumulation of wisdom with the idolatrous worship of power
through the exhibition of foreign artifacts. His comments
reveal the cultural gap between East and West that lends
the statues their resonant significance: from the Sheik's
perspective, a debasement from faith to idolatry. But the
true source of his wonder is not their exportation to London, but their excavation after so many years of oblivion:

God is great! Here are stones which have been buried ever
since the time of the holy Noah,—peace be with him! Perhaps
they were under ground before the deluge. I have lived on
these lands for years. My father, and the father of my father,
pitched their tents here before me; but they never heard of
these figures. For twelve hundred years have the true believ-
ers (and, praise be to God! all true wisdom is with them alone)
been settled in this country, and none of them ever heard of
a palace under ground. Neither did they who went before
them. But lo! here comes a Frank from many days' journey
off, and he walks up to the very place, and he takes a stick
(illustrating the description at the same time with the point
of his spear), and makes a line here, and makes a line there.
Here, he says, is the palace; there, says he, is the gate; and he
shows us what has been all our lives beneath our feet, without our having known any thing about it. Wonderful! wonderful! Is it by books, is it by magic, is it by your prophets, that
you have learnt these things? Speak, O Bey; tell me the secret
of wisdom. (2:70)

Abd-ur-rahman's speech contrasts the wisdom gained
through lineage and faith with the mimetically illustrated
magic of the western countries. For him, the wonder of
both Layard and his excavations stems primarily from
their incongruity with the Arabs' ancestral connection to
the land. The Sheik's contrasts of Layard's western
knowledge with his own people's Islamic faith and his

naive ascription of magic to European knowledge and power are, of course, staple tropes of Orientalist literature. As a narrative device, they establish a temporal and cultural dissonance that enables Layard to answer his queries with a redemptive history of the progress of civilization:

> The wonder of Abd-ur-rahman was certainly not without cause, and his reflections were natural enough. Whilst riding by his side I had been indulging in a reverie, not unlike his own, which he suddenly interrupted by these exclamations. Such thoughts crowded upon me day by day, as I looked upon every newly discovered sculpture. A stranger laying open monuments buried for more than twenty centuries, and thus proving,—to those who dwelt around them,—that much of the civilization and knowledge of which we now boast, existed amongst their forefathers when our "ancestors were yet unborn," was, in a manner, an acknowledgment of the debt which the West owes to the East. It is, indeed, no small matter of wonder, that far distant, and comparatively new nations would have preserved the only records of a people once ruling over nearly half the globe; and should now be able to teach the descendants of that people or those who have taken their place, where their cities and monuments once stood. (2:71–72)

The genealogy of civilization mapped out in this passage moves easily from a construction of origin and debt to one of telos and redemption. Layard's acknowledgment of the Eastern origins of civilization supports his claims for Western ascendancy, a position enacted in his excavations. The endeavors of the Ninevens achieve their value and glory only in their literal discovery by the English who are now positioned as masters and tutors of the former civilization's descendants. Introducing yet another definition of burden, Layard positions himself as both tutor and missionary, preaching not Christian doctrine, but providing "a short lecture upon the advantages of civilization and of knowledge." Layard conceives that "the exalted idea of the wisdom and power of the Franks" (2:72) secures him a position of safety and privilege among the Arabs. In this narrative, both the Sheik's wonder and

Layard's own indulgent reverie conspire to construct a tendentious cultural history rooted not in the ruins themselves, but in the act of excavation and appropriation. The burden and the song stand together.

If the statuary remains of the Nineven temple are transformed into burdens through their excavation and appropriation, then the edifice towards which they travel stands in apparent contrast to the temple whence they came. Considered as song, the architectural significance of temple and museum are differentiated by their compositional relation to their own conditions of production; the former born out of faith and devotion, the latter born out of skepticism and inquiry. Yet Layard's narrative reveals that their difference in meaning may depend just as much upon the subjective viewer. Concluding his account of the bull's removal and transportation, Layard revisits the temple before he has it reburied to protect it from the religious Arabs who would, he believes, destroy it for its idolatrous nature. The terms of his description reveal the gulf that separates him from the Ninevens who originally worshipped in its walls and the Arabs who now occupy the surrounding lands:

> We may wander through these galleries for an hour or two, examining the marvelous sculptures, or the numerous inscriptions that surround us. Here we meet long rows of kings, attended by their eunuches and priests,—there lines of winged figures, carrying fir-cones and religious emblems, and seemingly in adoration before the mystic tree. Other entrances, formed by winged lions and bulls, lead us into new chambers. In every one of them are fresh objects of curiosity and surprise. At length, wearied, we issue from the buried edifice by a trench on the opposite side to that by which we entered, and find ourselves again upon the naked platform. We look around in vain for any traces of the wonderful remains we have just seen, and are half inclined to believe that we have dreamed a dream, or have been listening to some tale of Eastern romance. Some, who may hereafter tread on the spot when the grass again grows over the ruins of the Assyrian palaces, may indeed suspect that I have been relating a vision. (2:92–93)

For the Western explorer, the Nineven temple becomes a museum of wonder and curiosity. Layard's comparison of the effect to a dream, vision, or tale of Eastern romance attests both to the Orientalist paradigms which inform his project and narrative and to the harmonizing and subli- mating use his imagination and reveries have brought to the ruins and fragments he has found. The romance told in the walls of the excavated temple seeks to convert the dissonance at the root of its representation by recasting the perceptive critique of the Arab Sheik as a naive ex- pression of wonder and admiration and supplanting it with a narrative of redemptive history and Western ascen- dancy.

Whereas Layard prefers the romance of the excavated temple, Rossetti glories in the irony of the national mu- seum. His poem capitalizes upon the disruption at the root of the burden's production as a form of aesthetic and archaeological contemplation. His argument demon- strates that dissonance both enables and confounds a mu- seum's ability to produce cohesive understandings of previous and foreign cultures. In his poetic reflections, the Babel of polyglot images and the burden of Nineveh reflect each other on the level of form. The bull itself is described as both a polyglot image and a trace of disrup- tion:

> A human face the creature wore,
> And hoofs behind and hoofs before,
> And flanks with dark runes fretted o'er.
> 'Twas bull, 'twas mitred minotaur;
>   A dead disbowell'd mystery;
> The mummy of a buried faith,
> Stark from the charnel without scathe,
> Its wings stood for the light to bathe, -
> Such fossil cerements as might swathe
>   The very corpse of Nineveh.
>
> (11–20)

Noting that "Some colour'd Arab straw-matting / Half- ripp'd, was still upon the thing" (21–22), Rossetti per- ceives in these traces of the burden's passage the occlu-

sion of any definite understanding of the cultural forces
which originally produced the image:

> What vows, what rites, what prayers preferr'd,
> What songs has the strange image heard?
> In what blind vigil stood interr'd
> For ages, till an English word
>   Broke silence first at Nineveh?
>
>   (26–30)

In his "Ode on a Grecian Urn," which these lines recall,
Keats interrogates the object's static images in order to
change the "silent form" into a "Sylvan historian." Yet
Keats's history, contending that "Heard melodies are
sweet, but those unheard / Are sweeter" (11–12), transforms historical difference back into aesthetic unity in
the poem's famous epigrammatic equation of truth and
beauty.[10] By contrast, Rossetti's historical interrogations
focus upon the artifact's context rather than its content,
making manifest the cultural disruption enabling his poetic reflections. The English word that breaks the silence
of Nineveh redeems the enigmatic form of the winged
bull both within a narrative of cultural progress and as a
sign of disruption. In both cases, the origin of the image
is less significant than the archaeological or linguistic act
which disturbs the image's entombment, bringing it into
the free-play of signs that constitutes the museum exhibition. Akin to the English word, the London sun in the
following stanza illuminates not the image, but its "recov-
er'd shadow," opening up its passage through time and
place as the site for imaginative restorations. Neither English word nor London sun produce stable meaning, but,
rather, enable Rossetti and the other visitors to the British Museum to reconstruct imaginatively the image's
presence at various biblical scenes (41–60) and to transform its signifying function into a museum artifact:

> Now, thou poor god, within this hall
> Where the blank windows blind the wall
> From pedestal to pedestal,
> The kind of light shall on thee fall
>   Which London takes the day to be.

Here cold-pinch'd clerks on yellow days
Shall stop and peer; and in sun-haze
Small clergy crimp their eyes to gaze;
And misses titter in their stays,
        Just fresh from "Layard's Nineveh."

Here, while the Antique-students lunch,
Shall Art be slang'd o'er cheese and hunch,
Whether the great R. A.'s a bunch
Of gods or dogs, and whether the Punch
        Is right about the P. R. B.
Here school-foundations in the act
Of holiday, three files compact,
Shall learn to view thee as a fact
Connected with that zealous tract,
        "Rome: Babylon and Nineveh."

                                        (61–80)

Within the polyglot Babel of the museum, the winged bull becomes an object of curiosity for the clerks, clergy, and ladies, a witness to aesthetic debate among the antiquarians and dilettantes, and an object of moral instruction for the young schoolchildren who are warned of the evils of idolatry, Roman or Babylonian. The relevancy of this warning for the fetishistic practices of the national museum remains implicit.[11]

This passage seems indebted to Byron's *The Curse of Minerva,* an earlier critique of similar acts of excavation and appropriation surrounding the British Museum. Rossetti's characterization of the burden's exhibition for clerks, ladies, dilettantes, and schoolchildren particularly recalls Byron's equally sarcastic portrait of the reception of the Elgin Marbles by "brawny brutes," "sauntering coxcombs," and "languid maid[s]." Byron's "calm spectator," who stands apart from the admiring crowd "in silent indignation mix'd with grief," would seem a prototype for Rossetti's ruminating observer of the various social dramas played out in front of the archaeological remains.[12] In *The Curse of Minerva,* Byron transforms Lord Elgin's activities into a symbol of British arrogance and rapine glory, disruptive activities whose power inevitably turns upon their agents. Rossetti's irony is similarly scathing, but by taking the decline of empire for granted and employing it in a meditation upon the unstable connections between power and representation, Rossetti offers a critique not only of nationalist illusions, but of the aesthetic ideologies enabling the institutional reproductions of these illusions. In the final stanzas of the poem, Byron's curse of endless disruption becomes Rossetti's burden of ironic signification. He follows his sarcastic dismissal of the interpretative practices enacted in the British Museum by his own reverie on the mystery of the object's origins and the irony of its exhibition alongside idols of competing faiths:

> Greece, Egypt, Rome,—did any god
> Before whose feet men knelt unshod,
> Deem that in this unblest abode
> An elder, scarce more unknown god
>   Should house with him from Nineveh?

(81–90)

All differences between the Egyptian, Greek, Roman, and now Assyrian antiquities are subsumed under their common function as "relics" to be appropriated in a variety of exhibitionary and interpretative practices. But this ironic logic of the burden's exhibition extends itself to the very Babel of polyglot which has incorporated it, destabilizing the museum's own claims to transcendental perspective or teleological significance. Layard's query ("Who can venture to foretell how their strange career will end?") is expanded upon in Rossetti's concluding stanzas:

> For as that Bull-god once did stand,
> And watch'd the burial-clouds of sand,
> Till these at last without a hand
> Rose o'er his eyes, another land,
>   And blinded him with destiny:
> So may he stand again; till now,
> In ships of unknown sail and prow,
> Some tribe of the Australian plough
> Bear him afar, a relic now
>   Of London, not of Nineveh.

> Or it may chance indeed that when
> Man's age is hoary among men,
> His centure is threescore and ten,—
> His furthest childhood shall seem then
>   More clear than later times may be:
> Who, finding in this desert place
> This form, shall hold us for some race
> That walk'd not in Christ's lowly ways,
> But bow'd its pride and vow'd its praise
>   Unto the god of Nineveh.
>
>   (171–200)

Rossetti perceives England's inevitable passage from power and the subsequent passage of its forms to alternative contexts and interpretations. But if Rossetti's premonitions destabilize any claims to semiotic permanence in the British Museum, they also turn retroactively to conclude the poem with a speculation on the burden's indeterminate origins: "O Nineveh, was this thy God, / Thine also, mighty Nineveh?" (209–10). As a burden of perpetual translation, the winged bull signifies only the endless acts of deferral at the root of historical origination. In its static pose of potential motion and trusted stability, unable to read its own markings, the bull becomes a symbol of its own fate and the exhibitionary mechanisms that have produced it as an object of contemplation. In Rossetti's poem, the burden seems to realize in its very form the calamitous conditions of its song.

For Layard, the British Museum supplants the Tower of Babel; for Rossetti, the two are completely identical. Opposite as these two relations may seem, both in effect negate cultural history even as they engage it. Layard anxiously asserts a romance of historical redemption that imperfectly converts the instability of meaning his own excavations have revealed. Recasting the temple into a museum for the Western explorer, Layard supplants the lesson of cultural instability he gleans as he watches the bull drift down the Tigris River. The course of history has run its route, and now exists only as a permanent exhibition, a display whose self-sufficient coherency defensively insists upon the absolute difference between origination and exhibition. Rossetti thoroughly rejects this romance, using a historically astute satire to ironically undermine the teleological narrative deployed by Layard and the British Museum. For Rossetti, the curse of Babel engenders not historical supremacy but perpetual calamity at the chorus of his culture's imperial song. In Rossetti's deconstructive irony, all is Babel and history merely an endless succession of difference and transformation. The exhibition offers the inquiring spectator only a heap of fragments in the face of which no understanding is possible. Thus are we left with objective ossification or subjective despondency; neither seems a particularly heartening approach to museum culture.

III

Lest we completely abandon ourselves to Layard's imperialist romance or Rossetti's skeptical despair, we may return to Shelley, whose phenomenological aesthetics negates neither Tower nor Museum, but holds them in productive dialogue. Understood as a representational valence between irony and romance, the conflation of the Tower of Babel and the British Museum provides an architectural correlative of the semiotic paradox characteristic of Shelley's poetics. In both his aesthetic and historical meditations and in his poetry, Shelley employs a skeptical idealism that transforms the curse of fragmentation into the burden of exhibition, producing artifacts whose incomplete and belated condition lie at the root of his imaginative sympathies. In so doing, he offers a sense of the poet as a creative curator, one who does not merely catalogue the remains of previous cultures from a presumed position of epistemological supremacy, but who fuses an aesthetic perception of identity with an historical awareness of difference. Shelley's metaphoric notion of poetry establishes both Tower and Museum as equally imperfect signifiers in a perpetual yet progressive chain of creation, destruction, and recuperation.

Shelley's own most famous ruin piece "Ozymandias" provides a telling contrast to Rossetti's latter poem. For

Shelley proves himself quite apt at critiquing the vanities of power through the ironies of exhibition and does so in a fashion that has proven more long lasting than many other analogous works of the period, Rossetti's included. It gains its power precisely because it recognizes that the ironies of exhibition do not merely undermine tyranny's delusions of perpetual hegemony, but can in turn empower the spectator to assume an active and critical agency in the production of meaning. Read as a figurative museum, Shelley's sonnet exhibits the ruined fragments of the Oriental king in a fashion both destructive and creative. Positing neither original ontological unity nor teleological redemption, Shelley nonetheless engages the reader in a phenomenological process of imaginative contemplation. What Rossetti's poem thematically critiques, Shelley's poem formally enacts; namely the transformation of a ruined fragment into a burden of poetic imagination.

Shelley's poem has so far stood the ravages of time, but its accompanying work has not been so fortunate. Shelley's work appeared in the 11 January 1818 edition of *The Examiner*, and Horace Smith's sonnet of the same name in the edition for 1 February. We may examine Shelley's sonnet as it then appeared alongside Smith's lesser-known work in order to better appreciate the critical reception it demands of its readers:

OZYMANDIAS

I met a Traveller from an antique land,
Who said, "Two vast and trunkless legs of stone
Stand in the desert. Near them, on the sand,
Half sunk, a shattered visage lies, whose frown,
And wrinkled lip, and sneer of cold command,
Tell that its sculptor well those passions read,
Which yet survive, stamped on these lifeless things,
The hand that mocked them, and the heart that fed:
And on the pedestal these words appear:
"My name is OZYMANDIAS, King of Kings."
Look on my works, ye Mighty, and despair!
No thing beside remains. Round the decay

Of that Colossal Wreck, boundless and bare,
The lone and level sands stretch far away.[13]

OZYMANDIAS

In Egypt's sandy silence, all alone,
  Stands a gigantic Leg, which far off throws
  The only shadow that the Desart knows:—
"I am great OZYMANDIAS," saith the stone,
  "The King of Kings; this mighty City shows
"The wonders of my hand."—The City's gone,—
  Nought but the Leg remaining to disclose
The site of this forgotten Babylon.
We wonder,—and some Hunter may express
Wonder like ours, when thro' the wilderness
  Where London stood, holding the Wolf in chace,
He meets some fragment huge, and stops to guess
  What powerful but unrecorded race
  Once dwelt in that annihilated place.[14]

By explicitly narrating the inevitable transformation of Britain's own structures of power into burdens of imaginative wonder, the argument of Smith's poem bears a closer resemblance to Rossetti's latter piece than does Shelley's. Both Smith and Shelley's sonnets differ from Rossetti's poem in terms of form, voice, and specificity of subject, yet all three offer a contemplative account of ruin that registers the vanity and impermanence of human endeavors and offers lessons for their contemporary age. Furthermore, all three connect these lessons to the disruptive effect of history upon systems of signification. By revealing the interdependence of power and language, all three demonstrate, in different modes, the consequential impermanence and indeterminacy of all social constructs of meaning. This is an especially ironic theme for the two sonnets whose chosen form, as Anne Janowitz has noted, is one traditionally linked with the transcendence of verbal art over the wasting of time.[15] Only Shelley's sonnet, however, has achieved at least such partial transcendence in the last nearly 180 years and this is due to the very same characteristics that mark it off as a *romantically* ironic poem. For what both Smith and Rossetti's poems thematically suggest, Shelley's poem enacts in its formal strategies of representation.

M. K. Bequette, the first critic to my knowledge to hold Shelley and Smith's sonnets up for comparison, sides firmly with Shelley's work as the superior. The very characteristics that Smith might plausibly have felt raised his poem above Shelley's are what diminish its poetic power in Bequette's judgment. Its historical and geographical specificity, its standard Petrarchan form, its schematic and expository moral message via the analogy between Babylon and London; all diminish the sonnet's power in Bequette's view: "The sonnet's effect is totally calculated, and as a result the reader can respond only unimaginatively to the programmed lesson Smith provides."[16] By contrast, Bequette praises Shelley's "rich and suggestive" sonnet through systematic opposition to Smith's failed efforts. Its imprecision of time and place, its formal fusion of octave and sestet, its descriptive detail of the ruin, and its refusal of explicit analogy: all give the scene "a solid physical reality" which surpasses its role as a vehicle for the moral message. More evocative than didactic, Shelley's sonnet demonstrates both the king's pride and the artist's skills, suggesting at least the possibility of creative transcendence. Consequently, it is the reader's judgment and not the poet's that motivates the ruins towards political and aesthetic lessons. As Bequette concludes, "[Shelley's] sonnet *invites* interpretation rather than imposes one and only one on the strange desert scene."[17] Of course, Bequette's evaluative criteria can be said simply to reproduce Shelley's privileging of critical recuperation as essential to the reception of art. As such, both Shelley's sonnet and Bequette's critical defense serve as models of a Romantic museum discourse concerned as much with aesthetic power as with historical disruption. Yet this attention to aesthetic reception strengthens rather than diminishes the historical lesson articulated more didactically by Smith and Rossetti. Like Bequette, Shelley's poetic voice has distanced itself from the subject, in turn achieving the same disinterested power ascribed to the sculptor who "well those passions

read, / Which yet survive." The space between loss and recovery in the sonnet's structure of meaning provides for
both critical analysis and poetic production; the text is
enabled by the very silences it conceals. In Smith's sonnet, as in Rossetti's latter poem, the act of recovery has
already been performed by the poetic voice, restricting
its ironic meditations to its theme. Shelley's poem, by
contrast, enacts its own conditions of articulation, positioning irony as a formal as well as thematic characteristic of the sonnet. The work's performative irony thus
enables its ideological critique as a mode of representation through the interpolation of a contemplating subject.

The figurative museum of Shelley's sonnet articulates
the statue as a burden whose meaning emerges from the
cursed conditions of its articulation. This irony is realized only in the reading subject who, through following
Shelley's "invitation" towards interpretation, constructs
meaning in the space of the exhibition's irony. As Janowitz puts it, "Ozymandias is thus memorialized three
times—once by the Egyptian sculptor, once by the Romantically ironic sonneteer, and once by the interpreting and
imaginative reader."[18] What survives this process of perpetual mediation and deferral is the sculptor's art, which
"well those passions read / Which yet survive, stamped on
these lifeless things" (6–7). The aesthetic power of the
piece itself does not so much overcome as reveal itself
through the historical ironies that frame its exhibition.
Indeed, the true skills and insight of the sculptor manifest themselves only through the wasting of time. The aesthetic identification joining reader, poet, traveler, and
sculptor is inextricable from the historical and cultural
shifts that divide them. Though this chain of creation, excavation, and exhibition undermines any claims to fixed
and determinate understanding, they do not, as Rossetti
would have it, undermine the potential for aesthetic encounter. By allowing the reader a participatory role in
the sonnet's creation of meaning, Shelley reveals a faith
in the dialectical power of artistic expression. While the
irony of the sonnet is directed against the tyrant's pride
and trust in the stable relation between language and
power, the ruination of signs enables a potential identi-

fication that transcends history even while it is revealed
through historical fluctuation. Framing the traveler's account of the ruin, Shelley transforms the curse of historical decay into a burden of critical reflection.

IV

The means by which Shelley enriches the ruined image
and suggests multi-dimensionality in his representational strategies may be understood as both an elevation
of artistic creation and the formulation of a dynamic cultural history. By locating meaning in a simultaneously
perceptive and creative act, "Ozymandias" formally exemplifies the model of poetic history that Shelley would
expound three years later in *A Defence of Poetry*. Fusing
poetic credo, cultural history, and political polemic,
Shelley's *Defence* is but one of many instances of a critical
art historiography that emerged in the early nineteenth
century. As Michael Podro has traced its development in
the German tradition, the critical history of art synthe-
sized the idealization of form promoted by Winckelmann
with the cultural and historical relativism promoted by
Herder. The result was a post-Kantian emphasis on artistic purpose that neither negated the contingencies of artistic production nor delimited its achievement to its own
cultural milieu, but viewed art as an imaginative bridge
between human freedom and the restraints of the material world.[19] Shelley's manifesto likewise synthesizes the
opposition between a contemplative and an active role
for art and thereby offers a model for retrieving the productions of the past without either effacing their alterity
through idealization or reducing them to archaeological
artifacts. Though manifestly concerned with the verbal
arts, Shelley's poetic treatise offers valuable insight into
the aesthetic and ideological dilemmas facing the British
Museum as it assumed a central role in what Tony Bennett has termed the "exhibitionary complex" shaping
Victorian imperial culture.[20] In privileging metaphorical
translation as both the origin and goal of cultural expression and transmission, Shelley formulates a critical histo-

riography that maintains difference in identity even as it asserts universal ideals by which artistic and ethical actions may be judged.

Shelley's aesthetic treatise offers a vision of cultural historiography that mediates between teleological idealism and irremediable contingency. Considered properly as a rejoinder to Peacock's "The Four Ages of Poetry," Shelley's *Defence* does not so much repudiate historical narratives of belated cultural reflection as seek to recast them as one stage of a dialectical process of inspired creation. Peacock's ironic history of the four stages of cultural development elevates rational comparison over imaginative synthesis. He uses a Viconian cyclical vision of historical narrative to promote skeptical philosophy and scientific inquiry at the expense of the fine arts. Peacock views poetry as secondary and functional and casts it as the effect of varying systems of power and belief, at first panegyric and mythological, but later merely decorative and nostalgic. His history moves from the iron age of kings and warriors to the golden age of statesmen and public institutions and on to the silver age of mercantile trade and philosophical refinement and the brass age of decadent luxury and barbarous despair. In each age, Peacock conceives a constantly diminishing role for poetry as skeptical inquiry and political institutions replace its philosophic and panegyric functions. Poetry becomes increasingly retrograde and irrelevant in modern society as evidenced by what Peacock takes to be the absurd illusions of his contemporary romantics in history's second age of brass. Their poetry, Peacock argues, "by rejecting the polish and the learning of the age of silver, and taking a retrograde stride to the barbarisms and crude traditions of the age of iron, professes to return to nature and revive the age of gold."[21] Against such irrational excesses of the poetic mind, Peacock praises a

> philosophical mental tranquillity which looks round with an equal eye on all external things, collects a store of ideas, discriminates their relative value, assigns to all their proper place, and from the materials of useful knowledge thus collected, appreciated, and arranged, forms new combinations

that impress the stamp of their power and utility on the real business of life. (17)

Bruce Haley has well characterized this philosophical tranquility as a sequential historical method that transforms things into thoughts and then collects, evaluates, and arranges these thoughts into novel combinations in order to comprehend and affect the larger world of social practice.[22] In Peacock's satirical cultural history, artistic expression has no transformational power, as the meaning of a work of art is inseparable from the social function for which it is produced. Once that social function is diminished to the point of virtual irrelevance, the poet is reduced to a curio-collector and his work to a cabinet of "disjointed relics of tradition and fragments of second-hand observation" (16). Peacock thus casts the philosopher and man of science as the more proper museum curators, privileging systematic arrangement over novel delight.

Shelley's more complexly dialectical response to Peacock's satire deploys no less an historical method, but one based in the supremacy of aesthetic effect, both within an artwork's own historical era, and upon the mind of the belated historian. Like Rossetti after him, Shelley recognizes the "heavy calamity" which lies as a burden at the chorus of poetic song. Poetic language emerges from a metaphoric ratio of difference, for "to be a poet is to apprehend the true and the beautiful, in a word the good which exists in the relation, subsisting, first between existence and perception, and secondly between perception and expression."[23] This metaphoric imagination is perceptive and creative, defined at the beginning of the *Defence* as "the expression of the Imagination," and thereby bound up in a temporal process of longing and anticipation. The numerous analogies Shelley deploys for the poetic act all speak to its ever-elusive origin. The lyre trembling "after the wind has died away" (480–81); the child singing and dancing "to prolong also a consciousness of the cause" (481); the "fading coal which some invisible influence, like an inconstant wind, awakens to transitory brightness" (504): all of these images speak to the absence and deferral at the root of the poet's song. "A Poet is a nightingale," Shelley writes, "who sits in darkness and sings to cheer its own solitude with sweet sounds; his auditors are as men entranced by the melody of an unseen musician, who feel that they are moved and softened, yet know not whence or why" (486). Shelley's willed analogy between the poet and the nightingale attests to the shared longing of poet and auditors in the metaphoric cycle joining existence, perception, and expression. As Jerrold E. Hogle has described this poetics of loss and deferral, "ideas, emotions, and faculties that lead to great poetry and all its progeny emerge from a process of transfer and substitution rather than from a first Unity or a grounding Presence."[24] The poet may "participate[] in the eternal, the infinite, and the one," but this participation is always one of exchange and translocation.

At the root of this cycle of perpetual translation lies an act of differentiation that constitutes both origin and metaphor. Shelley's famous distinction between contemplative reason and active imagination as particular modes of mental action upon the forms of the corporeal world offers complementary curatorial options for exhibitionary representation. Reason dwells upon comparison, imagination upon unity and it is the latter which allows us to glimpse the order that underlies the former:

> Reason is the enumeration of quantities already known; imagination is the perception of the value of those quantities, both separately and as a whole. Reason respects the differences, and imagination the similitudes of things. Reason is to Imagination as the instrument to the agent, as the body to the spirit, as the shadow to the substance. (480)

Though his generative metaphors privilege the latter terms for their original status, Shelley's alternatively inductive and deductive modes of comparison and unification work in tandem, constructing a tenor from the logic of its vehicle. Reason contemplates "the relations borne by one thought to another, however produced," but imagination actively transforms those thoughts "so as to colour them with its own light," producing new ideas "each containing within itself the principle of its own integrity" (480). The resultant synthesis is hence less an original unity perceived than a new order produced dialectically between subject and object. The integrity of imaginative ideas does not emerge *sui generis*, but always from an intentional act of integration. This act is born of the very rational differentiation it seeks to overcome and attests to the perpetual divergence at the root of origination.[25] The collectivist ideology that signifies similitude, agency, spirit, and substance only attests to the belatedness of its creation, depending upon reason's differentiation of reality for its subsequent imaginative synthesis, realizing unity only in its catalogue.

This metaphorical poetics gives rise to history through the very nature of aesthetic form. Akin to the mutually engendering relation of reason and imagination, poetic production and reception are merely two aspects of a poem's transitional meaning. Shelley forwards the conceit that "every original language near to its source is in itself the chaos of a cyclic poem: the copiousness of lexicography and the distinctions of grammar are the works of a later age, and are merely the catalogue and the form of the creations of Poetry" (482). Yet just as the paradox of an "original language near to its source" reveals poetry's always belated condition, so too the conjoining of "the catalogue and the form" reveals the inextricability of division and structure. Creation and perception are two moments of the same act of memorial longing continuously producing each other through the synthesizing powers of poetry, mutually generating the trajectory of cultural history. Love here takes its place as the means of connecting the world of human affairs to the realm of ideals in a peculiarly memorial logic:

> Poetry lifts the veil from the hidden beauty of the world, and makes familiar objects be as if they were not familiar; it reproduces all that it represents, and the impersonations clothed in its Elysian light stand thenceforward in the minds of those who have once contemplated them, as memorials of that gentle and exalted content which extends itself over all

thoughts and actions with which it coexists. The great secret of morals is Love; or a going out of our own nature, and an identification of ourselves with the beautiful which exists in thought, action, or person, not our own. (487)

By transforming objects into memorials, imaginative poetry allows for a transcendence of alterity and identification with a higher unity constructed through representation. Such memorials thus both transcend and embody temporality. They exceed their metonymic status as archaeological traces and metaphorically speak to a universal "indestructible order." But this unification of parts may only be realized by a future age. Such a memorial and redemptive logic insures that the true glory of any epoch will only be perceived in the traces left by its absence:

> In the infancy of the world, neither poets themselves nor their auditors are fully aware of the excellence of poetry: for it acts in a divine and unapprehended manner, beyond and above consciousness; and it is reserved for future generations to contemplate and measure the mighty cause and effect in all the strength and splendour of their union. (486)

Reception and creation are interchangeable poles of a historical sequence in which a poem's meaning resides only in the passage of time. In their quest to "reanimate . . . the sleeping, the cold, the buried image of the past" (505), poets conjoin loss and desire with representation, constructing a master narrative of memorial longing and redemptive hope. Shelley's ascription of the conscious enactment of organic unity to such "happier ages" as that of the ancient Greeks is matched (not equaled) by "those who are more finely organized . . . [who] may recognize [bucolic and erotic poetry] as episodes to that great poem, which all poets, like the co-operating thoughts of one great mind, have built up since the beginning of the world" (493). The metaphorical relation obtaining between expression and perception in Shelley's aesthetic reflections is thus historically realized both in its posited original inception and in its ultimate re-organization: in the temple and in the museum.

Though the former institution may be said, in the manner of "original languages" to be founded "near to its source," this proximity to an always-deferred origin does not bestow upon it any epistemological supremacy over the latter. The museum is not only a categorical organization, but also a formal expression of an imaginative age, and may thereby serve as an active site of social transformation. The curse of Babel severs poets and auditors from a direct enactment of the divine, exhibiting fragmentation as the constitutive condition of language and history. Its burden makes imperative the contemplation and measurement of an always unreachable union and the identification "with the beautiful which exists in thought, action, or person, not our own."

This necessity of identification exists not only in the realm of artistic reception and production. For Shelley, such imaginative sympathy translates by necessity into moral sympathy, engendering the perpetual progress of human society. As an inheritor of the ethical imperatives of the eighteenth-century aesthetic tradition, Shelley evidences a firm belief in the salutary effects of imaginative contemplation: "The connexion of scenic exhibitions with the improvement or corruption of the manners of men, has been universally recognized: in other words, the presence or absence of poetry in its most perfect and universal form has been found to be connected with good and evil in conduct and habit" (490). The ongoing transformation of the temple into the museum in cultural history is akin to the ongoing transformation of expression into contemplation in poetic metaphor. Both "enlarge[] the circumference of the imagination by replenishing it with thoughts of ever new delight, which have the power of attracting and assimilating to their own nature all other thoughts, and which form new intervals and interstices whose void for ever craves fresh food" (488). This self-perpetuating act of identification "strengthens that faculty which is the organ of the moral nature of man, in the same manner as exercise strengthens a limb" (488). Hence Shelley's cultural history of metaphorical transport is simultaneously a history of "man in society," joining the perception of "equality, diversity, unity, contrast, [and] mutual dependence" with "pleasure in sensation, virtue in sentiment, beauty in art, truth in reasoning, and love in the intercourse of kind." The perception of unity in diversity at the root of metaphorical imagination constitutes the intention of social consciousness and the design of cultural history: "The social sympathies, or those laws from which as from its elements society results, begin to develop themselves from the moment that two human beings coexist; the future is contained within the present as the plant within the seed" (481). Thus, Shelley is not content simply to praise the creative powers of the past, but ends the *Defence* with a prophecy of national revival. "The literature of England," he contends, "an energetic development of which has ever preceded or accompanied a great and free development of the national will, has arisen as it were from a new birth" (508). Sharing the Hellenistic faith in the connection between political liberty and artistic achievement, Shelley positions metaphorical imagination as the cornerstone of his poetic museum. Reading the "spirit of the age," as one of passion for freedom and renovation of human dignity, Shelley enshrines the achievements of his contemporaries and foresees that "our own will be a memorable age." Shelley's critical cultural history maintains an aesthetic and moral ideal inextricable from the course of history. For the contemplation of difference in identity at the root of metaphoric imagination insures the perpetual striving towards understanding and expression across cultures and throughout time. The burden of the curse of Babel, the disjunction between the temple and the museum, between the heavy calamity and the chorus of a song, neither negates nor redeems historical and cultural difference. Rather, it forms the foundation of moral and aesthetic imagination and the seed of cultural progression.

V

Once institutionalized, however, as Rossetti's poem reveals, such a burden can undermine the very structures it has helped to found. From Rossetti's position on the steps of the museum, we might turn and lift our heads to consider once more the resonance of Westmacott's sculptural representation of the progress of civilization. Westmacott emblematically traces humanity's emergence from "a rude savage state" to a religious contemplation of the world that is gradually refined into the sciences and the arts, a process whose culmination has produced the very institution the statuary now adorns. The Greek ideal, located irrevocably in the past, literally informs Westmacott's sculpture as several of the Elgin Marbles served as direct models for his work. This artistic appropriation introduces an ironic recognition of historical difference into the pediment's romantic iconography. As we have seen, maintaining the Elgin Marbles as symbols of ideal beauty conflicted repeatedly with the British Museum's exhibitionary arrangements of evolutionary narrative. Westmacott's statuary testifies to the tension between progressive historiography and aesthetic idealization that dominated discussions of the museum's integrity during the 1850s. In the wake of the Great Exhibition of 1851, the expansion of the National Gallery, and proposals for a new museum complex at Kensington, Parliament revisited the role of the British Museum in a series of inquiries in 1852–53 and again in 1857–58. In this context, the tensions between formal and archaeological evaluations of antiquities assumed an explicitly political context.

Westmacott's own curatorial practice had long provoked such contentions. Despite the theme of his pediment sculpture, he was often at odds with those among the museum's curators, particularly Edward Hawkins, director of the Department of Antiquities, and Edmund Oldfield, Hawkins's assistant, who wished to maintain a semblance of chronological coherency in the museum's displays. In 1834 he had sought permission from the Trustees "to intermix with the Townley Collection such other objects as might produce a suitable harmony of arrangement," and to place "statues of heroic size" in dramatic positions in the Front Hall.[26] In 1845 he had adopted a similarly aesthetic approach to the arrangement of the Lycian marbles from Xanthos much to the chagrin of their discoverer Charles Fellows who labeled Westmacott's arrangement an ignorant misrepresentation based purely on picturesque ideals. But it was the introduction of Layard's Assyrian statuary to the national museum, while considered by many as providing a "missing link" in the progressive development of Greek art, which brought these longstanding tensions to a head. Frederick N. Bohrer has explored the reception of the Assyrian statuary by the British Museum and the public culture at large in terms of a competition between spatial and temporal representation. Each offers a different version of 'presence' to overcome the aesthetic and historical gaps constructing the received objects as distinguishably foreign.[27] Though the competition between these two compensatory methods of exhibition led to an increased, if still imperfect, attempt at chronological interpretation, the testimony of many of its key players reveal the inextricability of these two approaches. While maintaining aesthetic excellence as a standard for appraising various works of antiquity, most of those involved with the museum pressed historical presentation as the method most suitable for a national institution.

In part the tensions between these two approaches were purely architectural, as Robert Smirke's newly constructed edifice proved immediately inadequate to house the museum's holdings in anything resembling a chronologically systematic fashion. Statuary from the various digs at Nineveh was already being relegated to the Front Hall and even to the outdoor colonnade and the situation was assuming a crisis proportion. Efforts to place the Assyrian sculptures and reliefs in a conveniently large room connecting the Greek and Lycian sculptures were repeatedly countered by those such as Hawkins who favored a chronologically systematic and thereby historically instructive arrangement. An imperfect compromise was finally reached whereby the Assyrian sculptures and reliefs were placed in a sequence of side galleries in a rough approximation of both their geographical location and chronological sequence. Visitors to the museum were thus led backwards in time, beginning with the Roman antiquities and travelling back through the varying stages of Greek and Lycian culture to the Assyrian works and then on to the Egyptian galleries.[28]

If this arrangement provided a degree of chronological system to the exhibitionary experience, it by no means alleviated the aesthetic tensions produced by the juxtaposition of Grecian and Assyrian art. The Parliamentary hearings regarding the National Gallery raised the possibility of transferring some or all of the British Museum's holdings in antiquities, particularly the Elgin Marbles, to the National Gallery's collection of European masters. Among the concerns repeatedly expressed during these hearings were such perennial issues as the facility and desirability of public access, the deleterious effects of the London air, and the proper organization of the museum's governing bodies. But at the heart of the testimony of those involved with the British Museum was the categorical integrity of the museum's antiquities. Though the testimony from the museum staff was almost entirely unanimous in the need to maintain the unity of the collections, their rationales reveal the inextricability of archaeological historicism and aesthetic formalism in the appreciation of the museum's holdings. Edmund Oldfield could proclaim that "it is incorrect to view the British Museum as a collection of works of art; it is in its primary character a collection of antiquities of the highest value as illustrative of history," but Antonio Panizzi's declaration, "I do not know where art begins and archaeology ends," was the more typical.[29] Most of those testifying at the hearings viewed aesthetic appreciation and historical understanding as two aspects of the same taste. Edward Hawkins declared the galleries as suitable "for the instruction of artists, and for the gratification of men of taste, and . . . of great assistance to the historian," and Charles Newton vehemently countered the separation of "archaeological research" and "aesthetic culture" in an extensive letter addressed to the Committee from Rhodes. "Museums," he observed, "are designed for the instruction and recreation, first, of the general public; secondly, of the artist by profession and of the student of art; and thirdly, of the archaeologist and historian. Why should not all these classes meet on common ground? In what respect do they hinder each other's study and enjoyment?"[30] Simultaneously a testimony to the subjective quality of interpretative distinctions and an insistence on a catholic policy of admission, Newton's remarks reveal the perpetration of the class issues which followed the museum's development from its very inception in the 1750s. Questions of public access and the behavior of the lower classes emerged in these hearings, as they had in almost every decade before. But though the crowds were sometimes associated with the dirt and dust of London as equally harmful to the welfare of the antiquities, the museum's civilizing function was now recognized as preeminent. In this context, the tension between aesthetics and archaeology was more than simply academic.

Intriguingly, it was Westmacott who came in for some of the most aggressive scrutiny during the Parliamentary hearings. Westmacott had advocated fusing the holdings of the National Gallery and the British Museum into a comprehensive collection so that "there should be a regular history as it were of the art; that you should begin with the Egyptian, go on to the Assyrian, and come down to the Grecian, Roman, and the lower ages."[31] Westmacott's suggestions were made in a full spirit of national improvement. Pointing to the purchase of the Townley Marbles as an example of beneficial acquisitions, he maintained that under their influence "our taste has improved, our manufactures have advanced; everything has shown, as clearly as possible, the connexion of the arts with everything that is civilised."[32] But the civilizing function of a comprehensive view of cultural history was not apparent to all. Richard Moncton Milnes inquired whether "the liberal introduction into the British Museum of works of earlier and oriental art, has had any effect upon the interest felt by the public with regard to the Elgin Marbles," a suggestion Westmacott denied. The inquiry continued however as Milnes expressed fear "that introducing freely into the institution objects of more occasional and peculiar interest, such for instance as the sculptures from Nineveh may deteriorate the public taste, and less incline them than they otherwise would be to study works of great antiquity and great art." Pressed on the point, Westmacott drew a distinction between "works for study" such as the Grecian statues and "prescriptive art" such as the Assyrian and Egyptian statues. The public, he insisted, "would look at the Nineveh Marbles and be thinking of their Bible at the time they were looking at them; they would consider them as very curious monuments of an age they feel highly interested in; but the interest in the Elgin marbles arises from a distinct cause; from their excellence as works of art."[33] Francis Haskell characterizes this exchange as "one of the most crucial artistic encounters of the century—a desperate attempt being made, in the interest of modern art, to preserve traditional and absolute standards of beauty from 'barbarian' contamination."[34] Ian Jenkins has rightly emphasized, however, that despite Westmacott's hierarchical distinctions between the Grecian and Assyrian artifacts, he joined with his colleagues at the museum in arguing against removing only the Elgin Marbles to the proposed National Gallery. He was perhaps able to maintain these seemingly contrary views between aesthetic idealism and historical comprehension due to his emphasis on the subjective interest of the viewer. "I do not think," he concluded, "that any consideration of the sculptures of Nineveh would affect a man who looked at the Elgin Marbles."[35]

Rossetti would prove him mistaken. In his revised version of "The Burden of Nineveh" for his *Poems* of 1870, he radically emended the opening stanza, moving from an equally-spread disdain for all of the Babel of polyglot images to a sequence of carefully structured distinctions:

> In our Museum galleries
> To-day I lingered o'er the prize
> Dead Greece vouchsafes to living eyes,—
> Her Art for ever in fresh wise
>   From hour to hour rejoicing me.
> Sighing I turned at last to win
> Once more the London dirt and din;
> And as I made the swing-door spin
> And issued, they were hoisting in
>   A winged beast from Nineveh.

$$(1-10)^{36}$$

Rossetti's revisions demarcate clearly between the aesthetic beauty of Greek art and the historical curiosity of the Assyrian statue. Though the Greek culture that produced such objects has deceased, "living eyes" retain its "prize," as its artistic accomplishment engenders perpetual aesthetic delight. All mention of Babel is excised as Rossetti distinguishes between the sacred space of the museum and the "dirt and din" of the London metropolis, a distinction manifestly effaced in the earlier version. Rossetti's original fusion of museum culture with urban chaos and semiotic confusion supported his broader critique of exhibitionary practice. His more cautious later version maintains his thematic meditation on the fate of ruins, but curtails it within narrower limits. His revisions help to protect the nationalized ideal from Milnes's feared "free introduction of more barbarous specimens," drawing a clear demarcation between the historical consciousness provoked by the burden of Nineveh and the aesthetic delight vouchsafed by the Grecian prize.

VI

But the introduction of the burden need not lead to such a conflict. Returning to Kenyon's introduction to Boulton's *Romance of the British Museum*, we can perhaps better appreciate his fusion of archaeological knowledge and aesthetic taste. His utopia fantasia of the "picture book of the history of man" *should* give us pause. As Layard's tendentious romance attests, the fusion of difference within the temporal framework of progressive history may be seen simply to maintain a sequence of privileged hierarchies between the center and the peripheries of power. As Johannes Fabian has argued, the universal frame of reference of evolutionary sequences may incorporate alterity only to further debase it as historically underdeveloped.[37] Certainly Layard's romance of origins and recovery reproduces the imperial relation between Britain and the Orient in the temporal relation between modernity and the past. Boulton's reproduction of the image of Babel as a frontispiece to his romance hardly suffices as a critically reflexive gesture, but the necessary fusion of irony and romance in curatorial practice had already been articulated at the very moment that the administration of the British Museum was assuming a more aggressively nationalist purpose.

As the debates surrounding the integrity of the British Museum's collections were emerging into the open in 1852, *The Museum of Classical Antiquities* published a lecture by Francis Pulsky "On the Progress and Decay of Art and on the Arrangement of a National Museum." Pulsky forwards an argument congruent with Kenyon's and oddly resonant with our contemporary concerns over multiculturalism:

> In the present state of knowledge, when we feel that there is a common link which connects the civilized nations of all ages, a museum cannot satisfy public expectation, which contains only some more or less important specimens of Greek, Etruscan, or Roman art. We see that Egyptian antiquities, excluded in the last century from the history of art, and considered only as curiosities, are now everywhere added to the public collections. Nay, the works of eastern nations, as the Persians, the Assyrians, and the Hindoos, even the productions of the yellow race of China and Japan, excite attention though despised by some artists from their unconformity with the Greek ideal. All these monuments of former civilization now claim a place worthier of them, than where they are at present, displayed side by side with the curiosities and instruments of the barbarous races of Africa and Oceania. Since the permanent place held by oriental civilization in the history of mankind is no longer questioned, we must bestow on its monuments also some attention.[38]

Though unable to include Africa and Oceania among the favored nations, Pulsky's argument nonetheless broadly expands the range of legitimate interest for a national museum. He achieves this inclusive vision by fusing an ironic historical assessment of the semiotics of the modern museum with a pluralistic vision of cultural legitimacy. In a single paragraph, Pulsky recognizes the historical role of dynasties, nations, and religions in producing the monuments of human history even as he constructs a realm of aesthetic power that transcends passions and ideologies by which such artifacts may be understood:

> It must be admitted, that but few understand the teaching of these monuments, few listen to the lessons revealed to us by the continuous series of works of art, for the noise of busy life renders the ear incapable of listening to the instructive voice proceeding from ages which are past. The passions which have whirled around those monuments are stilled; the dynasties and nations which raised them have disappeared; the gods to whom they were dedicated are forgotten; but whatever bore the stamp of genius is still the object of veneration; and what was grand or beautiful in centuries past, will continue to be so in ages to come. (13)

Repeating the logic of "Ozymandias," Pulsky here argues for the simultaneously antithetical and interdependent status of the realms of the aesthetic and the historical. Beauty unites what Time has severed, but it is a beauty only apparent through the evidence "stamped on those lifeless things." Where Shelley deployed the drama of this contradiction as the formal principle of his famous sonnet, Pulsky converts it into the organizing principle of a national museum.

For Pulsky, the very institution of the museum signifies a belated and skeptical relationship to artistic and cultural production. Deploying a cyclical narrative of repeated cultural development and decline homologous with Peacock's "Four Ages of Poetry," Pulsky traces art's recurrent emergence from faithful devotion and disintegration into luxurious adornment and melancholic nostalgia. But whereas Peacock marks the sequence of ages in terms of artistic production, Pulsky locates its manifestation in cultural reception. He traces the emergence of art in primitive societies as the offspring of religion, representing the struggles of gods, heroes, and kings, through its public and monumental function in the great republics of Greece and Rome:

> With such views of art, it is natural that the people of antiquity did not know those institutions which we designate by

the name of museums and sculpture galleries. The temples
and market-places, the theatres and circuses, the baths and
porticoes, constituted their galleries. In these public places
the works of art were displayed under the protection of religion, and by their perfection and beauty tended to confirm
and realize the mystic fables which they glorified. Art maintained a divine and elevated character; far from pampering
the luxury and ambition of private individuals, it became a
monument of public grandeur and devotion. (3–4)

Between the temple and the museum lies a historical
breach defined by the gap between public faith and private disbelief. In Pulsky's narrative, the degeneration of
belief combined with the increased power of the individual over the state produced in the ancient world a reified
and memorial relationship to artistic exhibition as art
works migrated from temples and squares to private galleries and villas. In its final stages of decline, under the
emperor Hadrian, Roman culture sought to recapture the
power of mythological art by reconciling philosophy and
fables, restoring the ancient temples and statues, and recasting the old religion as splendid festivals. Hadrian
decorated his villa at Tibur with reproductions of the
best of Roman, Greek, and Egyptian art, not simply as
"pompous decorations of his imperial seat," but as "monuments of his government, lasting evidence of his policy":

> His villa thus became a museum, but its influence proved un-
> availing. Hadrian added a brilliant page to the history of art,
> but he was unable to impart new life to the declining hea-
> thendom, the more so because he himself was a sceptical phi-
> losopher and did not believe in the gods whose altars he
> renewed. The restorer of the old creed died with words of
> sceptical philosophy upon his lips. (7)

As in Peacock's narrative, this curatorial age of brass rejects the sophistication of its modern era and looks back
to the age of myth and faith in order to restore the splendor of its golden age. But the breach is irreparable; the
museum is not the temple.

Out of this very skepticism Pulsky constructs his plan
for the national museum. Situating the nineteenth cen-

tury as another age of brass, irrevocably cut off from the faith of the middle ages and the glory of the Renaissance and dissatisfied with the princely ostentation of the seventeenth and eighteenth centuries, the modern nations find themselves in an analogous position as Hadrian, restoring the works of antiquity in a quest for public enlightenment. However, so long as the national museums of Europe resemble more closely the curiosity cabinets of the princely powers such nations have supplanted, the goals of true national development will not be reached. Pulsky notes that "in Naples, in Munich, in Berlin, and in London, great buildings have been erected as temples of art and antiquity," but complains that too often "the monuments appear as in a storehouse, where the objects are heaped together without feeling, and even here in London, the noblest productions of human genius are placed under the same roof with objects of natural history":

> We go from the masterworks of the Parthenon straight up to the stuffed seal and buffalo; and two monster giraffes stand as sentinels before the gallery of vases. Moreover, in the arrangement of the several works of art, we see no leading idea, no system carried out continuously. The only arrangement approaching to a system is a geographical one, where we find monuments of the same country placed together, but without any regard to chronology and style. The colossal figures of the Pharaohs are mixed with Greek works of the time of the Ptolomies, the monuments of the era of Hadrian with those of the time of Pericles. (11–12)

Such exhibitions "are noble proofs, therefore, of princely display, but they lack that civilizing influence on the people, which, if duly arranged, they might easily impart" (12). He, therefore, calls for the complementing of the collections with casts in an arrangement that strives towards a chronological and cultural comprehensiveness. Such a collection would be both instructive and inspiring to the public taste and allow the nation to understand itself in relation to the history of civilization.

Pulsky combines this historical consciousness with a

perception of universal beauty, made all the more beautiful for its universality:

> Such a collection would be the most convincing proof of the
> affinity of all civilized peoples, of the unity of mankind. We
> should see that the first beginning of art is the same with all
> nations, and though, from the peculiar circumstances of
> each, its development was carried out in different ways and
> under different forms towards perfection, yet we should be
> able to detect a close affinity and connexion between the
> masterpieces of every national art, clearly showing that the
> feeling of the beautiful is the same in all ages and in all coun-
> tries, and that the imitative arts of all nations, so soon as they
> break the thraldom of conventionality, which protected them
> in their infancy, but hindered their further development, are
> the most noble offspring of human genius, whether in Japan
> or Athens, whether on the Nile or the Arno, on the Euphrates
> or the Tiber. (15)

Pulsky's argument accords with Shelley's formulation
that "those who are more finely organized or born in a
happier age," are enabled to recognize all artistic production "as episodes to that great poem, which all poets,
like the co-operating thoughts of one great mind, have
built up since the beginning of the world."[39] Pulsky capitalizes upon the degeneration of public art not in the interest of teleological hierarchies, but in the service of an
aesthetic consciousness that recognizes unity in diversity, in art and in humanity.

As in the earliest assessments of the British Museum,
the national subject is positioned as a reconciliation of
difference and identity. Where its eighteenth-century ap-
praisals stressed spatial relations, their nineteenth-century reflections stress temporal. Yet these harmonious
visions are inherently unstable. Institutional incorpora-
tions of fragmentary bodies, both the museum and the nation promise individual and collective unification. Their
power derives neither in effacing or enforcing cultural
and historical distinctions, but in allowing a space for
subjective observation and imaginative reflection. Pulsky's essay contains a stern warning in the midst of its cultural and exhibitionary history:

The human mind requires not only to live like a child for the enjoyment of the present; it desires at once to act upon the future and to see into the past. A nation, which is not conscious of its position in the order of the world, remains but a subordinate member of the great human society, and will be overwhelmed sooner or later by races of a more powerful organization. If a civilized people become lifeless and decayed, and if a system of social relations begin to decline, the most certain evidence of their approaching decay is their increasing selfishness, when it cares only for the peace and prosperity of the present moment, closing its eyes to the future and forgetting the admonitions of the past. (14)

The burden of the curse of Babel is a burden to be borne. Pulsky's conflation of the human mind and the health of the nation constitutes a realization of Romantic nationalism as an aesthetic experience. Joining historical consciousness with social responsibility, Pulsky chastises self-absorption as a sign of naive infancy or degenerate decline. The encounter with the foreign establishes self-identity in time and place, but this need not lead to hierarchy and domination. Rather, it may constitute an ongoing valence between perception and creation in which the recollection of the past and the actions of the future are informed by an imaginative perception of unity and affinity. Although history has demonstrated the course this encounter took, the Romantic aesthetic experience within the utopian space of the museum bears the trace of alternative resolutions to the curse of alterity. These resolutions acknowledge the burden of history even as they posit an idealized realm of identity, apprehended if not achieved within the museum's walls.

Notes

ABBREVIATIONS

O. P.   Original Papers of the Trustees of the British Museum, consisting of various letters and reports, contained in the Museum's Central Archive.
AddMS Additional Manuscripts, British Library.

INTRODUCTION

1. J. Mordant Crook, *The British Museum* (New York: Praeger, 1972), 127.

2. AddMS 6179, f.55–56.

3. Whether conceived of as locations for learned or creative activities, as temples of memory meant to eternalize the deeds of great men or civilizations, or as structures set apart especially for collections, the idealized *musaea* of Renaissance and Baroque iconologies, as Marcin Fabianski has documented, were consistently represented as temples surrounded by Apollo and the muses or their symbolic equivalents. "Iconography of the Architecture of Ideal *Musaea* in the Fifteenth to Eighteenth Centuries," *Journal of the History of Collections* 2, no. 2 (1990): 95–134.

4. Earlier conceptions of the *musaea*, as Paula Findlen's genealogy of its Renaissance employment argues, had served to mediate between the private domain of contemplative study and the public realm of prestigious display under the epistemological rubric of encyclopedic knowledge manifested in material collection. "The Museum: Its Classical Etymology and Renaissance Genealogy," *Journal of the History of Collections* 1, no. 1 (1989): 59–78. Findlen's more recent *Possessing Nature: Museums, Collecting, and Scientific Culture in Early Modern Italy* (Berkeley: University of California Press, 1994) offers a superb study of late Renaissance and Baroque practices of collection and exhibition, as does Krzysztof Pomian, *Collectors and Curiosities: Paris and Venice, 1500–1800*, trans. Elizabeth Wiles-Portier (Cambridge: Polity Press, 1990). See also the indispensable collection, Oliver Impey and Arthur MacGregor, eds., *The Origins of Museums: The Cabinet of Curiosities in Sixteenth- and Seventeenth-Century Europe* (Oxford: Clarendon Press, 1985).

5. For statistics on recent attendance at the British Museum, see David M. Wilson, *The British Museum: Purpose and Politics* (London: British Museum, 1989), 106.

6. For the history of eighteenth-century cultural contests over British identity, see Linda Colley, *Britons: Forging the Nation 1707–1837* (New Haven: Yale, 1992). The most comprehensive history of the museum in European culture remains Germain Bazin's *The Museum Age*, trans. Jane van Nuis Cahill (New York: Universe, 1967), though more current works listed below have become equally indispensable.

7. As Crook notes, although the Louvre often stands as the model for the modern national museum, it was not a public, secular, and national museum until 1793, whereas the British Museum met all three criteria from the moment of its foundation forty years earlier (Crook, 34–38). Andrew McClellan's study of the early histories of the Luxembourg Gallery and the Louvre demonstrates the prolific discussion of curatorial theory in eighteenth-century France and the centrality of political doctrine in determining exhibitionary design. His identification of the Louvre, as it was formed under Napoleon, as "the archetypal state museum and model for subsequent national art museums the world over" (*Inventing the Louvre: Art, Politics, and the Origins of the Modern Museum in Eighteenth-Century Paris* [Cambridge: Cambridge University Press, 1994], 2) is certainly correct. But, as was so often the case with the institutions of the Enlightenment, the French theorized what the English had already established.

8. In the revised edition of *Imagined Communities*, Benedict Anderson identifies the museum, alongside the census and the map, as a key institution in linking colonial states with European nationalism. These institutions, Anderson argues, "profoundly shaped the way in which the colonial state imagined its dominion—the nature of the human beings it ruled, the geography of its domain, and the legitimacy of its ancestry." "For museums," he writes, "and the museumizing imagination, are both profoundly political" (London: Verso, 1991), 164, 178.

9. Carol Duncan, *Civilizing Rituals: Inside Public Art Museums* (London: Routledge, 1995).

10. Stephen Larrabee, *English Bards and Grecian Marbles: The Relationship Between Sculpture and Poetry Especially in the Romantic Period* (Port Washington, N.Y.: Kennikat Press, 1943).

11. Murray Krieger, *Ekphrasis: The Illusion of the Natural Sign* (Baltimore: Johns Hopkins University Press, 1992).

12. W. J. T. Mitchell, *Picture Theory: Essays on Verbal and Visual Representation* (Chicago: University of Chicago Press, 1994); James A. W. Heffernan, *Museum of Words: The Poetics of Ekphrasis from Homer to Ashbery* (Chicago: University of Chicago Press, 1992); Grant F. Scott, *The Sculpted Word: Keats, Ekphrasis, and the Visual Arts* (Hanover, N.H.: University Press of New England, 1994).

13. Philip Fisher, "A Museum with One Work Inside: Keats and the Finality of Art," *Keats-Shelley Journal* 33 (1984): 85–102; see also Fish-

er's more extensive consideration of museum culture *Making and Effacing Art: Modern American Art in a Culture of Museums* (Oxford: Oxford University Press, 1991); A. W. Phinney, "Keats in the Museum: Between Aesthetics and History," *Journal of English and Germanic Philology* 90, no. 2 (1991): 208–29; John Whale, "Sacred Objects and the Sublime Ruins of Art," in *Beyond Romanticism*, ed. Stephen Copley and John Whale (London: Routledge, 1992), 218–36.

14. This historical conjunction between the modern museum and the modern nation state is most dynamically explored in the various essays collected in Gwedolyn Wright, ed., *The Formation of National Collections of Art and Archaeology* (Washington, D.C.: National Gallery of Art, 1996; distributed by University Press of New England).

15. Francis Pulsky, "On the Progress and Decay of Art and On the Arrangement of a National Museum," *The Museum of Classical Antiquities* 5 (1852): 11.

16. James L. Larson, *Interpreting Nature: The Science of Living Form from Linnaeus to Kant* (Baltimore: Johns Hopkins University Press, 1994); Lynn L. Merrill, *The Romance of Victorian Natural History* (Oxford: Oxford University Press, 1989); Mary Louise Pratt, *Imperial Eyes: Travel Writing and Transculturation* (London: Routledge, 1992); Rhoda Rappaport, *When Geologists Were Historians, 1665–1750* (Ithaca: Cornell University Press, 1997); Harriet Ritvo, *The Platypus and the Mermaid and Other Figments of the Classifying Imagination* (Cambridge: Harvard University Press, 1997); Ann B. Shteir, *Cultivating Women, Cultivating Science* (Baltimore: Johns Hopkins University Press, 1996); see also the collections of essays gathered in *Victorian Science in Context*, ed. Bernard Lightman (Chicago: University of Chicago, 1997) and *Science and Imagination in Eighteenth Century British Culture*, ed. Sergio Rossi (Milan: Edizioni Unicopli, 1987).

17. Susan Stewart, *On Longing: Narratives of the Miniature, the Gigantic, the Souvenir, the Collection* (Durham, N.C.: Duke University Press, 1993), 156.

18. Richard Altick, *The Shows of London* (London: Belknap Press, 1978).

19. *Act for the Purchase of the Museum or Collection of Sir Hans Sloane,* 26 George II.

20. Edward Edwards, *Lives of the Founders of the British Museum with Notices of Its Chief Augmentors and Other Benefactors 1570–1870* (London, 1870; reprinted Amsterdam: Gerard Th. Van Heusden, 1969); Edward Miller, *That Noble Cabinet: A History of the British Museum* (London: Andre Deutsch, 1973); Crook, *British Museum*; A. E. Gunther, *The Founders of Science at the British Museum 1753–1900* (Suffolk, England: Halesworth, 1980); Ian Jenkins, *Archaeologists and Aesthetes in the Sculpture Galleries of the British Museum 1800–1939* (London: British Museum, 1992).

21. The implications of the conflation of visual and verbal culture and interpretation has been theorized eloquently by the many essays compiled in *Vision and Textuality*, ed. Stephen Melville and Bill Read-

ings (Durham, N.C.: Duke University Press, 1995). I am particularly indebted to Melville and Readings's fine introductory essay for helping me to think through the relation between poetic structure and aesthetic reflection. See also *Visual Culture: Images and Interpretations*, ed. Norman Bryson, Michael Ann Holly, and Keith Moxery (Hanover, N.H.: University Press of New England, 1994).

22. Here I am thinking most of the simultaneous institutional and epistemic genealogies found in such works as Donald Preziosi, *Rethinking Art History: Meditations on a Coy Science* (New Haven: Yale, 1989); Douglas Crimp, *On the Museum's Ruins* (Cambridge: MIT Press, 1993); and Tony Bennett, *The Birth of the Museum: History, Theory, Politics* (London: Routledge, 1995). The excellent collection of essays edited by Daniel J. Sherman and Irit Rogoff (*Museum Culture: Histories, Discourses, Spectacles* [Minneapolis: University of Minnesota Press, 1994]) also exemplifies this Foucauldian approach.

23. Here I have in mind such generous and astute curatorial reflections as Duncan, *Civilizing Rituals*; Susan M. Pearce, *Museums, Objects and Collections: A Cultural Study* (Washington, D.C.: Smithsonian Institution Press, 1992); and Alan Wallach, *Exhibiting Contradiction: Essays on the Art Museum in the United States* (Amherst, Mass.: University of Massachusetts Press, 1998). See also the many excellent essays from the conferences held in 1988 and 1990 at the International Center of the Smithsonian Institute and gathered in Ivan Karp and Steven D. Lavine, ed., *Exhibiting Cultures: The Poetics and Politics of Museum Display* (Washington, D.C.: Smithsonian Institution Press, 1991) and Ivan Karp, Christine Mullen Kreamer, and Steven D. Lavine, ed., *Museums and Communities: The Politics of Public Culture* (Washington, D.C.: Smithsonian Institution Press, 1992).

24. For important cultural histories of collecting in the European tradition, see, in addition to Findlen, *Possessing Nature*, and Pomian, *Collectors and Curiosities*; John Elsner and Roger Cardinal, ed., *The Cultures of Collecting* (Cambridge: Harvard University Press, 1994); Francis Haskell, *Rediscoveries in Art: Some Aspects of Taste, Fashion and Collecting in England and France* (London: Phaedon Press, 1976); Frank Hermann, *The English as Collectors: A Documentary Chrestomathy* (New York: Norton, 1972); Niels von Holst, *Creators, Collectors, and Connoisseurs* (New York: G. P. Putnam's Sons, 1967); Francis Henry Taylor, *The Taste of Angels: A History of Art Collecting From Rameses to Napoleon* (Boston: Little, Brown and Company, 1948); as well as the ongoing collection of essays in the *Journal of the History of Collections* (Oxford: Oxford University Press, 1989–).

25. John Elsner and Roger Cardinal, "Introduction," in *Cultures of Collecting*, 5. Though many of the essays collected in this anthology reinforce the distinction between the private collection and the public museum, the volume's overall emphasis on the incorporation of marginal and eccentric collecting belies this very distinction.

26. Jerome McGann, *The Romantic Ideology* (Chicago: University of Chicago Press, 1983).

27. Oscar Kenshur, *Dilemmas of Enlightenment: Studies in the Rhetoric and Logic of Ideology* (Berkeley: University of California Press, 1993); George Levine, "Introduction: Reclaiming the Aesthetic," in *Aesthetics and Ideology*, ed. George Levine (New Brunswick, N.J.: Rutgers University Press, 1994), 1–28; Thomas Pfau, "Reading beyond Redemption: Historicism, Irony, and the Lessons of Romanticism," in *Lessons of Romanticism*, ed. Thomas Pfau and Robert F. Gleckner (Durham, N.C.: Duke University Press, 1998), 1–37.

28. Terry Eagleton, *The Ideology of the Aesthetic* (Oxford: Basil Blackwell, 1990), 28.

CHAPTER 1: THE PLEASURES OF THE BRITISH MUSEUM

1. G. R. de Beer, *Sir Hans Sloane and the British Museum* (London: British Museum, 1953; reprint, New York: Arno Press, 1975), 109 (page citations are to the reprint edition).

2. Michel Foucault, *The Order of Things: An Archaeology of the Human Sciences* (New York: Vintage, 1973), 55.

3. Michael Hunter, *Establishing the New Science* (Woodbridge, Suffolk: Boydell Press, 1989), 123–55.

4. de Beer, *Sir Hans Sloane*, 109.

5. Mieke Bal, *Double Exposures: The Subject of Cultural Analysis* (London: Routledge, 1996), 4.

6. Ibid., 10.

7. Bennett, *Birth of the Museum*, 80.

8. Bennett notes that, in focusing exclusively on the designs and deliberations of museum promoters, directors, librarians, and curators, he excludes a consideration of "the degree to which such plans and projections were and are successful in organizing and framing the experience of the visitor or, to the contrary, the degree to which such planned effects are evaded, side-stepped or simply not noticed" (Ibid., 11).

9. Stephen Bann, *The Clothing of Clio: A Study of the Representation of History in Nineteenth-Century Britain and France* (Cambridge: Cambridge University Press, 1984), 78.

10. Among the best critical surveys of British aesthetic theory in the eighteenth century are George Dickie, *The Century of Taste: The Philosophical Odyssey of Taste in the Eighteenth Century* (Oxford: Oxford University Press, 1996); Walter John Hipple, Jr., *The Beautiful, the Sublime, and the Picturesque in Eighteenth-Century British Aesthetic Theory* (Carbondale, Ill.: Southern Illinois University Press, 1957); Samuel Holt Monk, *The Sublime: A Study of Critical Theories in Eighteenth Century England* (Ann Arbor: University of Michigan Press, 1960); and Robert E. Norton, *The Beautiful Soul: Aesthetic Morality in the Eighteenth Century* (Ithaca: Cornell University Press, 1995). See also the excellent anthology, Andrew Ashfield and Peter de Bolla, eds., *The Sublime: A Reader*

in British Eighteenth-Century Aesthetic Theory (Cambridge: Cambridge University Press, 1996).

11. *Longinus on the Sublime*, ed. D. A. Russell (Oxford: Clarendon Press, 1964), 86.

12. *The Poetical Works of Mark Akenside*, ed. Robin Dix (Madison and Teaneck: Farleigh Dickinson University Press, 1996), 85–174. Hereafter cited parenthetically in the text by book and line.

13. *Poetry and Prose of Alexander Pope*, ed. Aubrey Williams (Boston: Houghton Mifflin, 1969), 66.

14. See particularly Pomian, *Collectors and Curiosities*; Findlen, *Possessing Nature*; and Hunter, *New Science*.

15. Nicholas Thomas, "Licensed Curiosity: Cook's Pacific Voyages," in *Cultures of Collecting*, ed. Elsner and Cardinal, 118.

16. *Catalogue of King Charles the First's Collection of Pictures*, 1757, AddMS 38791, iv. Hereafter cited parenthetically in the text by page.

17. Crook, *British Museum*, 48.

18. Horace Walpole, *Aedes Walpolianae* (London, 1752), quoted in Herrmann, *The English as Collectors*, 83.

19. Walpole to Horace Mann, 18 June 1751, *The Yale Edition of Horace Walpole's Correspondence*, ed. W. S. Lewis (New Haven: Yale, 1937–83), 20:268, quoted in Cynthia Wall, "The English Auction: Narratives of Dismantlings," *Eighteenth-Century Studies* 31 (1997): 2.

20. Wall, "English Auction."

21. Quoted in Herrman, *English as Collectors,* 82.

22. In addition to the general histories of the British Museum, the most useful studies of Sloane are de Beer, *Sir Hans Sloane*; E. St. John Brooks, *Sir Hans Sloane: The Great Collector and his Circle* (London: Batchworth, 1954); and the sympathetically comprehensive Arthur MacGregor, ed., *Sir Hans Sloane: Collector, Scientist, Antiquary, Founding Father of the British Museum* (London: British Museum, 1994).

23. Edwards, *Lives of the Founders*, 296–97.

24. *The Correspondence of John Locke*, ed. E. S. de Beer, vol. 5 (Oxford, 1976–89), 128, quoted in Arthur MacGregor, "The Life, Character and Career of Sir Hans Sloane," in MacGregor, *Sir Hans Sloane*, 16.

25. de Beer, *Sir Hans Sloane*, 61.

26. Ibid., 96–97.

27. *The Diary of John Evelyn*, ed. E. S. de Beer, vol. 5 (Oxford, 1955) 48, quoted in MacGregor, "Sir Hans Sloane," 22.

28. Pratt, *Imperial Eyes*, 27.

29. Thomas Birch, "Memoirs relating to the Life of Sir Hans Sloane Bart. Formerly President of the Royal Society," AddMS 4241, quoted in MacGregor, "Sir Hans Sloane," 27.

30. Sloane diary for 16th April, 1691, quoted in dc Beer, *Sir Hans Sloane*, 110.

31. MacGregor, "Sir Hans Sloane," 26.

32. Z. C. von Uffenbach, *Merkwurdige Reisen durch Niedersachsen, Holland und Engelland* (Ulm, 1753–55), 3:247–51; translated in W. H. Quarrell and M. Mare, *London in 1710 from the Travels of Zacharias Conrad*

von Uffenbach (London, 1934) 185–88; reprinted as Appendix 1 in Mac-Gregor, "Sir Hans Sloane," 30–31.

33. *Gentleman's Magazine* 18 (July, 1748), 301–2.

34. 26 George II.

35. *A Description of Middlesex* (London, 1767) in Sir Frederick Madden [A collection of newspaper cuttings, views, etc. relating to the British Museum, 1755–1870] 4 vol., British Library.

36. Letter of Miss C. Talbot, 1756, AddMS 39311, f.83.

37. AddMS 4449.

38. AddMS 6179, f.32

39. Joseph Addison and Richard Steele, *The Spectator*, ed. Donald F. Bond (Oxford: Clarendon Press, 1965), 3:541.

40. William Hogarth, *The Analysis of Beauty*, ed. Ronald Paulson (New Haven: Yale University Press, 1997).

41. Addison and Steele, *Spectator*, 3:544.

42. Hogarth, *Beauty*, 28.

43. Francis Hutcheson, *An Inquiry into the Original of our Ideas of Beauty and Virtue; In Two Treatises*, 4th ed. (London, 1738), 17. Hereafter cited parenthetically in the text by page.

44. Adam Smith, *Essays on Philosophical Subjects*, ed. W. P. D. Wightman and J. C. Bryce (Oxford: Clarendon Press, 1980), 39–40.

45. Ibid., 51.

46. Edmund Burke, *A Philosophical Enquiry into the Origin of our Ideas of the Sublime and Beautiful*, ed. Adam Phillips (Oxford: Oxford University Press, 1990), 29.

47. Ibid., 66–67.

48. Ronald Paulson, *The Beautiful, Novel, and Strange: Aesthetics and Heterodoxy* (Baltimore: Johns Hopkins University Press, 1996), 49.

49. Addison and Steele, *Spectator*, 3:540–41.

50. Sir Richard Blackmore, *Essays upon Several Subjects* (London, 1716; reprint, New York: Garland, 1971), 36.

51. Joseph Priestley, *A Course of Lectures on Oratory and Criticism* (London, 1777; reprint, New York: Garland, 1971), 151.

52. O. P., 1:40.

53. Ibid.

54. Ibid.

55. O. P., 1:51.

56. Ibid.

57. Smith, *Essays*, 7.

58. Burke, *Sublime*, 140.

59. AddMS 6179, f.61.

60. *Hansard*, 1st ser., 3 (1805): 410.

61. AddMS 6179, f.61.

62. Pierre Jean Grosley, *A Tour to London, or, New Observations on England and its Inhabitants*, trans. Thomas Nugent (London, 1772), 2:23.

63. Madden, [British Museum], vol. 4.

64. O. P. 2:745–48.

65. Ibid., 745.

66. Ibid., 747.

67. *A View of the British Museum: or, A Regular Account Relating What is Most Remarkable and Curious to be Seen There. Collected from Several Authentic Reports. For the Benefit of Those Who Have a Mind to be Acquainted with the Principal Parts of It,* (London, 1760), 3.

68. Edmund Powlett, *The General Contents of the British Museum: With Remarks Serving as a Directory in Viewing That Noble Cabinet* (London, 1761), v. Hereafter cited parenthetically in the text by page.

69. This character is most likely based on Andrew Gifford, the museum's first Assistant Keeper of the Department of Manuscripts.

70. Rev. Warden Butler, "A Pleasing Recollection, or A Walk through the British Museum," AddMS 27276.

71. Powlett, *General Contents*, 64.

72. Alexander Thomson, *Letters on the British Museum* (London, 1767), 2. Hereafter cited parenthetically in the text by page.

73. Hogarth, *Beauty*, 17.

74. Burke, *Sublime*, 57.

75. B. Faujas Saint Fond, *Travels in England, Scotland, and the Hebrides* (London, 1799), 1:64. Hereafter cited parenthetically in the text by volume and page.

76. See the remarkable collection of titles in Edward F. Ellis, *The British Museum in Fiction: A Check-List* (Buffalo, N.Y.: n.p., 1981).

77. Tobias Smollett, *Humphry Clinker*, ed. James L. Thorson (New York: Norton, 1983), 96. Hereafter cited parenthetically in the text by page.

78. For a more comprehensive view of Smollett's novel in relationship to material collections, see Edward L. Schwarzschild, " 'I Will Take the Whole Upon My Shoulders': Collections and Corporeality in *Humphry Clinker" Criticism* 36, no. 4 (1994): 541–68.

79. *The Ambulator; or, The Stanger's Companion in a Tour round London* (London, 1774), 19. Hereafter cited parenthetically in the text by page.

80. O. P., 4:1366.

81. Addison and Steele, *Spectator*, 3:541.

82. Ibid., 3:541.

83. John and Andrew van Rymsdyk, *Museum Britannicum, Being an Exhibition of a Great Variety of Antiquities and Natural Curiosities Belonging to That Noble and Magnificent Cabinet, The British Museum* (London, 1778), ii.

84. Ibid., ix.

85. Ibid., ii.n.

86. Anthony Ashley Cooper, Third Earl of Shaftesbury, *Characteristics of Men, Manners, Opinions, Times*, ed. John M. Robertson (Indianapolis: Bobbs-Merrill Co., 1964), 279.

CHAPTER 2: WORDSWORTH IN THE MUSEUM

1. Powlett, *General Contents*, ix–x.

2. Ibid., ix.

3. *A Companion to every Place of Curiosity and Entertainment In and About London and Westminster* (London, 1767), 1.

4. *An Historical Account of the Curiosities on London and Westminster* (London, 1777), 3:2.

5. William Wordsworth, *The Letters of William and Dorothy Wordsworth: The Middle Years, 1806–1811,* ed. E. de Selincourt and Mary Moorman (Oxford: Clarendon Press, 1969), 1:148.

6. William Wordsworth, *Poetical Works,* ed. E. de Selincourt (Oxford: Clarendon Press, 1940), 3:18.

7. William Wordsworth, *Prose Works,* ed. W. J. B. Owen and Jane Worthington Smyser (Oxford: Clarendon Press, 1974), 2:353–354.

8. William Wordsworth, *The Prelude,* ed. Jonathan Wordsworth, M. H. Abrams, and Stephen Gill (New York: Norton, 1979). The 1805 *Prelude* hereafter cited parenthetically in the text by book and line.

9. Altick, *Shows,* 33.

10. Carl Philipp Moritz, *Travels of Carl Philipp Moritz in England in 1782* (London, 1795; reprint, London: Humphrey Milford, 1924), 68–69. Hereafter cited parenthetically in the text by page.

11. Burke, *Philosophical Enquiry,* 57. Hereafter cited parenthetically in the text by page.

12. Mortiz, *Travels,* 68. Hereafter cited parenthetically in the text by page.

13. Stewart, *On Longing,* 158.

14. See Edward Godfrey Cox, *A Reference Guide to the Literature of Travel* (Seattle: University of Washington Press, 1949), 3:93–94.

15. Grosley, *A Tour to London,* 1:191. Hereafter cited parenthetically in the text by volume and page.

16. "and a Mind / Infused through all the members of the world / Makes one great living body of the mass" (6.975–977). Virgil, *The Aeneid,* trans. Robert Fitzgerald (New York: Vintage, 1990), 185.

17. For the history of Westminster Abbey as a site of ideological identification in the eighteenth-century public sphere, see David Bindman, *Roubiliac and the Eighteenth-Century Monument: Sculpture as Theatre* (New Haven: Yale University Press, 1995).

18. *Longinus,* 14–15.

19. Burke, *Philosophical Enquiry,* 46–47. Hereafter cited parenthetically in the text by page.

20. Samuel Taylor Coleridge, *Collected Works,* ed. Carl Woodring (Princeton: Princeton University Press, 1990), 7.1:305. Hereafter cited parenthetically in the text by page.

21. Coleridge, *Collected Works,* 14.1:258–59.

22. Ibid., 259.

23. Coleridge's theories of the aesthetics of the state find a homologous counterpart in Ernesto Laclau and Lilian Zac's contention that "the principle of [political] organization is the point of crystallization of a tension, of an undecidable alternative *between* subject and object; it expresses itself *through* the objective and can only manage to do so by its dialectical reversal." "Minding the Gap: The Subject of Politics"

in *The Making of Political Identities*, ed. Ernesto Laclau (London: Verso, 1994), 12.

24. Steven Knapp, *Personification and the Sublime: Milton to Coleridge* (Cambridge: Harvard University Press, 1985), 82.

25. William Shenstone, "Ode to Memory," quoted in Butler, "Pleasing Recollection."

26. Frances Yates, *The Art of Memory* (Chicago: University of Chicago Press, 1966), 157–58.

27. John Locke, *An Essay Concerning Human Understanding*, ed. Alexander Campbell Fraser (New York: Dover, 1959), 1:193–94. Hereafter cited parenthetically in the text by volume and page.

28. Wordsworth, *Prose*, 1:131, 141.

29. Paul de Man, "The Rhetoric of Temporality," in *Blindness and Insight* (Minneapolis: University of Minnesota Press, 1983), 241.

30. Patricia Meyer Spacks, *An Argument of Images* (Cambridge: Harvard University Press, 1971), 144.

31. Clifford Siskin, "Personification and Community: Literary Change in the Mid and Late Eighteenth Century," *Eighteenth Century Studies* 15, no. 4 (1982): 377–78.

32. Ibid., 373.

33. Knapp, *Personification*.

34. *The Poems of Thomas Gray, William Collins, and Oliver Goldsmith*, ed. Roger Lonsdale (London: Longmans Annotated Poets, 1969), 54–63. Hereafter cited by line.

35. Though our readings differ on certain points, I am indebted in my analysis of Gray to Clark's erudition and insight. S. H. Clark, " 'Pendet Homo Incertus': Gray's Response to Locke," *Eighteenth-Century Studies* 24, no. 3 (1991), 273–92; no. 4 (1991), 484–503.

36. M. H. Abrams, "Structure and Style in the Greater Romantic Lyric," in *From Sensibility to Romanticism: Essays Presented to Frederick A. Pottle*, ed. Frederick W. Hilles and Harold Bloom (Oxford: Oxford University Press, 1965), 539. In this seminal essay, Abrams singles out the Eton College ode as the closest predecessor to the canonical romantic lyrics he surveys. He is pressed to consider Gray's "depersonalized" style as the determining factor distinguishing Gray's ode "from the free flow of consciousness, the interweaving of thought, feeling, and perceptual detail, and the easy naturalness of the speaking voice which characterize the Romantic lyric" (538–59). What is "depersonalized" is the style, or mode of representation, a registration of the lack of subjectivity as a mediating agency in the poem, the poetic voice assuming a polar as opposed to a central role.

37. Wordsworth, *Prose*, 3:34–35.

38. de Man, "Temporality," 207.

39. Wordsworth, *Poetical Works*, 5:339.

40. Mary Jacobus, *Romanticism, Writing, and Sexual Difference: Essays on The Prelude* (New York: Oxford University Press, 1989), 30.

41. Wordsworth, *Poetical Works*, 2:261–63. Hereafter cited parenthetically in the text by line.

42. Jacobus, *Romanticism*, 99.

CHAPTER 3: COMPOSITION AND ALIENATION

1. John Keats, *Complete Poems*, ed. Jack Stillinger (Cambridge: Belknap, 1978), 58. Hereafter cited parenthetically in the text by line.

2. William Hamilton, *Memorandum on the Subject of the Earl of Elgin's Pursuits in Greece* (London, 1811), 24.

3. Edward Daniel Clarke, *Travels in Various Countries of Europe, Asia and Africa* (London, 1811–13), 6:224.

4. Lord Byron, *Complete Poetical Works*, ed. Jerome McGann (Oxford: Clarendon Press, 1980), 2:191–92. Hereafter cited in the text by canto and line.

5. "And who marvels at such emotion?" Clarke asks rhetorically (*Travels*, sixth edition [London, 1817], 226).

6. Felicia Hemans, *Modern Greece* (London, 1817; reprint, New York: Garland, 1978). Hereafter cited in the text by line.

7. The amount of commentary on the Elgin Marbles, both scholastic and polemical, is immeasurable. The most useful and insightful works on the subject are A. H. Smith, "Lord Elgin and His Collection," *Journal of Hellenic Studies* 36 (1916): 163–372; William St. Clair, *Lord Elgin and the Marbles* (Oxford: Clarendon Press, 1967); Jacob Rothenberg, *"Descensus Ad Terram" The Acquisition and Reception of the Elgin Marbles* (New York: Garland, 1977); B. F. Cook, *The Elgin Marbles* (London: British Museum, 1984); Christopher Hitchens, *The Elgin Marbles: Should They Be Returned to Greece?* (London: Chatto & Windus, 1987); and Theodore Vrettos, *The Elgin Affair* (New York: Little Brown, 1997).

8. Ian Jenkins has provided thorough documentation of the exhibitionary installation of the Elgin Marbles since their purchase for the British Museum. Jenkins notes that their original arrangement was predominantly aesthetic, providing a line of sculptures and architectural fragments backed by metopes and friezes on the walls, all culminating in the Dionysus taken from the monument of Thrasyllus perched upon a column from the Parthenon. On either side of this figure stood the two reclining nudes from the Parthenon's pediment (Jenkins, *Archaeologists*, 75–101).

9. *Gentleman's Magazine* (London, Jan. 1817): 80.

10. *Hansard*, 1st ser., 34 (1816) 1028.

11. Ibid., 1031.

12. Ibid., 1030.

13. Ibid., 1034.

14. *Report from the Select Committee of the House of Commons on the Earl of Elgin's Collection of Sculpted Marbles* (London, 1816), 4.

15. John Henry Merryman, "Who Owns the Elgin Marbles?" *ART-News* (September, 1986): 107.

16. Keats, *Complete Poems*, 58.

17. Ibid.

18. Scott forwards the argument that Keats's sonnet "offers a complex revaluation of contemporary aesthetic response to the Elgin Marbles; it not only questions the process of artistic inspiration but

tempers the current enthusiasm over the proposed function of the statuary" (Scott, *Sculpted Word*, 67).

19. Noah Heringman attributes such a performative sensibility to "the experience of a pleasure as much sensory as ideal" in the materially fragmented stones which "generates a new model of aesthetic experience along with the beginning of a turn from elegiac sweetness to a kind of alienated sublimity in Keats's Hellenism" ("Stones so wonderous Cheap," *Studies in Romanticism* 37, no. 1 [1998]: 53–54). In concord with Heringman, I would emphasize Keats's thematic and formal articulation of the valence between symbolic union and figurative distance.

20. In a recent article, Gillen D'Arcy Wood employs Vrettos's recent scholarship concerning Elgin's illness and divorce to forward a compelling Freudian reading of his antiquarian pursuits. Following Freud's model of pathological melancholy, Wood argues that "Elgin's passion for the rescue of endangered antiquities is no longer for the objects themselves, either their beauty or cultural value, but for the insistent and repeated act of recovery itself, as a way of mastering the trauma of the loss of his nose and the further series of emasculating 'losses' which overtook him as a consequence: his wife, his fortune, his career and even, as a final indignity, his seat in the House of Lords" ("Mourning the Marbles: The Strange Case of Lord Elgin's Nose," *The Wordsworth Circle* 29 [1998]: 176).

21. Hamilton, *Memorandum*, 48.

22. The location of these works is unknown. A drawing based upon the "Theseus," now identified as either Heracles or Dionysus, is in the Pierpont Morgan Library. For more information on the provenance of these works, see Helmut von Erffa and Allen Staley, *The Paintings of Benjamin West* (New Haven: Yale, 1986), 439–41.

23. Hamilton, *Memorandum*, 50.

24. Benjamin Robert Haydon, *Autobiography* (New York, 1853), 1:89. Hereafter cited parenthetically in the text by volume and page.

25. John Barrell, *The Political Theory of Painting from Reynolds to Hazlitt* (New Haven: Yale, 1986).

26. For more on West and the academic tradition, see Ann Uhry Abrams, *The Valiant Hero: Benjamin West and Grand-Style History Painting* (Washington, D.C.: Smithsonian, 1985).

27. Sir Joshua Reynolds, *Discourses on Art*, ed. Robert R. Wark (New Haven: Yale, 1975), 134.

28. Ibid., 170.

29. Ibid., 90.

30. West's struggle with the ecumenical imperative of public institutions is less pronounced, most likely due to his own humble origins. Yet his promotion of the Grecian model is in part a rearguard action against "the innovations of caprice and fashion, to which the public is always prone" (John Galt, *The Life of Benjamin West* [London, 1820], 2:107) as well as a program to maintain royal patronage.

31. Ibid., 2:108.

32. Ibid., 2:98.

33. Ibid., 2:150–51.

34. Under West's presidency, following Reynolds, the Royal Academy became closely aligned with the British Museum. As President, West was an *ex officio* trustee of the museum whose expanding collection of Greco-Roman antiquities would serve as a storehouse of models for the academy's students throughout the nineteenth century. Indeed it was this alliance between the academy and the museum that served as a major justification for the national acquisition of the Elgin Marbles. The figures from the Parthenon were not to serve simply as objects of wonder for a general populace, but, as West hoped to exemplify in his compositions, as figures for the instruction and emulation of the British artist.

35. Allen Staley, *Benjamin West: American Painter at the English Court* (Baltimore: Baltimore Museum of Art, 1989), 94.

36. von Erffa and Staley, *Paintings*, 222.

37. Ibid., 359. See Hazlitt's review of "Mr. West's Picture of Christ Rejected," in *Complete Works*, ed. P. P. Howe (London: J. M. Dent, 1933) 18: 28–34.

38. Hamilton, *Memorandum*, 43–45.

39. Ibid., 51.

40. Ibid., 52.

41. Galt, *Benjamin West*, 2:150.

42. *British Review and London Critical Journal* (London, 1811): 45. Hereafter cited parenthetically in the text by page.

43. Benjamin Robert Haydon, *Diary* (Cambridge: Harvard University Press, 1960), 2:517.

44. Benjamin Robert Haydon, *Correspondence and Table Talk* (London, 1876), 1:255–56, quoted in Rothenberg, *Elgin Marbles*, 281.

45. Haydon, *Diary*, 1:280.

46. Roger J. Porter, " 'In *me* the solitary sublimity': Posturing and the Collapse of Romantic Will in Benjamin Robert Haydon," in *The Culture of Autobiography: Constructions of Self-Representation*, ed. Robert Folkenflik (Stanford, Calif.: Stanford University Press, 1993), 168–87.

47. Haydon, *Diary*, 5:561, quoted in Porter, "Romantic Will," 176.

48. Haydon, *Autobiography*, 1:82. Hereafter cited in the text by volume and page.

49. For a more thorough treatment of progressive historiography during the period, see David Spadafora, *The Idea of Progress in Eighteenth-Century Britain* (New Haven: Yale University Press, 1990).

50. James Thomson, *Poetical Works*, ed. J. Logie Robertson (London: Oxford University Press, 1965), 309–421. Hereafter cited in the text by book and line.

51. In their two classic readings of Byron's poem, Robert Gleckner and Jerome McGann situate it as an internalization of the traditions of topographical and progress poems as practiced by Thomson and Goldsmith, as well as his contemporaries Waller Rodwell Wright and Rich-

ard Polwhele. Unlike these earlier poets, Byron organizes the particulars of his travels not according to philosophical doctrine or conceptual integrity, but according to the psychological self-consciousness of the poetic persona. Robert F. Gleckner, *Byron and the Ruins of Paradise* (Baltimore: Johns Hopkins Press, 1967); Jerome McGann, *Fiery Dust: Byron's Poetic Development* (Chicago: University of Chicago Press, 1968).

52. Bruce Haley, "The Sculptural Aesthetics of *Childe Harold IV,*" *Modern Language Quarterly* 44, no. 3 (1983): 254.

53. Byron, *Poetical Works*, 2:508–12.

54. Larabee opines that Byron's writings on sculpture "mingled the language of the Academies with the new and 'romantic' theories of the imagination of Shelley and Wordsworth. With no feeling of strain he wrote of the Ideal Beauty of Neo-Classical and Academic tradition in one line, and in the next advanced an idea or theory stemming from Romantic aesthetics" (Larabee, *English Bards*, 162). As I hope this chapter demonstrates, easing the division between "neo-classical" and "romantic" allows us to perceive the necessity of subjective response in public art and exhibition.

55. Jerome McGann has pointed out that the eighteenth-century predecessors to Byron's work such as Thomson's *Liberty* and Goldsmith's *The Traveller*, "possess . . . a concern for a philosophic or conceptual integrity, a systematic wholeness whose objective validity (whether rational or symbolic or both) overarches and controls the final coherence of the poem. In poetry of this sort the poet is always a persona, or perhaps a prophetic voice, since his personal existence is kept subordinate to an informing principle, or idea. In *Childe Harold's Pilgrimage I–II*, however, the formal element is not conceptual, but unfolds out of the immediate and changing act of the poet's individual self-consciousness" (McGann, *Fiery Dust*, 105).

56. Byron, *Poetical Works*, 2:189.

57. Bernard Beatty, "Byron and the Paradoxes of Nationalism," in *Literature and Nationalism*, ed. Vincent Newey and Ann Thompson (Savage, Md.: Barnes & Noble, 1991), 152–62.

58. Byron, *Poetical Works*, 1:320–30. Hereafter cited parenthetically in the text by line.

59. Critics have recognized Hemans's poetry as offering a domestic ideology of nationalist sentiment which positions female melancholy as the central emotive fusion between past and present and between home and empire. Tricia Lootens reads Hemans's employment of patriotic heroines throughout her verse as simultaneously engendering and subverting representations of national identity. Situating female loss at the center of nationalist conceptions of self and country provides Hemans with a powerful emotional catalyst for poetic redemption; it also calls attention to the personal and public disruption at the root of nationalist rhetoric. ("Hemans and Home: Victorianism, Feminine 'Internal Enemies,' and the Domestication of National Identity," *PMLA* 109, no. 2 [1994]: 238–53). For Nanora Sweet, Hemans's adoption

of an aesthetics of the beautiful provides a feminine counterpoint to the masculine aesthetics of sublime monumentality and empire. Hemans's persistent location of artistic productivity in such emblematic figures as the flower and the ruin, for Sweet, as an articulation of an international and republican vision which counters the insular and imperial ("History, Imperialism, and the Aesthetics of the Beautiful: Hemans and the Post-Napoleonic Moment," in *At the Limits of Romanticism: Essays in Cultural, Feminist, and Materialist Criticism*, ed. Mary A. Favret and Nicola J. Watson [Bloomington: Indiana University Press, 1994], 170–84). While I see merit in both Lootens and Sweet's recent readings, a close examination of *Modern Greece* demonstrates how the feminine beautiful and the masculine sublime engage in a dialogue which implicates both in an apologia for British hegemony.

60. Hemans, *Modern Greece*, 65.
61. Ibid., 65.
62. Ibid., 65.
63. Ibid., 66.

CHAPTER 4: EKPHRASIS AND EMPIRE

1. William Wordsworth, *Poetical Works*, 3:232. Hereafter cited parenthetically in the text by line.
2. B. F. Cook, *The Townley Marbles* (London: British Museum, 1985), 15.
3. André Malraux, *The Voices of Silence*, trans. Stuart Gilbert (Princeton: Bolingen Press, 1978), 14.
4. Stephen Gill, *William Wordsworth: A Life* (Oxford: Oxford University Press, 1990), 372.
5. Altick, *Shows of London*, 434–54.
6. Ian Jenkins provides detailed information on the architectural and curatorial transformations surrounding the Townley Gallery in his sixth chapter (*Archaeologists and Aesthetes*, 102–39).
7. Cook, *Townley Marbles*, 7–26.
8. John Nichols, *Illustrations of the Literary History of the Eighteenth Century* (London, 1818), 3:725–26.
9. Ibid., 3:726.
10. Edwards, *Lives of the Founders*, 376.
11. Ibid., 376. Relating this same anecdote, Nichols forwards the argument that "this circumstance has a classical parallel":

When, as we learn from Pausanias, . . . the cunning Phryne wished to obtain from her lover Praxiteles his best work, she feigned that his workshop was on fire, and he exclaimed, "I am ruined if my Cupid or Satyr are destroyed." Thus, possessed of his real opinion as to the excellence of his own performance, she claimed his promise of giving her the best, which he had before left to the accident of her choice. Impressed with apprehensions of a total loss, Mr. Townley made a similar selection. (*Illustrations*, 3:727)

12. Nichols calls Zoffany's painting "a picture of exquisite finishing and truth of portrait, representing the smaller library, with several of the statues placed near Mr. Townley sitting, and d'Hancarville standing near him, as if spiritedly engaged in some subject of discussion" (*Illustrations*, 3:730).

13. Jenkins, *Archaeologists and Aesthetes*, 102–10.

14. Nichols, *Illustrations*, 3:722.

15. Ibid., 3:723.

16. Ibid., 3:733.

17. *Gentleman's Magazine* 80 (London, 1810): 209.

18. J. C. B. Richmond, *Egypt 1798–1952: Her Advance Towards a Modern Identity* (New York: Columbia University Press, 1977).

19. Altick, *Shows of London*, 237.

20. Edward Said, *Orientalism* (New York: Vintage, 1979), 118.

21. For more on the early nineteenth-century Egyptian Revival in Western European architecture and design, see James Stevens Curl, *Egyptomania: The Egyptian Revival: A Recurring Theme in the History of Taste* (Manchester: Manchester University Press, 1994), 107–52.

22. Timothy Mitchell, *Colonising Egypt* (Berkeley: University of California Press, 1988).

23. Robert Southey, *Letters from England* (London, 1807), quoted in *The Inspiration of Egypt: Its Influence on British Artists, Travellers and Designers, 1700–1900*, ed. Patrick Conner (Brighton: Croydon, 1983), 39–40.

24. *The British Museum: Egyptian Antiquities* (London, 1832), 1:4–5.

25. *Guide to the Beauties of the British Museum* (London, 1826), ii. Hereafter cited parenthetically in the text by page.

26. Johann Joachim Winckelmann, "Thoughts on the Imitation of the Painting and Sculpture of the Greeks," trans. H. B. Nisbet, in *German Aesthetic and Literary Criticism: Winckelmann, Lessing, Hamann, Herder, Schiller, Goethe*, ed. H. B. Nisbet (Cambridge: Cambridge University Press, 1985), 54.

27. Ibid., 60.

28. *Guide*, 14.

29. Scott, *Sculpted Word*, xi. This is the specific definition offered by James A. W. Heffernan (*Museum of Words*, 3), but it may serve as a focused definition of the object of most contemporary studies of the topic.

30. Gotthold Ephraim Lessing, "Laocoön, or On the Limits of Painting and Poetry," trans. W. A. Steel, in Nisbet, *German Aesthetic and Literary Criticism*, 58–133. Lessing's distinction between the temporality of the verbal and the spatiality of the visual has been both expanded and contested by these latter critics. In addition to Heffernan and Scott, see Krieger, *Ekphrasis*; Mitchell, *Picture Theory*; and Wendy Steiner, *The Colors of Rhetoric: Problems in the Relation Between Modern Literature and Painting* (Chicago: University of Chicago Press, 1982).

31. Keats, *Complete Poems*, 282–83. Hereafter cited parenthetically in the text by line.

32. See Heffernan (*Museum of Words*, 94–107) for a complete account of "Elegiac Stanzas" in the context of Wordsworthian ekphrasis.

33. William Wordsworth, *Poetical Works*, 4:120–25. Hereafter cited parenthetically in the text by line.

34. In the notes to the poem in the Cornell Wordsworth, Jared Curtis argues that Wordsworth is more likely referring to a painting (William Wordsworth, *Last Poems, 1821–1850*, ed. Jared Curtis [Ithaca: Cornell University Press, 1999], 269–70), yet the similarities between the pencil sketch and details in Wordsworth's poem would seem to point to this sketch as a likely source.

35. Matthew C. Brennan, "Wordsworth's 'Lines Suggested by a Portrait from the Pencil of F. Stone' 'Visible Quest of Immortality'?" *English Language Notes* 35, no. 2 (1997): 33–44.

36. Scott, *Sculpted Word*, 124–31.

37. *Yarrow Revisited and Other Poems* contains two other ekphrastic pieces in addition to the three poems discussed. The sonnet "Picture of Daniel in the Lion's Den, at Hamilton Place" offers an ambiguous meditation on both the painting's location and content, finding in the stillness of the painting's lions "a more enduring fear" than offered by "those that roam at large / Over the burning wilderness" (6–7). More intriguing is the later sonnet "To the Author's Portrait. Painted at Rydal Mount, by W. Pickersgill, Esq., for St. John's College, Cambridge":

> Go, faithful Portrait! and where long hath knelt
> Margaret, the saintly Foundress, take thy place;
> And, if Time spare the colours for the grace
> Which to the work surpassing skill hath dealt,
> Thou, on thy rock reclined, though kingdoms melt
> And states be torn up by the roots, wilt seem
> To breathe in rural peace, to hear the stream,
> And think and feel as once the Poet felt.
> Whate'er thy fate, those features have not grown
> Unrecognised through many a household tear,
> More prompt, more glad to fall than drops of dew
> By morning shed around a flower half-blown;
> Tears of delight, that testified how true
> To life thou art, and, in thy truth, how dear!

Less a description of the painting's content and more a speculation on its fate, this sonnet prophesies the painting's elegiac effect in future years after the poet's death. Maintaining the volume's general privileging of memory over re-visitation, the sonnet foresees the painting's power growing in its ability to evoke the "pleasing melancholy" of recollection. Yet, even this praise of the pictorial image is predicated upon its belated reception and verbal testimonial.

38. James Douglas Merriman, *The Flower of Kings: A Study of the Arthurian Legend in England Between 1485 and 1835* (Lawrence: Kansas University Press, 1973), 158–67.

39. Wordsworth, *The Prelude*, 1850, 1.168–71.

40. *Guide*, 13.

41. David Spurr, *The Rhetoric of Empire: Colonial Discourse in Journalism, Travel Writing, and Imperial Administration* (Durham, N.C.: Duke University Press, 1993), 32.

CHAPTER 5: BABEL'S CURSE AND THE MUSEUM'S BURDEN

1. *Shelley's Poetry and Prose*, ed. Donald H. Reiman and Sharon B. Powers (New York: Norton, 1977), 484. Hereafter cited in the text by page.

2. Here I differ from the emphasis in Timothy Webb's argument that Shelley viewed all translation as inevitably a failure, useful only for personal poetic exercise and public moral imagination. I choose rather to follow his acknowledgement that all acts of aesthetic reception are translations insofar as they involve "transplanting the thoughts of another into our own mind," an essential act of "imaginative sympathy." *The Violet in the Crucible: Shelley and Translation* (Oxford: Clarendon Press, 1976), 21. My reading of this image is obviously indebted to Paul de Man's well-known treatment of Hölderlin's analogy between words and flowers in "The Intentional Structure of the Romantic Image," in *The Rhetoric of Romanticism* (New York: Columbia University Press, 1984), 1–17.

3. W. H. Boulton, *The Romance of the British Museum* (London: Sampson, Low, Marston & Co., 1930), vii–viii.

4. See, for example, Anne Mellor's formulation of Romantic irony as "a form or structure that simultaneously creates and decreates itself," an endless process of destroying and creating metaphysical ideals and epistemological convictions that "bear with them the seeds of their own destruction." *English Romantic Irony* (Cambridge: Harvard University Press, 1980), 5. See also David Simpson's discursive analysis of Romantic irony as "the studied avoidance . . . of determinate meanings . . . the refusal of closure . . . and the consequent raising to self-consciousness of the authoritarian element of discourse . . ." (*Irony and Authority in Romantic Poetry* [Totowa, N.J.: Rowman and Littlefield, 1979], 190.)

5. Ian Jenkins (*Archaeologists and Aesthetes*) has traced the competition between aestheticism and archaeology governing the British Museum's Department of Antiquities throughout the nineteenth century, a competition that witnessed the gradual assertion of chronological arrangement over the more picturesque practices I have been emphasizing throughout this book.

6. Dante Gabriel Rossetti, "The Burden of Nineveh," *Oxford and Cambridge Magazine* (1856): 512–16. Hereafter cited parenthetically in the text by line.

7. Carl Woodring, "The Burden of Nineveh," *The Victorian Newsletter* 63 (1983): 12.

8. C. J. Gadd, *The Stones of Assyria* (London: Chatto and Windus, 1936), 38, quoted in Jenkins, *Archaeologists and Aesthetes*, 157.

9. Austen Henry Layard, *Nineveh and its Remains* (New York: George P. Putnam, 1849), 2:85–86. Hereafter cited parenthetically in the text by volume and page.

10. Keats, *Complete Poems*, 282–83.

11. James Swafford has called attention to this irony in relation to Layard's narrative. "Layard, British Idolatry, and Rossetti's 'The Burden of Nineveh,' " *ANQ* 3, no. 1 (1990): 11–12.

12. Byron, *Poetical Works*, 1:320–30, lines 181–206.

13. *Examiner* 524 (11 Jan., 1818): 24.

14. *Examiner* 527 (1 Feb., 1818): 73.

15. Anne Janowitz, "Shelley's Monument to Ozymandias," *Philological Quarterly* 63, no. 4 (1984): 477–91.

16. M. K. Bequette, "Shelley and Smith: Two Sonnets on Ozymandias," *Keats-Shelley Journal* 26 (1977): 30.

17. Ibid., 31.

18. Janowitz, "Shelley's Monument," 489.

19. Michael Podro, *The Critical Historians of Art* (New Haven: Yale University Press, 1982).

20. Bennett, *Birth of the Museum*, 59–88.

21. Thomas Love Peacock, *The Four Ages of Poetry*, ed. John E. Jordan (Indianapolis: Bobbs-Merrill, 1965), 10–11. Hereafter cited parenthetically in the text by page.

22. Bruce Haley, "Shelley, Peacock, and the Reading of History," *Studies in Romanticism* 29, no. 3 (1990): 441.

23. Shelley, *Poetry and Prose*, 482.

24. Jerrold E. Hogle, "Shelley's Poetics: The Power as Metaphor," *Keats-Shelley Journal* 31 (1982): 159.

25. Paul de Man's account of Romantic imagery in general: "it is always constitutive, able to posit regardless of presence but, by the same token, unable to give a foundation to what it posits except as an intent of consciousness" ("Structure," 6).

26. Miller, *Noble Cabinet*, 196.

27. Frederick N. Bohrer, "The Times and Spaces of History: Representation, Assyria, and the British Museum," in *Museum Culture*, ed. Sherman and Rogoff, 197–222.

28. For more detail on the arrangement of antiquities during this period, see Jenkins, *Archaeologists and Aesthetes*, 158–67.

29. House of Commons, "Report of the Select Committee on the Management of the National Gallery," *Parliamentary Papers, 1852–53*, XXXV, 640; House of Commons, "Report of the Commissioners on the Site for the National Gallery," *Parliamentary Papers, 1857, Session 2*, XXIV, 78.

30. *Parliamentary Papers, 1852–53*, XXXV, 829.

31. Ibid., 689.

32. Ibid., 691.

33. Ibid., 692–93.

34. Francis Haskell, *Rediscoveries in Art: Some Aspects of Taste, Fashion and Collecting in England and France* (Ithaca: Cornell, 1976), 102.

35. *Parliamentary Papers, 1852–53*, XXXV, 693.

36. Dante Gabriel Rossetti, *Poems* (London, 1870), 170–79.

37. Johannes Fabian, *Time and the Other: How Anthropology Makes Its Object* (New York: Columbia University Press, 1983), 26.

38. Pulsky, "National Museum," 12. Hereafter cited parenthetically in the text by page.

39. Shelley, *Poetry and Prose*, 493.

Works Cited

Abrams, Ann Uhry. *The Valiant Hero: Benjamin West and Grand-Style History Painting.* Washington, D.C.: Smithsonian, 1985.

Abrams, M. H. "Structure and Style in the Greater Romantic Lyric." In *From Sensibility to Romanticism: Essays Presented to Frederick A. Pottle,* edited by Frederick W. Hilles and Harold Bloom, 527–60. Oxford: Oxford University Press, 1965.

Acts and Votes of Parliament Relating to the British Museum. London, 1824.

Addison, Joseph and Richard Steele. *The Spectator.* Edited by Donald F. Bond. Oxford: Clarendon Press, 1965.

Akenside, Mark. *The Poetical Works of Mark Akenside.* Edited by Robin Dix. Madison and Teaneck: Farleigh Dickinson University Press, 1996.

Altick, Richard. *The Shows of London.* London: Belknap Press, 1978.

Ambulator, The, or, The Stranger's Companion in a Tour round London. London, 1774.

Anderson, Benedict. *Imagined Communities: Reflections on the Origin and Spread of Nationalism.* Rev. ed. London: Verso, 1991.

Ashfield, Andrew and Peter de Bolla, eds. *The Sublime: A Reader in British Eighteenth-Century Aesthetic Theory.* Cambridge: Cambridge University Press, 1996.

Bal, Mieke. *Double Exposures: The Subject of Cultural Analysis.* London: Routledge, 1996.

Bann, Stephen. *The Clothing of Clio: A Study of the Representation of History in Nineteenth-Century Britain and France.* Cambridge: Cambridge University Press, 1984.

Barrell, John. *The Political Theory of Painting from Reynolds to Hazlitt.* New Haven: Yale University Press, 1986.

Bazin, Germain. *The Museum Age.* Translated by Jane van Nuis Cahill. New York: Universe, 1967.

Beatty, Bernard. "Byron and the Paradoxes of Nationalism." In *Literature and Nationalism,* edited by Vincent Newey and Ann Thompson, 152–62. Savage, Md.: Barnes & Noble, 1991.

Bennett, Tony. *The Birth of the Museum: History, Theory, Politics.* London: Routledge, 1995.

Bequette, M. K. "Shelley and Smith: Two Sonnets on Ozymandias." *Keats-Shelley Journal* 26 (1977): 29–31.

Bindman, David. *Roubiliac and the Eighteenth-Century Monument: Sculpture as Theatre*. New Haven: Yale University Press, 1995.

Blackmore, Sir Richard. *Essays upon Several Subjects*. London, 1716. Reprint, New York: Garland, 1971.

Bohrer, Frederick N. "The Times and Spaces of History: Representation, Assyria, and the British Museum." In *Museum Culture: Histories, Discourses, Spectacles*, edited by Daniel J. Sherman and Irit Rogoff, 197–222. Minneapolis: University of Minnesota Press, 1994.

Boulton, W. H. *The Romance of the British Museum*. London: Sampson, Low, Marston & Co., 1930.

Brennan, Matthew C. "Wordsworth's 'Lines Suggested by a Portrait from the Pencil of F. Stone' 'Visible Quest of Immortality'?" *English Language Notes* 35, no. 2 (1997): 33–44.

British Museum. *The British Museum: Egyptian Antiquities*. London, 1832.

Brooks, E. St. John. *Sir Hans Sloane: The Great Collector and his Circle*. London: Batchworth, 1954.

Bryson, Norman, Michael Ann Holly, and Keith Moxery, eds. *Visual Culture: Images and Interpretations*. Hanover, N.H.: University Press of New England, 1994.

Burke, Edmund. *A Philosophical Enquiry into the Origin of our Ideas of the Sublime and Beautiful*. Edited by Adam Phillips. Oxford: Oxford University Press, 1990.

Butler, Rev. Warden. "A Pleasing Recollection, or A Walk through the British Museum." AddMS 27276.

Byron, Lord. *Complete Poetical Works*. Edited by Jerome McGann. Oxford: Clarendon Press, 1980.

Clark, S. H. " 'Pendet Homo Incertus': Gray's Response to Locke." *Eighteenth-Century Studies* 24, no.3 (1991), 273–92; no. 4 (1991), 484–503.

Clarke, Edward Daniel. *Travels in Various Countries of Europe, Asia and Africa*. London, 1811–13.

Coleridge, Samuel Taylor. *Collected Works*. Edited by Carl Woodring. Princeton: Princeton University Press, 1990.

Colley, Linda. *Britons: Forging the Nation 1707–1837*. New Haven: Yale, 1992.

A Companion to every Place of Curiosity and Entertainment In and About London and Westminster. London, 1767.

Cook, B. F. *The Elgin Marbles*. London: British Museum, 1984.

———. *The Townley Marbles*. London: British Museum, 1985.

Cox, Edward Godfrey. *A Reference Guide to the Literature of Travel*. Seattle: University of Washington Press, 1949.

Crimp, Douglas. *On the Museum's Ruins*. Cambridge: MIT Press, 1993.

Crook, J. Mordant. *The British Museum*. New York: Praeger, 1972.

Curl, James Stevens. *Egyptomania: The Egyptian Revival: A Recurring Theme in the History of Taste.* Manchester, Vt.: Manchester University Press, 1994.

De Beer, G. R. *Sir Hans Sloane and the British Museum.* London: British Museum, 1953. Reprint, New York: Arno Press, 1975.

De Man, Paul. "The Rhetoric of Temporality." In *Blindness and Insight.* Minneapolis: University of Minnesota Press, 1983.

———. "The Intentional Structure of the Romantic Image." In *The Rhetoric of Romanticism.* New York: Columbia University Press, 1984.

Dickie, George. *The Century of Taste: The Philosophical Odyssey of Taste in the Eighteenth Century.* Oxford: Oxford University Press, 1996.

Duncan, Carol. *Civilizing Rituals: Inside Public Art Museums.* London: Routledge, 1995.

Edwards, Edward. *Lives of the Founders of the British Museum with Notices of Its Chief Augmentors and Other Benefactors 1570–1870.* 1870. Reprint, Amsterdam: Gerard Th. Van Heusden, 1969.

Eagleton, Terry. *The Ideology of the Aesthetic.* Oxford: Basil Blackwell, 1990.

Ellis, Edward F. *The British Museum in Fiction: A Check-List.* Buffalo, N.Y.: n.p., 1981.

Elsner, John, and Roger Cardinal, eds. *The Cultures of Collecting.* Cambridge: Harvard University Press, 1994.

Fabian, Johannes. *Time and the Other: How Anthropology Makes Its Object.* New York: Columbia University Press, 1983.

Fabianski, Marcin. "Iconography of the Architecture of Ideal *Musaea* in the Fifteenth to Eighteenth Centuries." *Journal of the History of Collections* 2, no. 2 (1990): 95–134.

Findlen, Paula. "The Museum: Its Classical Etymology and Renaissance Genealogy." *Journal of the History of Collections* 1, no. 1 (1989): 59–78.

———. *Possessing Nature: Museums, Collecting, and Scientific Culture in Early Modern Italy.* Berkeley: University of California, 1994.

Fisher, Philip. "A Museum with One Work Inside: Keats and the Finality of Art." *Keats-Shelley Journal* 33 (1984): 85–102.

———. *Making and Effacing Art: Modern American Art in a Culture of Museums.* Oxford: Oxford University Press, 1991.

Foucault, Michel. *The Order of Things: An Archaeology of the Human Sciences.* New York: Vintage, 1973.

Galt, John. *The Life of Benjamin West.* London, 1820.

Gill, Stephen. *William Wordsworth: A Life.* Oxford: Oxford University Press, 1990.

Gleckner, Robert F. *Byron and the Ruins of Paradise.* Baltimore: Johns Hopkins Press, 1967.

Gray, Thomas, William Collins, and Oliver Goldsmith. *The Poems of*

Thomas Gray, William Collins, and Oliver Goldsmith. Edited by Roger Lonsdale. London: Longmans Annotated Poets, 1969.

Grosley, Pierre Jean. *A Tour to London; or, New Observations on England and Its Inhabitants.* Translated by Thomas Nugent. London, 1772.

Guide to the Beauties of the British Museum. London, 1826.

Gunther, A. E. *The Founders of Science at the British Museum 1753–1900.* Suffolk: Halesworth, 1980.

Haley, Bruce. "The Sculptural Aesthetics of *Childe Harold IV.*" *Modern Language Quarterly* 44, no. 3 (1983): 251–66.

———. "Shelley, Peacock, and the Reading of History." *Studies in Romanticism* 29, no. 3 (1990): 439–61.

Hamilton, William. *Memorandum on the Subject of the Earl of Elgin's Pursuits in Greece.* London, 1811.

Haskell, Francis. *Rediscoveries in Art: Some Aspects of Taste, Fashion and Collecting in England and France.* Ithaca, N.Y.: Cornell, 1976.

Haydon, Benjamin Robert. *Autobiography.* New York, 1853.

———. *Diary.* Cambridge: Harvard University Press, 1960.

Hazlitt, William. *Complete Works.* Edited by P. P. Howe. London: J. M. Dent, 1933.

Heffernan, James A. W. *Museum of Words: The Poetics of Ekphrasis from Homer to Ashbery.* Chicago: University of Chicago Press, 1992.

Hemans, Felicia. *Modern Greece.* London, 1817. Reprint, New York: Garland, 1978.

Hermann, Frank. *The English as Collectors: A Documentary Chrestomathy.* New York: Norton, 1972.

Heringman, Noah. " 'Stones so Wonderous Cheap.' " *Studies in Romanticism* 37, no. 1 (1998): 43–62.

Hipple, Walter John, Jr. *The Beautiful, the Sublime, and the Picturesque in Eighteenth-Century British Aesthetic Theory.* Carbondale: Southern Illinois University Press, 1957.

An Historical Account of the Curiosities of London and Westminster. London, 1777.

Hitchens, Christopher. *The Elgin Marbles: Should They Be Returned to Greece?* London: Chatto & Windus, 1987.

Hogarth, William. *The Analysis of Beauty.* Edited by Ronald Paulson. New Haven: Yale University Press, 1997.

Hogle, Jerrold E. "Shelley's Poetics: The Power as Metaphor." *Keats-Shelley Journal* 31 (1982): 159–97.

Holst, Niels von. *Creators, Collectors, and Connoisseurs.* New York: G. P. Putnam's Sons, 1967.

Hunter, Michael. *Establishing the New Science.* Woodbridge, Suffolk: Boydell Press, 1989.

Hutcheson, Francis. *An Inquiry into the Original of our Ideas of Beauty and Virtue; In Two Treatises.* 4th ed. London, 1738.

Impey, Oliver and Arthur MacGregor, eds. *The Origins of Museums: The Cabinet of Curiosities in Sixteenth- and Seventeenth-Century Europe.* Oxford: Clarendon Press, 1985.

Jacobus, Mary. *Romanticism, Writing, and Sexual Difference: Essays on The Prelude.* New York: Oxford University Press, 1989.

Janowitz, Anne. "Shelley's Monument to Ozymandias." *Philological Quarterly* 63, no. 4 (1984): 477–91.

Jenkins, Ian. *Archaeologists and Aesthetes in the Sculpture Galleries of the British Museum 1800–1939.* London: British Museum, 1992.

Karp, Ivan, and Steven D. Lavine, eds. *Exhibiting Cultures: The Poetics and Politics of Museum Display.* Washington, D.C.: Smithsonian Institution Press, 1991.

Karp, Ivan, Christine Mullen Kreamer, and Steven D. Lavine, eds. *Museums and Communities: The Politics of Public Culture.* Washington, D.C.: Smithsonian Institution Press, 1992.

Keats, John. *Complete Poems.* Edited by Jack Stillinger. Cambridge: Belknap, 1978.

Kenshur, Oscar. *Dilemmas of Enlightenment: Studies in the Rhetoric and Logic of Ideology.* Berkeley: University of California Press, 1993.

Knapp, Steven. *Personification and the Sublime: Milton to Coleridge.* Cambridge: Harvard University Press, 1985.

Krieger, Murray. *Ekphrasis: The Illusion of the Natural Sign.* Baltimore: Johns Hopkins University Press, 1992.

Laclau, Ernesto and Lilian Zac. "Minding the Gap: The Subject of Politics." In *The Making of Political Identities*, edited by Ernesto Laclau, 11–39. London: Verso, 1994.

Larrabee, Stephen. *English Bards and Grecian Marbles: The Relationship Between Sculpture and Poetry Especially in the Romantic Period.* Port Washington, N.Y.: Kennikat Press, 1943.

Larson, James L. *Interpreting Nature: The Science of Living Form from Linnaeus to Kant.* Baltimore: Johns Hopkins University Press, 1994.

Layard, Austen Henry. *Nineveh and its Remains.* New York: George P. Putnam, 1849.

Lessing, Gotthold Ephraim. "Laocoön, or, On the Limits of Painting and Poetry." Translated by W. A. Steel. In *German Aesthetic and Literary Criticism: Winckelmann, Lessing, Hamann, Herder, Schiller, Goethe*, edited by H. B. Nisbet, 58–133. Cambridge: Cambridge University Press, 1985.

Levine, George. "Introduction: Reclaiming the Aesthetic." In *Aesthetics and Ideology*, edited by George Levine, 1–28. New Brunswick, N.J.: Rutgers University Press, 1994.

Lightman, Bernard, ed. *Victorian Science in Context.* Chicago: University of Chicago, 1997.

Locke, John. *An Essay Concerning Human Understanding.* Edited by Alexander Campbell Fraser. New York: Dover, 1959.

Longinus. *Longinus on the Sublime*. Edited by D. A. Russell. Oxford: Clarendon Press, 1964.

Lootens, Tricia. "Hemans and Home: Victorianism, Feminine 'Internal Enemies,' and the Domestication of National Identity." *PMLA* 109, no. 2 (1994): 238–53.

MacGregor, Arthur, ed. *Sir Hans Sloane: Collector, Scientist, Antiquary, Founding Father of the British Museum*. London: British Museum, 1994.

McClellan, Andrew. *Inventing the Louvre: Art, Politics, and the Origins of the Modern Museum in Eighteenth-Century Paris*. Cambridge: Cambridge University Press, 1994.

McGann, Jerome. *Fiery Dust: Byron's Poetic Development*. Chicago: University of Chicago Press, 1968.

———. *The Romantic Ideology*. Chicago: University of Chicago Press, 1983.

Madden, Sir Frederic. [A collection of newspaper cuttings, views, etc. relating to the British Museum, 1755–1870], British Library.

Malraux, André. *The Voices of Silence*. Translated by Stuart Gilbert. Princeton: Bolingen Press, 1978.

Mellor, Anne. *English Romantic Irony*. Cambridge: Harvard University Press, 1980.

Melville, Stephen, and Bill Readings, eds. *Vision and Textuality*. Durham, N.C.: Duke University Press, 1995.

Merrill, Lynn L. *The Romance of Victorian Natural History*. Oxford: Oxford University Press, 1989.

Merriman, James Douglas. *The Flower of Kings: A Study of the Arthurian Legend in England Between 1485 and 1835*. Lawrence: Kansas University Press, 1973.

Merryman, John Henry. "Who Owns the Elgin Marbles?" *ARTNews* (September, 1986): 100–109.

Miller, Edward. *That Noble Cabinet: A History of the British Museum*. London: Andre Deutsch, 1973.

Mitchell, Timothy. *Colonising Egypt*. Berkeley: University of California Press, 1988.

Mitchell, W. J. T. *Picture Theory: Essays on Verbal and Visual Representation*. Chicago: University of Chicago Press, 1994.

Monk, Samuel Holt. *The Sublime: A Study of Critical Theories in Eighteenth Century England*. Ann Arbor: University of Michigan Press, 1960.

Moritz, Carl Philipp. *Travels of Carl Philipp Moritz in England in 1782*. London, 1795. Reprint, London: Humphrey Milford, 1924.

Nichols, John. *Illustrations of the Literary History of the Eighteenth Century*. London, 1818.

Nisbet, H. B., ed. *German Aesthetic and Literary Criticism: Winckelmann,*

Lessing, Hamann, Herder, Schiller, Goethe. Cambridge: Cambridge University Press, 1985.

Norton, Robert E. *The Beautiful Soul: Aesthetic Morality in the Eighteenth Century.* Ithaca: Cornell University Press, 1995.

Paulson, Ronald. *The Beautiful, Novel, and Strange: Aesthetics and Heterodoxy.* Baltimore: Johns Hopkins University Press, 1996.

Peacock, Thomas Love. *The Four Ages of Poetry.* Edited by John E. Jordan. Indianapolis: Bobbs-Merrill, 1965.

Pearce, Susan M. *Museums, Objects and Collections: A Cultural Study.* Washington, D.C.: Smithsonian Institution Press, 1992.

Pfau, Thomas. "Reading beyond Redemption: Historicism, Irony, and the Lessons of Romanticism." In *Lessons of Romanticism,* edited by Thomas Pfau and Robert F. Gleckner, 1–37. Durham, N.C.: Duke University Press, 1998.

Phinney, A.W. "Keats in the Museum: Between Aesthetics and History." *Journal of English and Germanic Philology* 90, no. 2 (1991): 208–29.

Podro, Michael. *The Critical Historians of Art.* New Haven: Yale University Press, 1982.

Pomian, Krzysztof. *Collectors and Curiosities: Paris and Venice, 1500–1800.* Translated by Elizabeth Wiles-Portier. Cambridge: Polity Press, 1990.

Pope, Alexander. *Poetry and Prose of Alexander Pope.* Edited by Aubrey Williams. Boston: Houghton Mifflin, 1969.

Porter, Roger J. " 'In *me* the solitary sublimity': Posturing and the Collapse of Romantic Will in Benjamin Robert Haydon." In *The Culture of Autobiography: Constructions of Self-Representation,* edited by Robert Folkenflik, 168–87. Stanford, Calif.: Stanford University Press, 1993.

Powlett, Edmund. *The General Contents of the British Museum: With Remarks Serving as a Directory in Viewing That Noble Cabinet.* London, 1761.

Pratt, Mary Louise. *Imperial Eyes: Travel Writing and Transculturation.* London: Routledge, 1992.

Preziosi, Donald. *Rethinking Art History: Meditations on a Coy Science.* New Haven: Yale, 1989.

Priestley, Joseph. *A Course of Lectures on Oratory and Criticism.* London, 1777. Reprint, New York: Garland, 1971.

Pulsky, Francis. "On the Progress and Decay of Art and On the Arrangement of a National Museum." *The Museum of Classical Antiquities* 5 (1852): 1–15.

Rappaport, Rhoda. *When Geologists Were Historians, 1665–1750.* Ithaca: Cornell University Press, 1997.

Report from the Select Committee of the House of Commons on the Earl of Elgin's Collection of Sculpted Marbles. London, 1816.

Reynolds, Sir Joshua. *Discourses on Art*. Edited by Robert R. Wark. New Haven: Yale, 1975.

Richmond, J. C. B. *Egypt 1798–1952: Her Advance Towards a Modern Identity*. New York: Columbia University Press, 1977.

Ritvo, Harriet. *The Platypus and the Mermaid and Other Figments of the Classifying Imagination*. Cambridge: Harvard University Press, 1997.

Rossetti, Dante Gabriel. "The Burden of Nineveh." *Oxford and Cambridge Magazine* (1856): 512–16.

————. *Poems*. London, 1870.

Rossi, Sergio, ed. *Science and Imagination in Eighteenth Century British Culture*. Milan: Edizioni Unicopli, 1987.

Rothenberg, Jacob. *"Descensus Ad Terram": The Acquisition and Reception of the Elgin Marbles*. New York: Garland, 1977.

Said, Edward. *Orientalism*. New York: Vintage, 1979.

Saint Fond, B. Faujas. *Travels in England, Scotland, and the Hebrides*. London, 1799.

Schwarzschild, Edward L. " 'I Will Take the Whole Upon My Shoulders': Collections and Corporeality in *Humphry Clinker*." *Criticism* 36, no. 4 (1994): 541–68.

Scott, Grant F. *The Sculpted Word: Keats, Ekphrasis, and the Visual Arts*. Hanover, N.H.: University Press of New England, 1994.

Shaftesbury, Anthony Ashley Cooper, Third Earl of. *Characteristics of Men, Manners, Opinions, Times*. Edited by John M. Robertson. Indianapolis: Bobbs-Merrill Co., 1964.

Shelley, Percy Bysshe. *Shelley's Poetry and Prose*. Edited by Donald H. Reiman and Sharon B. Powers. New York: Norton, 1977.

Sherman, Daniel J., and Irit Rogoff, eds. *Museum Culture: Histories, Discourses, Spectacles*. Minneapolis: University of Minnesota Press, 1994.

Shteir, Ann B. *Cultivating Women, Cultivating Science*. Baltimore: Johns Hopkins University Press, 1996.

Simpson, David. *Irony and Authority in Romantic Poetry*. Totowa, N.J.: Rowman and Littlefield, 1979.

Siskin, Clifford. "Personification and Community: Literary Change in the Mid and Late Eighteenth Century." *Eighteenth Century Studies* 15, no. 4 (1982): 371–401.

Smith, A. H. "Lord Elgin and His Collection." *Journal of Hellenic Studies* 36 (1916): 163–372.

Smith, Adam. *Essays on Philosophical Subjects*. Edited by W. P. D. Wightman and J. C. Bryce. Oxford: Clarendon Press, 1980.

Smollett, Tobias. *Humphry Clinker*. Edited by James L. Thorson. New York: Norton, 1983.

Spacks, Patricia Meyer. *An Argument of Images*. Cambridge: Harvard University Press, 1971.

Spadafora, David. *The Idea of Progress in Eighteenth-Century Britain*. New Haven: Yale University Press, 1990.

Spurr, David. *The Rhetoric of Empire: Colonial Discourse in Journalism, Travel Writing, and Imperial Administration*. Durham, N.C.: Duke University Press, 1993.

Staley, Allen. *Benjamin West: American Painter at the English Court*. Baltimore: Baltimore Museum of Art, 1989.

St. Clair, William. *Lord Elgin and the Marbles*. Oxford: Clarendon Press, 1967.

Steiner, Wendy. *The Colors of Rhetoric: Problems in the Relation Between Modern Literature and Painting*. Chicago: University of Chicago Press, 1982.

Stewart, Susan. *On Longing: Narratives of the Miniature, the Gigantic, the Souvenir, the Collection*. Durham, N.C.: Duke University Press, 1993.

Swafford, James. "Layard, British Idolatry, and Rossetti's 'The Burden of Nineveh,'" *ANQ* 3, no. 1 (1990): 11–12.

Sweet, Nanora. "History, Imperialism, and the Aesthetics of the Beautiful: Hemans and the Post-Napoleonic Moment." In *At the Limits of Romanticism: Essays in Cultural, Feminist, and Materialist Criticism*, edited by Mary A. Favret and Nicola J. Watson, 170–84. Bloomington: Indiana University Press, 1994.

Taylor, Francis Henry. *The Taste of Angels: A History of Art Collecting from Rameses to Napoleon*. Boston: Little, Brown and Company, 1948.

Thomas, Nicholas. "Licensed Curiosity: Cook's Pacific Voyages." In *The Cultures of Collecting*, edited by John Elsner and Roger Cardinal, 116–36. Cambridge: Harvard University Press, 1994.

Thomson, Alexander. *Letters on the British Museum*. London, 1767.

Thomson, James. *Poetical Works*. Edited by J. Logie Robertson. London: Oxford University Press, 1965.

Van Rymsdyk, John and Andrew van Rymsdyk. *Museum Britannicum, Being an Exhibition of a Great Variety of Antiquities and Natural Curiosities Belonging to That Noble and Magnificent Cabinet, The British Museum*. London, 1778.

A View of the British Museum: or, A Regular Account Relating What is Most Remarkable and Curious to be Seen There. Collected from Several Authentic Reports. For the Benefit of Those Who Have a Mind to be Acquainted with the Principal Parts of It. London, 1760.

Von Erffa, Helmut and Allen Staley. *The Paintings of Benjamin West*. New Haven: Yale University Press, 1986.

Vrettos, Theodore. *The Elgin Affair*. New York: Little Brown, 1997.

Wall, Cynthia. "The English Auction: Narratives of Dismantlings." *Eighteenth-Century Studies* 31 (1997): 1–25.

Wallach, Alan. *Exhibiting Contradiction: Essays on the Art Museum in the United States*. Amherst: University of Massachusetts Press, 1998.

Webb, Timothy. *The Violet in the Crucible: Shelley and Translation*. Oxford: Clarendon Press, 1976.

Whale, John. "Sacred Objects and the Sublime Ruins of Art." In *Be-

yond Romanticism, edited by Stephen Copley and John Whale, 218–36. London: Routledge, 1992.

Wilson, David M. *The British Museum: Purpose and Politics.* London: British Museum, 1989.

Winckelmann, Johann Joachim. "Thoughts on the Imitation of the Painting and Sculpture of the Greeks." Translated by H. B. Nisbet. In *German Aesthetic and Literary Criticism: Winckelmann, Lessing, Hamann, Herder, Schiller, Goethe,* edited by H. B. Nisbet, 31–54. Cambridge: Cambridge University Press, 1985.

Wood, Gillen D'Arcy. "Mourning the Marbles: The Strange Case of Lord Elgin's Nose." *The Wordsworth Circle* 29, no. 3 (1998): 171–77.

Woodring, Carl. "The Burden of Nineveh." *The Victorian Newsletter* 63 (1983): 12–14.

Wordsworth, William. *The Letters of William and Dorothy Wordsworth: The Middle Years, 1806–1811,* edited by E. de Selincourt and Mary Moorman. Oxford: Clarendon Press, 1969.

———. *Poetical Works,* edited by E. de Selincourt. Oxford: Clarendon Press, 1940.

———. *The Prelude,* edited by Jonathan Wordsworth, M. H. Abrams, and Stephen Gill. New York: Norton, 1979.

———. *Prose Works,* edited by W. J. B. Owen and Jane Worthington Smyser. Oxford: Clarendon Press, 1974.

———. *Yarrow Revisited and Other Poems.* London, 1835.

Wright, Gwendolyn, ed. *The Formation of National Collections of Art and Archaeology.* Washington: National Gallery of Art, 1996; distributed by University Press of New England.

Yates, Frances. *The Art of Memory.* Chicago: University of Chicago Press, 1966.

Index

Page numbers in italics are illustration pages

280